Travel and Tourism

Third edition

Travel and Tourism
Tutor's Manual

Patrick Lavery

To accompany this book, a tested set of exercises, cases,
notes and other materials to help
tutors extend and support their students' learning

ISBN 1 85450 435 5

Travel and Tourism
A North-American-European perspective
Patrick Lavery & Carl Van Doren

Overview of the industry and the role of private/public sectors
in the UK, USA and Europe.
Level introductory, beginners plus on higher education courses.
32, Book, 224pp, 1 85450 125 9

Travel and Tourism

Patrick Lavery

Third edition

ELM Publications

This third edition of **Travel and Tourism** is published November 1996 by ELM Publications, Seaton House, Kings Ripton, Huntingdon, Cambs, PE17 2NJ.

Tel: 01487 773254   Fax: 01487 773359

Printed by St Edmundsbury Press, Bury St Edmunds, Suffolk, England.

Bound by Woolnough Bookbinding, Express Works, Church Street, Irthlingborough, Northants, England.

ISBN 1 85450 199 2

British Library Cataloguing-in-Publication Data. A catalogue record for this publication is available from The British Library.

Contents

List of Tables

List of Figures

About the Author

Professor Patrick Lavery was Pro Vice Chancellor at the University of Humberside and formerly Head of Tourism at Bournemouth University. He has taught at the Universities of Liverpool and London and for several years was responsible for tourism planning with a Metropolitan County Council. He has acted as a consultant/advisor to the European Commission since the early 1980s. He has worked for public and private sector tourism interests in many parts of the world and has written several books and produced many papers and reports on tourism issues over the past 25 years.

Acknowledgements

My particular thanks go to Mrs Bobbie Branson for her patience and care in typing all the amendments and revisions to the third edition of *Travel and Tourism*. I would also like to thank my publisher Sheila Ritchie for commissioning the book and her encouragement to produce an updated version from the second edition. Finally I must give special thanks to my wife Alma for her encouragement and patience over the past six months.

Without their combined assistance and support this book would not have been revised and updated.

Introduction

This new and enlarged third edition provides an update on developments in the field of travel and tourism in the 1990s and considers issues that will be of importance to the industry between 1995 and the year 2000 and beyond. Many of the chapters have been completely rewritten and take account of developments in technology and in the structure and management of the industry which have emerged during the 1990s.

This book has also been rewritten with the aim of assisting students who wish to acquire General National Vocational Qualifications (GNVQ's) at both intermediate and advanced level and who, therefore, require a knowledge and understanding of the tourist industry.

Each chapter sets out the learning objectives contained within that chapter, and also includes further reading and exercises. A Tutor's Guide has also been produced to accompany this book, and this provides an opportunity for students to develop performance criteria and to build up portfolios of evidence which will demonstrate their acquisition of skills of knowledge and understanding of the tourist industry. This book will help to develop students' knowledge and understanding of the components and functioning of the travel and tourism industry, and of its products and services. It will also make students aware that tourism organisations operate as businesses and will consider concepts, including marketing and promotion. By following up the exercises at the end of each chapter, and in particular those linked to the tutor's pack, students will be able to demonstrate evidence of performance in the core skills area which they require for GNVQ's.

Chapter 1

The Tourism Industry

Learning Objectives:
After reading this Chapter and some of the references and tackling one of the assignments you should have a clear idea of:
- the nature of the tourist industry;
- some data sources about trends in domestic and international tourism.

Introduction: What is Tourism?
Although tourism has existed in a limited form since the Middle Ages, the first definition of the term 'tourist' was made almost 50 years ago by the Council of the League of Nations, (LN, 1937) and subsequently ratified in 1963 by the United Nations (IUOTO, 1963). The term 'tourist' was taken to mean any person travelling for a period of twenty-four hours or more in a country other than that in which he or she usually resides, for the purpose of leisure, business, family, friends, meeting mission. To this was added the term 'excursionist' to cover people staying less than twenty-four hours in the country visited (Lickorish, 1958).

However, neither definition covers domestic tourism and for this reason the phenomenon should be best described using a Tourism Society definition:

Tourism is the temporary short-term movement of people to destinations outside the places where they normally live and work, and their activities during their stay at these destinations; it includes movement for all purposes as well as day visits or excursions.
D Airey, 1981

Tourism then is a unique phenomenon. Unlike other products the tourism product has to be consumed on the spot and the industry is designed to move the market to the product; and in this regard is quite unlike any other form of economic activity. However, tourism is not just an economic phenomenon. It can have social, political and environmental consequences. So tourism is not a simple phenomenon and the types of 'tourist' and the reasons for them being tourists are not always readily apparent. Tourism is rather like the elephant. It is easier to recognise than to define.

What then are the characteristics of tourism? It involves travelling to a destination away from home for the purposes of leisure and pleasure. Tourists may stay in their holiday destination for days or weeks or hours – but in general their activities on arrival are similar – for example sight-seeing, relaxing on a beach, sport, shopping, enjoying the local cuisine or like pursuits. Often it involves buying a 'package' and this may cover everything from the return journey home to the resort as well as accommodation, meals and organised activities during the stay there.

The industry has developed to meet all the needs of the tourist, and in sequence these are:

  i. Developing tourist destinations/attractions;
  ii. Promoting and selling these;
  iii. Transporting tourists from their home area/country to the tourist resort;
  iv. Providing them with accommodation during their stay;
  v. Developing additional leisure activities and tours during their stay;
  vi. Making goods and selling souvenirs of their visits, local crafts and produce;
  vii. Transporting them home again.

The Tourist Industry
The tourist industry can then be divided into four main sectors, each of which has some responsibility for part or all of these activities. These sectors are:

● **Travel**: including travel agents, tour operators, airlines, cruise companies, coach companies, railways, taxis, tourist guides, couriers, reservations and sales staff.

- **Accommodation, catering and related services**: hotels with all their staff from receptionists to chamber maids, chefs and cooks, waiters/waitresses, bar staff, porters, caravan/camping staff, self-catering enterprises, restaurants and cafes.
- **Leisure facilities and entertainment**: these will include theatres, museums, art galleries, theme parks, zoos, wildlife parks, sports centres, gardens, historic houses, country parks, cinemas.
- **Tourist organisations**: whose aim is to market and monitor the quality and development of the tourist area. These will range from national and regional tourist bodies to staff at local tourist information centres.

It is already clear that the industry is a complex one and it includes many different kinds of occupation - all designed to meet the needs of the tourist. By any standards, tourism is a major industry. For example, in 1994 it was estimated that in Britain some 1.5 million people worked directly or indirectly connected with tourism. There are also many seasonal jobs in the tourist industry. The following facts give some indication of the scale of the industry.

- In 1993 Britain attracted 19 million overseas tourists, who spent over 9.2 billion dollars.
- In 1991 over 19 million Britons had summer holidays abroad.
- An airline buying a new aircraft, such as the airbus A340, will probably be spending about £770 million on this purchase.
- The *Oriana*, the new flag ship of the P&O cruise fleet, cost £200 million and will carry 1,975 passengers.
- The Channel Tunnel cost £8.4 billion.
- In 1994 there were over 528 million international tourism arrivals world-wide, worth over $321 billion (WTO 1995).
- France is the world's number one tourist destination and received over 59 million visitors in 1992.

Although the industry employs large numbers of people, it mainly consists of small, often family-run businesses such as hotels, guest houses, restaurants and taxi services. At the other end of the scale there are a

Figure 1.1: Real Spending by Overseas Visitors to the UK 1985-1994

This chart shows total spending by overseas visitors to the UK (excluding fare payments to British carriers) expressed in constant 1984 prices. Constant prices are obtained by adjusting current tourist spending to take account of annual inflation in the general index of retail prices (all items).

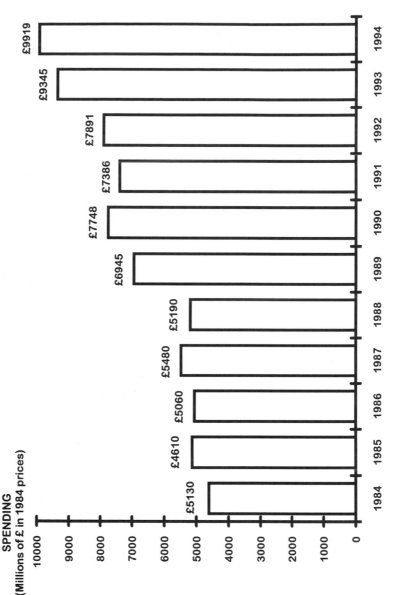

SPENDING
(Millions of £ in 1984 prices)

Calculations from Business Monitor Series; Overseas Travel and Tourism
Source: International Passenger Survey; adults and children resident abroad

4

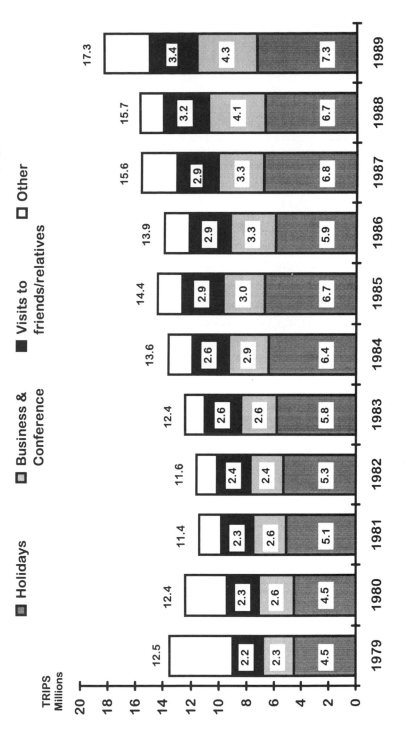

Figure 1.2: Numbers of Visitors to the UK from Overseas 1979-1989

This chart shows the number of visits to the UK, in millions, in total and for each main purpose.

Holidays

Business & Conference

Visits to friends/relatives

Other

TRIPS Millions

Totals from Business Monitor Series (HMSO)
Source: International Passenger Survey; adults and children resident abroad

5

limited number of very large companies, such as British Airways or American Express, with many thousands on their payrolls.

To sum up, the tourist industry is a complex one and contains many small businesses; it is one of, if not **the,** world's major industries. In Britain earnings from tourism through spending by overseas visitors rose from £95 million in 1954 to £190 million in 1964; rose steadily again to over £900 million in 1974; and rose again to over £9 billion in 1993. (BTA *Annual Reports*)

Domestic Tourism
Although we tend to think of travel and tourism in terms of holidays and travel abroad, there is a major and growing domestic industry in the UK catering for both overseas visitors to Britain and to British nationals on holiday, as well as day visitors to tourist areas within the UK. Domestic tourism has grown significantly over the past 10 years, from 114 million visits in 1984 to 141 million in 1994 (BTA 1995), though again with some peaks and troughs. Earnings from domestic tourism grew from £1.8 billion in 1984 to over £8.4 billion in 1994 (ETB 1995).

For British holidaymakers staying in the, UK the seaside has remained the main attraction over the past 30 years, and about two-thirds of domestic holidays are still taken at the seaside (BTA). However, the nature, timing and duration of these domestic holidays has changed, as Chapter 2 outlines.

For overseas visitors, the UK holiday is often part of a larger 'package' tour covering several destinations in Europe. The UK travel and tourism industry is catering for a largely affluent clientele who are attracted to a limited number of tourist destinations and who are primarily in Britain for sight-seeing and visiting cultural centres. For example, such overseas visitors would concentrate on an itinerary that covered London – Oxford – Stratford – Chester – Lake District, and perhaps would visit Scotland and return via the east coast taking in York and Cambridge on their return leg to London. The English Tourist Board and the regional boards, as well as many local authorities, all help to promote domestic tourism. In this context it is typically the mixed economy in action. The 'industry' which is largely made up of firms in the private sector, relies for much of its promotion and marketing activity on these public sector organisations. This particular issue is covered at greater length in Chapters 8 and 10.

In 1993 19.2 million overseas visitors came to Britain and amongst them spent £9.26 billion in Britain. As Table 1.1 shows, the USA provides the greatest number of overseas visitors from a single country, closely followed by France and Germany. (BTA 1994)

In 1993 British holiday-makers in Britain spent over £12 billion and made a total of over 90 million trips. (ETB 1994) The pattern of visits was much the same as in recent years with just under half being spent at the seaside, over one fifth in the countryside and the remainder in towns and cities. The pattern of visits was much the same in that holidays accounted for 47 per cent of all visits, business travel for 21 per cent and visit to friends and relatives 20 per cent. The main impetus to encourage the growth of the domestic tourist industry came in 1969 with *The Development of Tourism Act* which set up the British Tourist Authority and Tourist Boards for England, Scotland and Wales, with the responsibility for promoting the development of tourism to and within Great Britain. The consequences of this Act and the role of these boards are discussed at greater length in Chapters 3 and 9 of this book, but the significance here is that, for the first time, the government of the day recognised the importance of the domestic tourist industry, and its contribution both to employment and the balance of payments.

International Tourism
This refers to travel across national boundaries and may involve visits to one or several other countries. If we analyse the pattern of tourist flows on a world scale, it is clear that the industry is a major economic activity. International travel arrivals amount to over 500 million and world spending for international travel amounts to over $300 billion. (WTO 1994) In the developing countries, international tourism accounts for about one-third of their service trade. It is one of the fasting growing industries in the world and between 1974 and 1980 international tourism trade grew faster than world trade generally. Between 1961 and 1981 the world total of international tourism arrivals quadrupled. However, although the rate of growth of

international tourism has been dramatic, the potential for growth is still substantial. The reason for this is that most of this activity in recent decades has been confined to Europe, which accounts for 61 per cent of international tourism arrivals, and the Americas which account for 22 per cent of arrivals. The rest of the world accounts for less than 20 per cent of arrivals. Chapter 4 discusses in much greater detail the recent trends in international tourism and developments in world travel over the past decade.

Table 1.1: Overseas Visitors to UK: numbers (by market countries/areas) 1979 to 1989

Year	North America	Western Europe EEC	Other	All Countries
1979	2,196	6,605	3,685	12,486
1980	2,082	6,755	3,584	12,421
1981	2,105	6,021	3,325	11,452
1982	2,135	6,054	3,446	11,636
1983	2,836	6,078	3,550	12,464
1984	3,330	6,292	4,022	13,644
1985	3,797	6,557	4,095	14,449
1986	2,843	6,941	4,112	13,897
1987	3,394	7,731	4,445	15,566
1988	3,272	8,148	4,380	15,799
1989	3,481	8,960	4,896	17,338

Source: *International Passenger Survey*

The development of international tourism has produced two types of country – the generating country who provides the tourist, and the receiving country who attract and play host to the tourist. A few countries, such as Britain, fall into both categories, but most are either one type or the other. Generally, the tourist generating countries are those with advanced economies, high standards of living, available disposable income, greater spending power and a general system of paid annual holidays. The most important tourist generating countries are the United States, West Germany, Japan and the United Kingdom. The host countries have a low cost of living, attractive scenery and climate, are usually readily accessible and have a good public image. Over the past 20 years as the host countries such as Spain, Italy and Greece have developed their tourist industry, so the beaches and main resort areas have grown, to the extent that often they reach saturation point, and face competition from developing countries which are turning to tourism as a major source of income. Recent years have seen the development of new tourist areas outside of Europe with lower price levels and less tourist saturation.

Given that international tourism is the largest single item in foreign trade, the balance of trade between tourism generating and receiving countries can be a significant element in encouraging economic development. Table 1.2 shows international tourist receipts and expenditures, based on figures supplied by the Organisation for Economic Co-operation and Development (OECD). In Europe, Austria, France, Greece, Italy and Spain all have net surpluses in their balances of payments, while Germany, the Netherlands, Belgium and the Scandinavian countries have the most marked deficits. Outside of Europe, Japan has the most substantial net deficit and North America has a marked imbalance in its tourist trade. Tourism should be regarded as a trade product in that all countries can use the income from international tourism to create new jobs and to buy additional goods and services which they otherwise might not be able to afford. In Britain the tourist industry, unlike some other industries, has stood up well to the world recession and has, not only maintained, but improved its position as a major earner of foreign currency for the UK. In 1993 Britain received over 19.2 million overseas visitors and they generated foreign currency earnings, including fares paid to British carriers on travel tourism from Britain, which amounted to over £9 billion. (ETB 1994) One good example of how trade follows tourism can be seen by foreign visitor spending in British shops. These 19 million visitors are potentially additional customers for British shops, and visitor spending on footwear and textiles amounts to over £600 million each year, which is equal to almost half of all British footwear and textile exports.

9

Table 1.2: Trends in International Tourist Receipts in Real Prices

	1987 = 100					Relative share in percentage of total	
	1988	1989	1990	1991	1992	1991	1992
Austria	109.0	121.0	126.0	130.3	125.3	7.6	7.0
Belgium-Luxembourg	111.2	103.7	102.0	99.2	101.7	2.0	1.9
Denmark	102.5	101.5	120.1	126.4	127.3	1.8	1.8
Finland	107.5	106.7	103.2	106.9	122.8	0.6	0.6
France	112.1	136.8	140.3	149.2	160.4	11.7	12.0
Germany [5]	106.2	111.8	114.1	112.0	107.1	5.7	5.2
Greece	101.9	84.2	87.6	72.7	95.6	1.1	1.3
Iceland	115.1	125.1	142.9	132.6	117.5	0.1	0.1
Ireland	113.6	125.9	141.2	146.8	143.9	0.8	0.8
Italy [4]	97.4	93.2	126.3	114.6	126.0	9.2	9.6
Netherlands	103.0	116.2	115.2	134.8	148.5	2.4	2.5
Norway	106.2	98.0	98.6	106.1	118.3	0.9	0.9
Portugal	105.9	114.4	119.5	115.2	97.2	1.6	1.3
Spain	101.6	94.1	86.1	86.2	86.7	8.4	8.1
Sweden	105.3	112.7	106.7	94.0	98.6	1.3	1.3
Switzerland	102.6	108.4	106.5	107.4	110.8	3.8	3.8
Turkey	133.4	126.4	124.7	95.2	126.4	1.1	1.4
United Kingdom	95.3	98.4	101.0	91.1	90.6	6.1	5.8
EUROPE [1]	104.3	108.0	113.1	111.4	115.3	66.1	65.3
Canada	104.5	104.3	108.9	106.2	107.1	2.8	2.7
United States	121.2	141.2	159.0	171.6	185.4	26.6	27.4
NORTH AMERICA	118.8	135.9	151.8	162.2	174.1	29.3	30.1
Australia [3]	129.3	113.0	124.2	130.1	144.9	1.8	2.0
New Zealand [2]	163.6	155.3	165.4	165.3	171.0	0.8	0.8
Japan	123.2	141.4	163.3	141.0	136.3	1.9	1.8
AUSTRALASIA-JAPAN [1]	132.1	131.3	146.8	140.1	145.3	4.6	4.6
OECD [1]	108.7	115.2	123.1	123.9	129.7	100.0	100.0

1. After correcting for the effects of inflation in each country. For the regional and OECD totals, the receipts of the individual countries are weighted in proportion to their share in the total expressed in dollars.
2. Changes of series in 1986 and 1987.
3. Change of statistical coverage in 1987.
4. Break of series in 1990 due to the liberalisation of capital movements.
5. The data relate to the territory of the Federal Republic of Germany prior to 3rd October 1990. Since July 1990, data include all transactions of the former German Democratic Republic with foreign countries.

Source: OECD Reports

10

Data Sources on Tourism

Clearly, the movement of people between countries and within countries generates a demand for tourism, which consists of a range of goods and services provided by both the public and private sector. The income from the sale or purchase of these goods and services may be a major source of foreign or domestic revenue. When many industries or economic activities are examined, detailed statistical data are available on the production, export and import of hundreds of physical goods, often on a monthly basis. Yet data on tourism are scarce, often unreliable and not consistently compiled. Part of the reason for this is the substantial time lag which exists between the initial expansion of a sector and the collection of adequate data for that sector. For example it was not until well into this century that detailed statistics on manufacturing industries became available in many developed countries, although the industrial revolution had transformed the manufacturing sector during the 19th century.

Obtaining reliable detailed and accurate information is an essential part of research connected with tourism. Research is becoming increasingly important so that tourist boards and firms can identify new markets and determine what their customers want, both now and in the future. Given the importance of tourism as both a source of income and employment, it is clear that the public and private sector need to have detailed statistics on many aspects of tourism. For example, national governments collect data on tourist arrivals, countries of origin, visitor spending, mode of travel, purpose of visit and length of stay. All of this data analysed over time is used to provide forecasts concerning the growth or decline of the tourist industry. It is also important for firms to be able to plan their marketing strategies and to measure the effectiveness of their existing policies and products.

International Tourism Surveys: The main sources of data on international tourist flows and the characteristics of international tourism are the annual reports of the World Tourism Organisation (WTO) and those produced by the Organisation for Economic Co-operation and Development (OECD), as well as detailed reports published by the Economist Intelligence Unit (Travel and Tourism Analyst).

Figure 1.3: Employment Related to Tourism and Leisure

(Figures include restaurants, pubs, nightclubs, hotels and other tourist accommodation as well as libraries, museums and sports facilities)

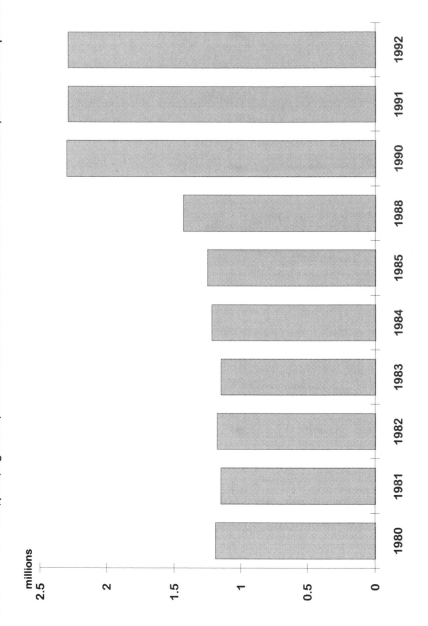

The Purpose, Scope and Function of this Book

The National Council for Vocational Qualifications has now issued details of mandatory units and core skills units for general national vocational qualifications offered by BTEC, City & Guilds and RSA examination boards. For students who are not taking this route and are perhaps studying tourism at HND or degree level this may be the first time they are dealing with this subject as part of the curriculum. The overall aim of this book is to provide a broad understanding of tourism studies and the travel and tourism industry. It is intended to provide a clear insight into the operations and characteristics of the tourist industry, and the role of the private and public sector in developing tourism, both in the UK and on the international scene. It is largely based on examples drawn from British experience, although where possible material from a range of international sources is used, because clearly tourism is essentially a world-wide phenomenon.

In order to provide a sound base for understanding tourism, it is not sufficient to concentrate solely on business skills in the private sector or on planning and administration in the public sector. For this reason the book does not focus on specific disciplines such as Business Studies, Law, Geography: subject areas play a supporting role. The focus is on tourism. The purpose of this book is to highlight the interactions between the different sectors of the travel and tourism industry and between components of the product consumed by tourists. This book therefore focuses on five main themes:

- The study of tourism and its social, economic and environmental components.

- Providing an understanding of the operation of the private and public sector of the travel and tourism industry, and the way they interact.

- The factors that motivate tourists and that influence the tourist market.

- The impact of tourism on the economy and on the environment.

- New and emerging forms of tourism, particularly since the mid 1980s.

ASSIGNMENTS

1. Using visitor surveys, reports and annual statistics, investigate the changes in the patterns of international and domestic tourism between 1974 and 1994 as they affect the UK.

2. You are employed by a national tourist office to produce a 750 word entry into a major tourism periodical. The task will, therefore, require you to include within your copy the following information:

   (a) main resorts/visitor attractions;

   (b) transport provision;

   (c) amenity/entertainment;

   (d) assessment of market;

   (e) other factors, including climate.

   You will be assessed according to the effectiveness of the 'copy' that you produce and the quality of examples that you use in your entry.

Chapter 2

The Development of the Tourist Industry

Learning Objectives:
After reading this Chapter and some of the references contained within it, you should understand how the industry has grown and developed; the form that the early tourist industry took; and the trends in travel and tourism in Britain since 1945.

Introduction
Throughout the ages man has travelled in search of new places, new lands, new cultures and experiences. History offers many examples, from Greek and Roman literature to Marco Polo, or Chaucer's pilgrims who were familiar with the famous shrines of Europe. For hundreds of years travel for the sake of pleasure was the prerogative of the rich, because those who travelled needed an income to free their time for such purposes. For the majority of the population of Britain and Europe the feast days of the Church, i.e. holy-days, were their only break from work. Only those who were educated and prosperous and aware of foreign places engaged in such travel. It was only through trade or wars that most people visited distant places. Maps were crude or non-existent. Roads were bad, and risks abounded. Even in the late nineteenth century Robert Louis Stephenson commented on travelling in central France:

> *A traveller of my sort was a thing hitherto unheard of in that district. I was looked on with contempt, like a man who should project a journey to the moon, yet with a respectful interest, like one setting forth for the inclement Pole.*

The Development of Mass Tourism
What changed this pattern? How did tourism, once the exclusive activity of the rich and well to-do, become an accepted part of life for the ordinary man and woman? To find the answer to these questions we must consider the requirements for travel and tourism. First, people must

have the free time available and second, they must have the disposable income to spend. Thirdly, travel must be safe, reliable and relatively cheap. There must be attractions which travellers know of and which they wish to visit, and a range of amenities, especially accommodation, must be available. All of these conditions need to exist if mass tourism is to develop.

The Industrial Revolution from the mid-eighteenth century was the catalyst which brought all these conditions into being. Scientific inventions, new industrial processes and new methods of production of manufactured goods changed society, first in Britain and then in America and Europe. An agricultural revolution formed part of this dynamic change, improving the productivity of crops and animal husbandry and providing new wealth for industrial development. With the development of the steam engine and coal as a source of power, new manufacturing districts grew up on the coalfields of the north and midlands of England and central Scotland. The application of coal and coke to smelting iron, and later steel, accelerated this process. The reduction in the death rate through medical and public health improvements led to a steady growth in the population of England and Wales, from 5½ millions in 1702 to 9 millions in 1801.

The Growth of Spas as Resort Towns
During the eighteenth century spa towns in England developed as places of resort for the rich and well to do, their seal of approval usually being a Royal visit. Conventional medicine vouched for the curative properties of their mineral waters, which though brackish and often foul-smelling, were drunk as well as bathed in. Bath is the best known of these, with a reputation dating from Roman times.

The visits to Bath by King William in 1695 and Queen Anne in 1702 and 1703 set the seal on this as a fashionable place of resort. The town hired Beau Nash in 1705 to provide a range of entertainments during the 'season', although he also ensured that the city developed good roads, good accommodation for the visitor and set an example that many other towns were to copy. The medicinal reputation of the mineral waters was of prime importance for would-be spas and the distribution of mineral springs was therefore the earliest locational influence on these centres. Thus, Scarborough developed as a spa town from 1627 (Lennard, 1931), and it was not until much later that its seaside location was to influence its long-term development as a resort.

The growth and spread of wealth among society encouraged more people to follow the fashion for taking mineral waters. By the mid-eighteenth century there were many spas, often of a purely local reputation, ranging from Bath at the height of fashion and the social scene, to Buxton, Leamington, Tunbridge Wells, Malvern and Gilsland. Epsom in fact came into being as a spa, and thereafter developed as a venue for horse racing with the Derby and the Oaks. By 1733 it was reported that the season at Scarborough had attracted almost one thousand of the nobility and the gentry. (Smollett, *Humphrey Clinker*). It was clear that by the mid-eighteenth century the now fashionable nature of this 'season' was an indication that the function of the larger spa towns was changing from that of a purely health resort to an important social centre, where the leisured classes could spend their time.

During the second part of the eighteenth century, there was a growth in small seaside 'watering places'. Sea bathing is depicted in an engraving of the South Bay, Scarborough (1735) and this print is the earliest record of bathing machines being used. In the eighteenth century sea bathing was recommended for gout and the medicinal value of sea water was given an added impetus by the publication of a *Dissertation concerning the Uses of Sea Water in Diseases of the Glands* by Dr Russel in 1753. The learned doctor also lived in Brighton and his advocacy of the virtues of sea water no doubt encouraged the growth of that resort. The arrival of the Prince of Wales in 1784 accelerated the growth of the town as a fashionable resort, just as royal visits to Bath had some eighty years earlier. In 1760 Brighton consisted of a large village with a population of 2,000. By 1820 it had over three thousand houses, a population of over 24,000 and more than 10,000 visitors a year. During the late-eighteenth century many other coastal towns realised the potential of their seaside location and Lewis' *Topographical Dictionary* of 1835 lists dozens of former hamlets and small fishing villages, from Bognor Regis to Rhyl, that were transformed as seaside watering places.

Figure 2.1: Sketch Diagram of a Typical Seaside Resort

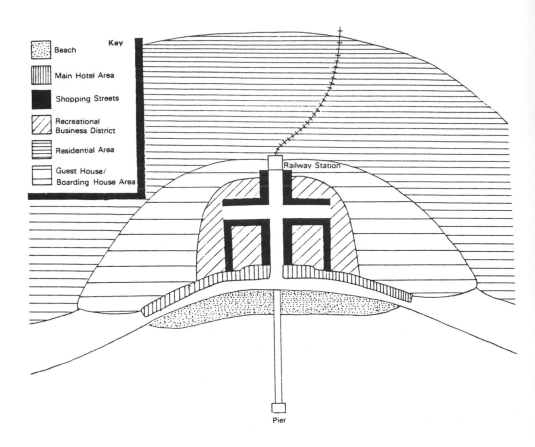

Key

Beach

Main Hotel Area

Shopping Streets

Recreational
Business District

Residential Area

Guest House/
Boarding House Area

Railway Station

Pier

Travel was still restricted to coach or horseback and most of these resorts were one or two days' journey from the major towns and cities. They were still resorts for a very limited section of society. To most of the working population they were remote and unknown places. The development of paddle steamers on the Thames in the early nineteenth century made the Kent coast resorts easily accessible to London for the first time. Almost 100,000 people were landed from London steamers on Margate pier in 1830. (Patmore, 1972).

18

Figure 2.2: Origin of Visitors Resident in Keswick August Bank Holiday Week 1877

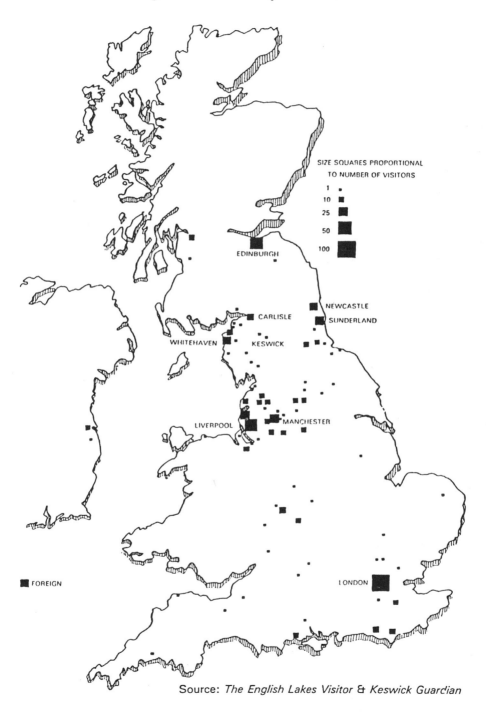

Source: *The English Lakes Visitor & Keswick Guardian*

The diffusion of wealth from the industrial and agricultural revolution brought more spending power to more of the population. In Britain the enclosure of agricultural land, and the growth of industrial towns, saw a mass migration from the countryside to the cities. At the end of the eighteenth century, the population of England and Wales was 9 million. In 1851 it was 22 million and by 1901 had grown to 38 million. During this period, the system of production changed from hand crafts to machine crafts; from small into large factories, with the workers housed in nearby housing developments; and by the mid-nineteenth century, over half of the population lived in the major towns.

The Growth of Seaside Resorts in Victorian England

The transport system was transformed by the invention of the railway and its spread throughout Britain between 1832 and 1870. For the first time, fast, cheap and readily accessible passenger transport was available to most of the country's population. Enterprising developers and railway companies promoted links between the growing industrial cities and the coastal resorts and, with improved accessibility, these prospered and rapidly grew in size. For example, the London, Tilbury and Southend Railway was opened and the population of the resort grew from 4,000 to 20,000 in 1901. Its present day population is over 150,000 and it receives over 6 million visitors a year, many of them still day trippers from London. The same pattern occurred at Brighton, Southport, Blackpool and many other, now familiar, coastal resorts. For example Brighton's population grew from 24,000 in 1820 to 99,000 in 1881 with the most rapid growth following the opening of the main London to Brighton line in 1841.

For the Victorian masses day excursions were the norm, rather than long holidays, although the diffusion of wealth and the growth of a middle class anxious to escape for a time from the industrial towns and cities introduced a wider spectrum of people to these resorts. This, in turn, led to a wider range of accommodation and amenities being offered.

Similarly in Europe once the railways linked the expanding industrial cities with the Mediterranean coast of France and Italy, the select resorts of the upper classes were newly discovered by the growing middle classes anxious to emulate aristocratic fashions. In 1865 the railway arrived at Nice, and two years later at Menton (Burnet, 1963) leading, in the period from 1865 to 1914, to the appearance of a number of thriving resorts along the Riviera coast which transformed it into the premier holiday region of France.

Some resorts had originally developed piers to accommodate visitors arriving by paddle steamer, but the practice of taking the sea air for health and relaxation, encouraged many resorts to build one, if not more, piers. The form and layout of most seaside resorts reflects both their development during the railway age and the strong attraction of the sea front. Most expanded parallel to the sea front with relatively little development inland. The main beach or promenade took over and copied the earlier spa promenade, replacing the pump room as a focus of social life. Having arrived by train for a day visit or longer stay, the resort was the self-contained provider of all the visitor's needs, from accommodation to entertainment. Most of the land and buildings associated with the tourism industry are located in a zone between the railway station and the sea front, with the prime frontal locations usually occupied in almost unbroken succession by the larger hotels. This pattern still persists today.

During the period between 1740 and 1840, the Lake District had been 'discovered' and, due largely to the accounts of eighteenth century travellers and poets, an appreciation of the 'wild' scenery of the area became fashionable. Within Britain it was in the Lake District more than anywhere else that the idea of a touring holiday developed. As early as 1793 it was reported that the number of strangers making the tour of the Lakes who frequented Keswick, 'amounted to no less than 1,540'. (Brittain, 1802).

On the 5th July 1841 Thomas Cook organised his first rail excursion for one shilling return, and by the 1870s all the railway companies ran regular cheap day excursions to the seaside. In 1871 the Bank Holiday Act provided four public holidays a year and, after this date, the extended family holiday at the seaside became more common.

The early attraction of the Alpine resorts as part of the eighteenth century Grand Tour, and the growth of winter sports and mountaineering in the late nineteenth century, led to the spread of winter sports resorts in the Alpine districts of France, Switzerland, Italy and Austria. (Defert, 1958).

The appearance of a large middle class with the Industrial Revolution in Britain also provided a supply of potential tourists who were predominant in nineteenth century Europe. Cross channel traffic increased from 100,000 per annum in the 1830s to over 500,000 per annum in the 1890s. The major tourist countries of Europe had an unprecedented boom in the 1920s when France, Switzerland and Italy each received well over 1 million visitors (Lickorish, 1958). By 1930 over 1,500,000 British travelled to the Continent.

Mass Tourism
At the beginning of this chapter time and money were mentioned as constraints on participation in tourism. By the beginning of the twentieth century most people still had limited opportunities for tourism and the factory system allowed few days off outside the statutory holidays.

During the 1920s and 1930s holidays with pay became more common and in 1925 the Ministry of Labour estimated that 1½ million manual workers received holidays with pay. In 1938 the Holidays with Pay Act gave a new stimulus to mass tourism, and by June 1939 over 11 million workers received holidays with pay (Brunner, 1945) and almost one person in three went away from home for a holiday. By 1945 80 per cent of the workforce received holidays with pay. (Patmore, 1972).

New types of holiday were developed in inter-war Britain, among them camping and youth hostelling. Membership of the YHA rose from 6,439 in 1931 to 83,418 in 1939. The membership of the Camping Club of Great Britain rose from 3,000 in 1933 to 7,000 in 1935. In 1937 Billy Butlin promoted the first holiday camp at Skegness and, by 1939, there were 200 such camps scattered around the coasts of Britain catering for 30,000 holidaymakers a week during the season. (Brunner, 1945). Thus, during the 1930s, through the holidays with pay movement, tourism no longer remained the preserve of the rich and well-to-do. It became an accepted activity for the majority of Britain's population.

The years following the Second World War saw a gradual growth in tourist activity. The geographic scale of the War had broken down international barriers and introduced great social changes. Those returning from the War expected greater opportunities, better living standards and more activity in their lives. This was to affect the scale of both domestic and international tourism.

Post-1945 Domestic Tourism
There was no sudden dramatic change in the pattern of domestic tourism, although the numbers spending a holiday away from home continued to increase as the population of Britain grew and more of the workforce had holidays with pay. There was little change in the pattern of tourist destinations. More than two thirds of all main holidays were taken at the seaside. Holiday camps were replacing the traditional resort as a basis for a self-contained 'package' catering for all the visitors' needs. Public transport was still popular in 1951 and only 25 per cent travelled by car. The Festival of Britain in 1951 and the Coronation of Elizabeth the Second in 1953 gave an impetus to the development of new tourist facilities. The Government introduced a grant scheme to provide financial help (albeit limited) to hotels catering for overseas visitors and in the 1956 Distribution of Industry Act, which gave the Treasury powers to make loans or grants in areas of high unemployment, hotels were included for the first time. It was during this period of the mid to late 1950s that the then British Travel Association attempted to encourage holidays in Britain with a co-operative scheme in which the British resorts and industry took part. This was designed to extend the holiday season and to encourage more people to visit Britain's holiday resorts.

The number of visitors to Britain from overseas also grew rapidly during the 1950s from 203,000 in 1946 to 1.7 million in 1960. Initially 69 per cent of these foreign visitors arrived by sea and 31 per cent by air. But the dramatic growth in air travel during the 1960s reversed these figures. From the development of holidays with pay in the 1930s to the growth of overseas visitors during the 1950s and 1960s, the domestic tourist industry came of age. Within the space of thirty years there emerged a major industry employing hundreds of thousands of people and producing many millions of pounds for the national economy. It is a very large and complex industry often with linkages between hotel groups, travel companies, transport operators, promotional agencies and tourist boards.

Figure 2.3: Overseas Visitors to United Kingdom 1946 – 1970

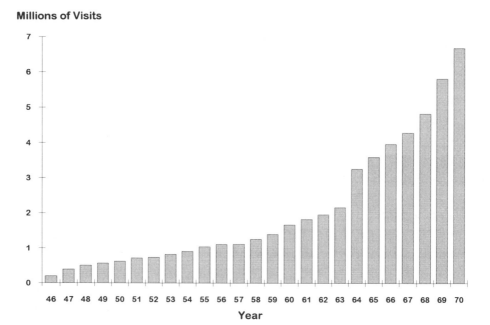

Millions of Visits

Year

Foreign Tourism
Until the late 1950s the bulk of the British took their main holiday in the UK, often at a seaside resort, and usually during July and August. There had been little change in the nature of the holiday destination for over 100 years. In 1951 only 1½ million out of a total population of 50 million Britons chose to go abroad for their holidays, (British Travel Association, 1970) spending £60 million in the process.

By 1970 5.75 million Britons took their holidays abroad spending £470 million. Over 25 per cent of these holidaymakers were aged between 16 and 24. In 1950 France was the most popular holiday destination, attracting 40 per cent of the Britons taking foreign holidays. The most dramatic change during this period was the tremendous growth in the popularity of Spain. Of the 5.75 million Britons taking foreign holidays in 1970, nearly one-third went to Spain.

What brought about this dramatic growth in foreign holidays? The immediate post war years were a period when there were many surplus aircraft and highly trained aircrews who wished to continue flying in civilian life.

Technological improvements in aircraft and engine design during the 1950s helped to reduce the relative cost of air travel. The cost of travel to a foreign country is a key element in its attractiveness as a holiday destination, together with the level of accommodation and general living costs that exist there. Between 1950 and 1968 the cost of a high season return from London to New York almost halved in price, and almost every route operated showed a marked reduction in the cost of air travel during this 18-year period.

To have the means to travel is not enough. There needs to be enough air services between the tourist generating countries (such as Britain) and the tourist receiving countries (such as Spain or Italy) to meet the peak season travel demands. Two trends emerged during this period. First, average aircraft seating capacity almost doubled for intra-European flights and almost trebled for transatlantic routes. Second, in Britain private airline companies were allowed by the Government to develop and to set up in competition with the State airlines. By the early 1960s the potential airline traveller to Spain or Greece, for example, could travel as an independent passenger on a scheduled or chartered flight as part of an inclusive group tour, or as an inclusive tour passenger on a scheduled flight in the mid and late 1950s.

It was the development of chartered flights which transformed the pattern of annual holidays for millions of British tourists. Foreign travel, for so long the prerogative of the rich, became easily accessible to the general population. In the early 1950s tour operators began to market package tours to the Continent linking up with private airlines such as Laker Airways and, by the early 1960s, Spain and the Mediterranean were being promoted and developed as holiday destinations for millions of Britons. The tour operators for the first time put together a foreign holiday 'package' covering travel, accommodation, meals and sometimes other items at an inclusive price. By chartering aircraft and filling every seat, the operator could keep travel costs down and, by making block bookings in particular hotels, could also provide accommodation at competitive prices. During the 1960s extensive tracts of the Costa Brava and Costa Blanca in Spain, and in the 1970s the Languedoc-Rousillon coast, were developed to meet this tourist boom. Today there are many kinds of holiday package and as many different holiday destinations. The sun, sea and sand package of the summer months is replaced by the sun, snow and skiing package over the Christmas – Winter period.

Throughout the 1960s to the 1980s individual income levels continued to grow and levels of car ownership in Britain grew from 2 million in 1950 to 17.7 million in 1981. By 1980 39 per cent of overseas travel to Western Europe used the Channel ferries – much of this traffic being private cars. The escalation in petrol prices, following the 1973 Arab-Israeli conflict, caused a temporary downturn in this trend, but by the early 1980s the number of Britons taking their cars on Continental holidays was again increasing. The development of motorway links to the Channel ports in Britain and similar improvements on the autoroutes in France, Belgium and Holland brought many more European resorts within driving distance from Britain, and this too – together with the easing of EEC frontier controls – made foreign travel much easier and attractive.

Even the recession from the late 1970s has failed to halt the demand for foreign holidays. In 1982, despite massive growth in unemployment, 8 per cent more Britons travelled abroad and spent 20 per cent more. (TAC *Anatomy of UK Tourism*).

In Britain the Government took the first steps to a national policy for tourism with the Development of Tourism Act in 1969. It established a British Tourist Authority, English, Scottish and Wales Tourist Boards with powers to provide loans and grants for hotel development schemes; to encourage the provision and improvement of tourist amenities and facilities; and to promote Britain as a tourist destination for overseas visitors. The results of this Act and the development of public sector tourism in Britain are discussed at greater length in Chapter 8. Its importance in this context is that, by the 1970s, the Government recognised the growing importance of the tourist industry, both as an employer of labour and as a major contributor to the national economy.

Other trends in tourism are beginning to emerge as new fashions and new holiday concepts appear. Time-sharing, villa holidays, Club 18 to 30, golfing holidays, trips to China, India or the West Indies, all highlight the importance of travel in our lives and the inventiveness of companies to develop and market new types of holiday product. These developments are discussed in Chapter 14.

The final chapter of this book looks at (in some detail) new developments that have emerged in the tourist industry over the last decade and includes activities such as timeshare, resort hotels, special interest holidays and new emerging tourist destinations. As air travel has become in real terms relatively cheaper and technology has enabled aircraft to carry more passengers at greater speeds, the world as it was in the 1960s has shrunk, and tourists will now readily contemplate trips to China or Australia or to more unique destinations in the Far East. These developments are discussed in the final chapter.

ASSIGNMENT
On the basis of tourist data showing trends in domestic and international tourism between 1950 and 1990, provide a summary of the main changes which have taken place during this period and outline the main causes of these changes in travel patterns and in tourist destinations.

Chapter 3

The Structure of the Tourist Industry in Britain

Learning Objectives:
After reading this Chapter you should understand the nature of, and linkages between, the different sectors of the tourist industry within Britain and their importance to the national economy.

Introduction
The demand for tourism, which has grown steadily over the past 45 years, is a demand for a range of goods and services which are provided by both the private and public sectors of the national economy. The private sector provides much of the accommodation and visitor attractions, the public sector provides much of the existing infrastructure, especially the transport facilities, and undertakes much of the tourism marketing activity. Within the tourist industry there is a great degree of interdependence between the private and public sectors, and the structure of the industry clearly reflects this characteristic. The tourist industry in Britain directly employs over 1.4 million people, and earns over £9 billion a year from spending by overseas visitors. Within Britain the industry serves two key markets. Firstly, it seeks to meet the needs of overseas tourists and, secondly, Britons taking a holiday within the United Kingdom (domestic tourism). Within the private sector this is also an important sector of the industry which serves to meet the needs of British holiday makers seeking holidays overseas (outgoing tourism).

The Tourism Product
The tourist product is the resort or historic town, the beaches, scenery, mountains, historic sites, theme parks, museums and other similar attractions. It is also the stock of accommodation that provides for the needs of the tourist. The difference between the tourist industry and other industries is that tourist goods and services, unlike other goods and

services, are not transported to their users but instead the users are transported to where the product exists, and production and consumption take place there. The industry consists of three main sectors:

1.   Suppliers of Tourist Services, Facilities and Attractions
There are five main types of activity within this general classification. These include accommodation, restaurants and cafes, conference facilities, passenger transport, car hire, motoring organisations, and tourist attractions and entertainment.   Between them these activities employ over 200,000 people with accommodation and catering being the dominant sectors. The firms involved in these activities are often small in size and are usually private companies, although some of the tourist attractions and transport facilities are in the quasi-public sector.

The main occupations in the tourist services sector are:

Service Staff in Hotels and Guest Houses
These consist of waiters and waitresses, chambermaids, porters and bar staff, and together they account for about 65,000 jobs in the UK domestic tourist industry. Traditionally much of this work force is seasonal and there is a substantial movement between jobs.

Managers In Hotels
There are about 50,000 general managers throughout the UK, many being working owners of small hotels and guest houses. Of these about 7,000 are front-of-house or specialist managers, usually employed by the larger hotel chains. The accommodation sector has been expanding steadily over the last 15 years, in line with the development of the tourist industry and the increase in conference business in the main resorts. (Chapter 7 examines the accommodation sector in more detail and discusses recent developments).

Travel Agency Staff
Counter and reservations staff in travel agencies are mainly employed by high street retail travel agencies, and this sector of the market is growing as some companies, such as Thomas Cook, increase the number of their high street branches. Currently about 14,000 people are employed in this

sector. In addition about 2,000 to 2,500 management jobs exist in the travel agency/tour operations business in the UK.

Tourist Attractions

There are over 50,000 people working in a wide variety of tourist attractions in Britain, ranging from seaside amusement arcades and shows to stately homes, museums and galleries and theme parks. Some of these, especially those located in seaside resorts, are seasonal whilst others may be open all year, attracting local people on day or half-day visits as well as touring visitors.

2. Travel Operations Staff

This covers British Rail, cross-Channel ferry operators and the airlines who deal with both domestic tourism and outgoing tourism. The airlines experienced a period of steady expansion during the 1970s and 1980s reflecting the overall growth in tourist travelling by air, and the increasing use of air charters, especially from the regional airports. The British airlines and overseas carriers employ over 4,000 managers in the UK and overall about 60,000 people are employed by the major airlines.

The ferry operations also saw a growth in traffic during this period and in the late 1970s some newcomers came on the scene, such as Sally Lines (from Ramsgate) and Olau Line (from Sheerness).

About 10,000 people are employed in the passenger management services, with about 4,000 stewards and attendants.

About 6,000 people are involved in coach tour operations, mainly in small firms with less than 30 employees. De-regulation of the coach industry in the autumn of 1986 provided new opportunities for expansion of coach touring and opened up more routes for competition. (Chapter 6 provides an overview of recent developments in the passenger transport sector).

3. Destination Management and Administration

It is an interesting aspect of the tourist industry in that, although it consists mainly of private sector firms and organisations, much of the promotional work for the tourist destinations within the UK is done by public sector bodies. In 1969, following *The Development of Tourism Act*, a British Tourist Authority was established together with three boards responsible for England, Scotland and Wales. (This Act and subsequent developments are discussed more fully in Chapter 8). There has also been a growth in tourism promotion at local authority level, and not just in the main seaside resorts. Many towns in holiday areas now operate tourist information centres and have an interest in tourism because of its job creation potential. There are now over 1000 staff in management positions in these organisations. In addition, there are now over 700 Tourist Information Centres (TIC's) in the UK and over 1000 people are employed in clerical and administrative jobs in this sector of the industry.

Very often the destination organisation (especially the National and Regional Tourist Boards) will have commercial members, who provide an important source of revenue income, supplementing that received directly from central government. It is notable that in recent years the governmental contribution towards tourism promotion and development has been steadily reduced, with a view from central government that the private sector ought to become more involved in tourist promotion and development generally.

Trade/Professional Organisations
A variety of organisations have evolved to represent the many different interests which make up the tourist industry. They are mainly organised on a sectoral basis, for example, covering the hotel sector, there are the Hotel, Catering and Institutional Management Association (HCIMA), the British Hotels Restaurants and Caterers Association and, covering travel, there are the Chartered Institute of Transport (CIT), the Institute of Travel and Tourism (ITT) and the Association of British Travel Agents (ABTA). In some tourist regions groups of tourist attractions have combined forces to market their product collectively. For example, in Cornwall 24 centres have formed the Cornwall Association of Tourist Attractions.

The general aim of these bodies is to represent the particular interests of their members, to promote certain standards of service and to act as a lobby to government.

Some professional organisations, such as the HCIMA, ABTA and the ITT (Institute of Travel and Tourism) are concerned about education and training for the industry, and the provision of a suitable range of courses to meet the industry's needs. Other important groups include BITOA (British Incoming Tour Operators Association), CAA (Civil Aviation Authority) and TOSG (Tour Operators Study Group).

However each of these bodies represents an individual sector of the industry and no single organisation exists to speak for the interests of the industry as a whole. Even the professional associations are mainly concerned with relatively narrow needs. Thus, ABTA is concerned about training for travel agency/tour operations work, HCIMA with catering and hotel or institutional management. There is a clear need for an overall body to integrate the industry and to present a single voice to central government, with a unified view of the education and training needs of the industry.

The Domestic Tourist Industry
This consists of two sets of activities:

- *Tourist arrivals in Britain:* In 1993 over 19.2 million overseas tourists came to Britain, spending over £9 billion. Between 1975 and 1995 the level of spending by foreign tourists to Britain has increased almost ten fold, from £1.25 billion to almost £10 billion.

- *Holidays by the British within the UK:* In 1993 they made over 90 million trips and spent over £12.4 billion on tourism within the UK. Over two thirds of domestic holidays were spent in the countryside or at the seaside, with the latter accounting for nearly half of all trips made.

These two elements of the domestic market have given rise to quite different holiday preferences and patterns of behaviour and, for this reason, are discussed separately. For example overseas visitors tend to concentrate on London and the immediate environs and Scotland; whilst for UK holiday makers the main domestic destination is the West Country.

Overseas Tourists

In 1993 64 per cent of overseas visitors came from European Union countries, a further 18 per cent from North America and the remainder, in approximately equal proportions, from Australia/New Zealand, Africa, and the Middle East, as well as the Far East. The main gateways for overseas visitors are the two airports close to London – Gatwick and Heathrow – and the channel ports of Dover and Folkestone. The concentration of these gateways close to London helps to enhance its position as Britain's main tourist destination for overseas visitors. In 1992 London accounted for 54 per cent of all overseas tourism to the UK.

The overseas visitors and British visitors complement each other. So the overseas visitors concentrate on London and the small number of historic towns and cities, whereas the British holiday makers taking domestic holidays still prefer to visit the seaside.

Outside of London and the South East, Scotland attracts more overseas visitors than any other tourist region, particularly North American tourists who account for about 40 per cent of overseas visitors to Scotland.

The typical overseas tourist will aim to visit several major cities in Britain, and about a third of foreign tourists come on inclusive tours. A typical inclusive tour will include several days in London with a 'milk run' which takes in Bath, Stratford on Avon, Chester, the Lake District, Edinburgh and returns by the east coast via York or Cambridge to London. About half of overseas visitors are tourists on holiday, about one-fifth are on business and one-fifth visiting friends and relations. Six out of ten arrive by air – a proportion that has remained very stable over the past decade.

The bulk of overseas visitors arrive between July and September and this seasonal concentration, together with a heavy focus of visits on London and on a small number of historic towns and cities, presents a planning problem for the national and regional tourist boards who promote Britain as a tourist destination. There is a need to market the 'shoulder months' and to promote new venues/new locations for overseas visitors, so that the peak season pressure on London's tourist resources can be eased. This will also help to spread the benefits and the income from overseas visitors to the local economy over a greater part of the year.

Figure 3.1: Destination of all Tourism Trips 1994
(Millions of Trips)

Source: British Tourist Authority, 1994

The British Tourist Authority promotes tourism to Britain from overseas and concentrates in particular on target marketing and promotional efforts aimed at, for example, the youth market, the senior citizen market and special interest markets. Over the past decade, the British Tourist Authority has increasingly undertaken joint promotional ventures with the private sector tourist industry to market Britain as a destination. This has included airlines, tour operators and hotel groups. The BTA also promotes a campaign to attract tourists over the shoulder months with its 'operation off peak', and this approach is discussed in more detail in Chapter 10 which deals with the marketing of travel and tourism.

Throughout the 1980s the total number of holidays taken by the British population increased steadily, from 46.75 million in 1982 to 53.75 million in 1992. However, this overall growth masks a slow but gradual decline in the numbers taking holidays of four nights or more in Britain, compensated by a strong growth in the numbers taking holidays abroad.

Over the past 30 years the proportion of the adult population in Britain taking holidays of at least four nights or more has remained steady at about 60 per cent, with the remaining population unable or unwilling to take such holidays. Given the static nature of the overall market, it is clear that growth can only arise from the same population taking more frequent holidays, or from growth in one sector such as foreign holidays, which will always be at the expense of the domestic market.

Outgoing Tourism
After the growth in the UK outbound market in the late 1980s, the first few years of the 1990s has seen important changes against the background of a recession in the British economy. Perhaps the most important change has been the steady swing away from organised holiday packages towards independent travel, reflecting both a dissatisfaction with a holiday package, its quality and value for money, as well as a greater preference for organising independent holidays. Outgoing tourism from the UK continued to grow during the 1980s despite the effects of the downturn in the economy. The number of trips abroad doubled from over 15 million in 1980 to over 31 million in 1990. Expenditure by UK residents on holidays abroad more than trebled over this decade.

The last 5 five years have seen some interesting trends in the UK out-bound market. Since 1991 war has broken out in the Balkans and the once thriving Yugoslav market has gone. Also tensions in the Middle East, particularly following the Gulf War, continued to affect confidence of travel. Moreover, the decline in the value of the pound after its withdrawal from the exchange rate mechanism in September 1992, caused severe problems for tour operators, with an effective 15 per cent to 20 per cent devaluation against other currencies. The most dramatic change in the UK outbound market was the sudden decline in trips to Yugoslavia, which experienced an 80 per cent drop in the volume of travel between 1987 and 1991 and which is no longer a holiday destination.

Table 3.1: Summer Holidays Abroad: Main Destinations and Changes, 1988-9
(visits abroad by UK residents; '000)

Destination	1988	1989	1991	% change 1991/88
France	3,093	4,007	4,742	53.3
Spain	4,691	4,222	3,194	-31.9
Italy	699	863	777	11.1
Greece	1,406	1,344	1,390	-1.1
Netherlands	610	671	825	35.2
Germany	779	927	974	25.0
Portugal	763	676	711	-6.8
Republic of Ireland	1,096	1,188	1,274	16.2
Gibraltar/Malta/Cyprus	534	718	618	15.7
Total	13,671	14,616	14,505	6.1
USA	849	1,121	1,158	36.4
Other[a]	3,938	3,993	3,435	-12.8
Total	18,458	19.730	19,098	3.5

[a] Includes the Middle East and other West Europe plus long haul destinations
Source: IPS

About three quarters of UK outbound travel is to the European Union countries, with France and Spain dominating the market. As table 3.1 shows, travel to France by British holiday makers increased by 39 per cent between

1987 and 1991, while travel to Spain decreased by 35 per cent during the same period. This suggests that, as there is little growth in the proportion of the total UK population taking holidays, increase in travel to a particular foreign destination is almost certainly going to be at the expense of another outbound destination. Not only do British holiday makers appear to be less inclined to visit Spain, but there was a decline in the numbers travelling to Italy, Greece and Austria during this same period. The USA saw the most dramatic growth during this period, with a 63 per cent increase in the number of UK visitors between 1987 and 1991.

Most UK holiday makers who travel to Spain, Greece and Portugal go for beach-based holidays, as do many of those who travel to France, the Netherlands and the USA. However, because of the long-haul nature of North American travel, UK holiday makers stay on average twice as long in the USA (20 days or more) compared with visits to European destinations.

Within Europe the winners appear to be France, whose market share grew by 39 per cent between 1981 and 1991, and Malta/Cyprus which saw a 10 per cent growth in market share during the same period. Evidence from the international passenger survey indicates that the British public is retreating from the traditional sun, sea and sand inclusive tour holiday, and Spain has suffered most from this change. For example, the number of UK residents taking holidays in Spain declined from 4.6 million in 1988 to 3.1 million in 1991 a drop of 32 per cent. The UK outbound market is discussed more fully in the next Chapter, International Tourism: an overview.

Distribution of the Tourist Industry in Britain
If the tourist product is the resort or the historic town or a mix of natural or man-made attractions, it follows that the industry that services this product will be concentrated in quite specific locations which are associated with tourism. From the large, brash seaside resorts, such as Blackpool or Brighton, to the quiet inland villages such as Grasmere or Bourton on the Water, they all have one feature in common – a large part of their economy is bound up with catering for and entertaining visitors.

Resorts in general are peripheral – both in Britain and in Western Europe generally – and most have a coastal location. The popularity of seaside

Figure 3.2: A Typical 'Milk Run' for Overseas Visitors

holidays in Britain, France and Spain has long established the pre-eminence of coastal towns as centres for the tourist industry. In Europe over 90 per cent of resorts have a coastal location. Added to these are two other types of resort – the capital cities such as London, Paris or Rome – whose position as centres of government, business and culture make them major attractions in their own right and secondly, towns with historic and cultural associations, such as Stratford on Avon or York, Heidleberg, or Oxford.

The traditional resort town shows a pattern of land use that is often centred on the 'resort' function of the town. Thus, the traditional seaside resort shows a pattern of land use and layout that is repeated world-wide. Buildings with a tourism function and the associated infrastructure of the resort are often concentrated in a relatively narrow sector of the town, usually along the coastal/beach front strip, particularly opposite the main pier, amusement area or casino – with a gradual decline in tourist activity away from the main centres of interest. Most seaside resorts expanded parallel to the sea front with relatively little development inland, a pattern repeated from Blackpool to Ocean City. The townscape of most resorts reflects their history of rapid development with a great influx of capital investment in the form of hotels, entertainment complexes, amusement parks, promenades and piers, all of which are so familiar to us today.

In Britain most resorts were well established by the late nineteenth century. For tourists up to the 1960s the most popular form of travel was by rail and, having arrived by train, the resort was generally a self-contained provider of all the visitor's needs from accommodation to entertainment. Tourists were not mobile and tended to spend most of their holiday within the resort. This is reflected in the layout of the seaside resort, with the railway station, the main shopping and tourist streets leading to or along the sea-front, where often there is a promenade and pier. Along this sea-front are grouped the hotels and boarding houses, shops and entertainment areas.

Although this range of land use can still be identified, the types of tourists who visit the resorts and patterns of tourism within the UK are quite different to when many of the resorts were in their heyday. Today's tourists, if they are from overseas, will be visiting several resorts, perhaps staying a short time in each, and will be highly mobile. Most domestic holiday makers arrive by car and more often tend to use resorts for short-break holidays in Spring or Autumn as a supplement to an annual holiday abroad. They have quite different wants and objectives compared with the tourist of twenty or thirty years ago. To begin with they are much more mobile, most arrive by car and are much more curious about the surrounding area, and they are generally more affluent and discriminating. Seaside resorts in general have had to adapt to this new kind of tourist, and to more fierce competition from abroad or from alternative forms of tourist destination within the UK. In response, some groups of resorts have formed consortia to market their product more effectively. One of the best known of these in the UK is the Torbay area which uses the slogan 'The English Riviera'.

Since the 1960s the UK seaside resorts have seen a decline in their share of the long-stay holiday market, due to the growth of competitive package holidays to the Mediterranean. One of the overriding issues facing many traditional resorts is that they need to invest in improving and developing their amenities and infrastructure to meet the changing needs of tourists in the 1990s and beyond. The resort authorities need to identify development opportunities; they need to consider ways and means of increasing their share of the tourist market; of attracting commercial investment and of promoting the resort as a destination. Often the key element in their development strategy is the provision of all-weather leisure attractions, such as the multi million pound Sandcastle Development in Blackpool or the International Leisure Centre in Bournemouth.

New types of tourist destination have also emerged. Some are industrial towns that have cleverly packaged their surrounding hinterland, often exploiting historical or literary associations. For example, Bradford expresses its links with the Bronte sisters, whilst South Tyneside promotes itself as 'Catherine Cookson Country'. Other attractions are based on Britain's rich and pioneering industrial heritage, such as the Ironbridge Museum at Coalbrookdale, which traces the story of iron and steel making, or the North of England Open Air Museum at Beamish.

The Beamish Museum, which covers over 300 acres, has recreated a microcosm of industrial life in north-east England as it was in the 19th century.

Since their creation in the late 1940s the 10 national parks of England and Wales have attracted growing numbers of tourists – although they often contained long-established resorts such as Keswick (Lake District), Buxton (Peak District) or Tenby (Pembrokeshire). More recently, some of the national parks have seen the growth of time-share developments – an issue discussed in more detail in Chapter 13.

There is a shortage of data for domestic tourism, and the annual reports of the OECD on *Tourism Policy and International Tourism* (OECD) indicate that among the member countries of that organisation only three, the United States, Canada and the UK, carry out annual surveys of their domestic tourist market. Most of the remaining countries either carry out periodic market research directed at the domestic industry or their major foreign market, or they undertake sectoral studies of the tourist industry, often on a one-off basis. The limitations of data on domestic tourism are particularly significant when we consider that about 90 per cent of world tourism is domestic tourism.

ASSIGNMENT

Using the standard industrial classification which is attached to census data, in your library you will find national census data for 1971 and 1991. Carry out an analysis of the changing nature of employment in the tourist industry in Britain over the past 20 years.

● What sectors of the industry have shown the greatest change?

● Explain why you think these changes have occurred in this way.

Chapter 4

International Tourism: An Overview

Learning Objectives:
After reading this Chapter and the range of source material referred to in it, and undertaking one or more of the assignments, you should understand:
- The nature and scope of international tourism;
- The distribution of international tourism;
- The factors that influence its development;
- Its importance in the world economy.

Introduction
Tourism is the largest industry in the world and, by any definition, the most international activity. International tourism, that is travel for holiday or pleasure from one country to another, is not a new phenomenon and can be traced back to Greek and Roman times. As the previous chapter has indicated, international tourism has grown rapidly through the 19th and early 20th centuries, but in terms of sheer volume of tourists travelling abroad, mass tourism is a relatively recent development which has only emerged since the late 1950s. This chapter provides a brief account of recent trends in international tourism and assesses its impact on the world's economy. It also provides an analysis of the factors that have affected, and are likely to continue to affect, the future expansion of international tourism.

Data Sources on International Tourism
The most comprehensive set of statistics on international tourism is published by the Organisation for Economic Co-operation and Development based in Paris. This organisation, which was established in 1960, represents most of the advanced industrial nations of the world and includes among its members all of the European countries, the United States, Japan, New Zealand and Australia. The OECD publishes an

annual report called *Tourism Policy and International Tourism in OECD Member Countries* and this contains a wide range of detailed returns on tourist flows and expenditure for all the OECD member states. The first half of each annual report includes a country by country update on government policy and action related to tourism. Although this OECD data provides much valuable information on international tourist flows, it must be used carefully. Each member state makes a count of all foreign visitors as they enter their country and this recorded under the 'arrivals'. If for example an English tourist is en route overland for Austria he could be recorded as an 'arrival' in France, Germany and Switzerland before he reaches his main tourist destination. So it is important to treat 'arrivals' statistics with caution. Moreover, no checks are made on the purpose of the visit, and few countries collect detailed information on the international travel patterns of their own population.

In Britain the international passenger survey is undertaken by the Office of Population Censuses and Surveys for the UK's Department of Employment, the Central Statistical Office and the Home Office. A full set of returns is published quarterly and annually in the Department of Trade and Industry's *Business Monitor Series*. The IPS produces estimates of UK residents travelling abroad and is based on a stratified random sample of passengers entering and leaving the UK on the principal air and sea routes. Normally around 160 to 170 thousand interviews are conducted annually.

Since 1947 the World Tourism Organisation has produced a year book of tourist statistics, and since 1966 the WTO has produced an *Annual Economic Review of World Tourism*. Both publications provide a valuable overview of world trends in tourism.

The Economist Intelligence Unit publishes *International Tourism Quarterly* which was renamed *International Tourism Reports* in 1986, which provides detailed country and regional profiles of tourism. The EIU also publishes a major journal *Travel and Tourism Analyst* on a bi-monthly basis. This is an invaluable source of data on international tourism and developments. Each issue contains five studies which focus on particular sectors of the industry:

- A study of transport issues.

- A study of a major out-bound market.

- A study of an individual market segment.

- Accommodation/financial services/leisure industry studies.

- A fifth study which addresses a variety of other subjects relevant to the industry.

In addition, each issue contains a database on the structure of the tourism industry in key countries and a commentary on recent developments in the industry world-wide.

One of the problems faced when dealing with international travel and tourism statistics is that there are great differences between international organisations and individual countries in the coverage and the methods of data collection. The four main international organisations dealing with the collection of travel and tourism data are the United Nations Statistical Office (UNSO), the World Tourism Organisation (WTO), the International Civil Aviation Organisation (ICAO) and the International Air Transport Association (IATA). These four bodies use six different classifications for world tourism regions. The Department of Trade and Industry in the UK groups tourism origin and destination countries into four regions, whilst the US Travel and Tourism Administration uses nine regions world-wide. This variation in systems of regionalisation means that data on tourist flows within and between regions must be treated with caution.

General Trends in International Tourism
As Table 4.1 shows, the growth in world tourist arrivals between 1950 and 1993 has been declining with each successive decade, from an annual percentage increase of 10.6 per cent in the period 1950 to 1960 to a figure of 3 per cent between 1990 and 1993. This slowing down in the rate of growth of world tourism suggests that in the near future we may well reach a point where the main tourist generating countries have reached saturation point. When this situation occurs, it is likely that National Tourist Organisations will only increase or retain their share of the world

tourism market at the expense of another tourist destination. This all points to a very fierce battle for market share among national tourist organisations over the years ahead. In 1983 receipts from international tourism amounted to over $100 billion. By 1993 this figure had trebled to just over $300 billion. Although international tourism has grown dramatically over the past thirty years, the bulk of the demand, which accounts for four fifths of the world total, is concentrated in Europe and North America. However, there has been a slight decline in their share of the world total from 82 per cent in 1980 to 76 per cent in 1992. This reflects the increasing share of tourist arrivals from developing countries each year, in particular from the Asia Pacific region whose market share has increased from 7.3 per cent in 1980 to 12.7 per cent in 1992. The East Asia/Pacific region also showed the fastest average annual rate of increase in arrivals between 1980 and 1992. (9.36 per cent)

Table 4.1: Tourist Activity Trends

	World Tourist Arrivals	
	Historical Growth rates 1950-1993	
	Annual percentage increase	Average annual percentage increase
1950-1960	174.2	10.6
1960-1970	139.2	9.1
1965-1970	46.9	8.0
1970-1980	73.6	5.7
1975-1980	29.5	5.3
1980-1990	59.3	4.8
1985-1990	39.1	6.8
1990-1993	9.1	3.0

Source: WTO 1994

The world's top tourism spenders are listed in Table 4.2. They are headed by the United States, ranked number one, followed by Germany, Japan, United Kingdom, Italy and France. Between them they account for over 50 per cent of all world tourism expenditure in 1992.

Table 4.2: World's Top Tourism Spenders

Country	Tourism Expenditure (US $million) 1992	Rank (1992)
United States	39,872	1
Germany	37,309	2
Japan	26,837	3
United Kingdom	19,831	4
Italy	16,617	5
France	13,910	6
Canada	11,265	7
Netherlands	9,330	8
Austria	8,371	9
Taiwan	7,098	10
World Total	275,911	

Source: WTO, 1994

Tourist Generating Countries

Although tourism is now a world-wide phenomenon, the main tourist generating countries are concentrated in North America and Europe. Two countries in particular, Germany and the United States, account for over 28 per cent of all world tourism spending, and about 40 per cent of tourist arrivals. Europe and North America account for 75 per cent of the entire movement of international tourist arrivals. (WTO 1995) This pattern has remained fairly constant over the past 20 years, although Japan is now becoming more important as a tourist generating country. Table 4.2, which is based on WTO statistics, emphasises the predominance of the United States and Europe on the world scene. The main tourist generating countries have five common characteristics.

- Their domestic population has the disposable income to spend on foreign holidays.
- They have a level of awareness of foreign holidays, through literature, the media and promotional campaigns.
- They have the infrastructure to package, sell and organise foreign travel.
- They have the free time to take holidays.
- Their geographical characteristics are such that they have a variety of destinations which are either in close proximity or accessible.

In the early 1990s Europe alone took up over 60 per cent of international tourist arrivals. The strength of Europe both as a generator and receiver of tourists is due to the following factors:

- More than half the population takes a period of paid holidays and leisure every year.
- European incomes are higher than incomes of many regions of the world, and there is a comparable system of paid leave, increasingly removal of frontier controls, protection of tourists and a commitment by national governments to tourism development generally.
- There is a large and well established tourist industry and infrastructure.
- There are a wealth of natural, cultural and historical attractions.
- Because of its size, distances between countries in Europe are relatively small. In addition, there is a comprehensive road, rail and air network which makes travel quick and easy. Europeans are highly mobile, with a high level of cars on a ship.

Within Europe, in the period between 1965 and 1995, there has been a redistribution of tourist demand, with Britain, Spain and France showing the greatest growth in income from international tourism. Between 1965 and 1995 the number of overseas visitors to Britain increased by 600 per cent, and to France by a similar amount. For the same period, Europe as a whole saw its receipts increase from over £3 billion in the mid sixties to over £150 billion in 1994. (WTO 1985) Eighty per cent of international travel in Europe is due to intra-European travel. This is particularly the case in the main European tourist destinations, where intra-regional arrivals accounted for 91 per cent of international arrivals to Italy and 95 per cent to Spain.

Although the tourist industry in Europe is continuing to grow in both volume terms and in value, tourism in other parts of the world is growing faster. In 1960 international visits to Europe accounted for 72 per cent of world tourism. In 1994 this figure had dropped to 60 per cent. There has been a similar fall in Europe's share of revenue from world tourism which has fallen from 60 per cent in 1960 to 50 per cent in 1994. The World Tourism Organisation predicts that Europe will continue to lose market share, and this may be down to maybe 50 per cent of all world travel by the year 2010. (See Table 4.3).

Table 4.3: International Tourist Arrivals Trends in Regional Market Share 1980-1993 (%)

Region	1980	1993	Change	
Europe	65.96	59.29	-6.67	↓
Middle East	2.8	1.44	-0.64	↓
South Asia	0.79	0.69	-0.10	↓
Americas	21.33	21.30	-0.03	↓
Africa	2.55	3.57	1.02	↑
East Asia/Pacific	7.28	13.71	6.42	↑

Source: WTO

Table 4.4: Arrivals of Tourists from Abroad by Regions

Region	Arrivals ('000)		Average annual rate of increase	Share of World Total (%)	
	1980	1992	1980-1992	1980	1992
Africa	7,337	17,471	7.5	2.5	3.6
Americas	61,387	101,137	4.25	21.3	21.0
East Asia/Pacific	20,961	61,306	9.36	7.3	12.7
Europe	89,830	290,219	3.6	65.9	60.27

Source: WTO 1994

One reason for this changing market share is very rapid economic growth in Asia during the 1980s. In East Asia and the Pacific region there were over 26.5 million tourist arrivals in 1984 (WTO 1986). By 1994 this had grown to over 70 million arrivals. During the period between 1990 and 1995 tourist arrivals in this region have grown at an average annual rate of 9.5 per cent (WTO 1994) The main tourist destinations within the region are Singapore, Hong Kong, Fiji and Samoa. This growth has been fuelled by a new emerging middle class in the fast growing economies of the Pacific rim countries who wish to take holidays within the East Asia and Pacific region. There is also an inbuilt threat to Europe's tourism in that a number of new Asian resorts have been developed over the last decade, and the steady decline in air fares and growth in long haul travel has encouraged European tourists to seek more exotic destinations in resorts in Thailand, Malaysia and elsewhere in the region.

Figure 4.1: International Tourism Demand Historical Growth Rates 1950-1993

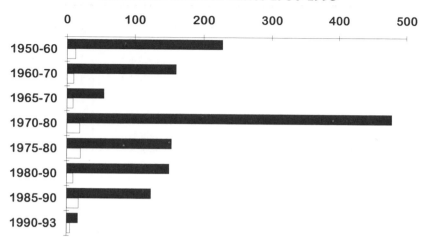

■ Annual percentage increase □ Average annual percentage increase

Source: WTO 1994

In Africa there has been an equally rapid growth due to developments in international tourism, with arrivals of tourists from abroad increasing from 1.3 million in 1964 to over 17 million in 1993 (WTO 1994). In the period between 1985 and 1990 the average annual percentage increase of tourism receipts amounted to 15 per cent. By far the bulk of arrivals have been to resorts on the Mediterranean coast of North Africa, which largely accounts for the growth in international tourism to the continent in the 1980s and early 90s. With the emergence of the new South Africa, there has been a steady growth in tourists visiting southern Africa, and this is expected to continue rapidly throughout the remaining 1990s.

The growth in international tourism in Africa was encouraged by increased promotion and the development of inclusive tours designed to attract tourists from Europe and North America. Between 1964 and 1994 receipts from international tourism to Africa grew from $256 million US to over $6.5 billion US. The most rapid period of growth was during the 1970s when tourism receipts grew at an average annual rate of over 18 per cent. (WTO 1994).

Table 4.5: Countries with Highest Receipts per Tourist and with Highest Expenditure per Trip Abroad

Highest Receipts per Tourist				
Rank		Country	Average receipt per tourist arrival US$	
1985	1992		1985	1992
1	1	Denmark	1,035.1	2,452.4
8	2	Japan	540.9	1,706.1
2	3	Australia	929.1	1,533.6
4	4	Belgium	675,.7	1,258.7
3	5	United States	699.3	1,206.4
7	6	Korea, Rep.	549.8	1,012.7
6	7	Singapore	606.3	955.6
12	8	Thailand	480.3	940.2
9	9	Hong Kong	530.6	864.2
10	10	Newtherlands	498.9	827.2
14	11	Italy	349.6	826.3
15	12	Austria	335.2	776.6
11	13	United Kingdom	492.8	738.2
13	14	Germany	374.3	725.0
17	15	Switzerland	264.3	597.7
16	16	Spain	296.6	559.6
5	17	Turkey	664.6	555.7
20	18	France	216.1	419.5
19	19	Portugal	227.9	418.8
18	20	Canada	235.6	385.3
Highest Expenditure per Trip Abroad				
Rank		Country	Average expenditure per trip abroad US$	
1985	1992		1985	1992
1	1	Norway	2,884.4	8,062.5
4	2	Japan	972.9	2,276.1
3	3	Australia	1,268.5	1,754.8
2	4	Taiwan	1,687.1	1,684.0
9	5	Netherlands	515.8	992.6
15	6	Italy	247.4	938.9
6	7	United States	7076.4	908.3
8	8	France	516.2	822.6
10	9	Sweden	313.5	666.1
13	10	Germany	284.9	602.2
12	11	United Kingdom	294.7	586.1
11	12	Belgium	308.5	567.2
5	13	Mexico	827.1	544.2
7	14	Austria	547.0	537.0
14	15	Switzerland	283.6	535.1

Source: WTO 1994

In Japan the domestic tourist industry is having to deal with the long term increase in the value of the yen against other international currencies, and arrivals figures have remained fairly static at over 2 million per year during the early 1990s. In contrast, the Japanese outbound market is very strong with over 7 million Japanese taking overseas holidays in 1994.

Within the world of international tourism, Table 4.5 (see page 50) shows those countries with the highest receipts per tourist arrival and those countries with the highest expenditure per trip abroad (WTO 1994). Denmark received the highest receipts per tourist with over $2000 per arrival, closely followed by Japan, Australia, Belgium and the United States. In terms of the highest spending countries, Norway comes top in ranking with over $8000 per trip abroad, followed, after a large gap, by Japan with over $2000, Australia and Taiwan each with over $1500 per trip abroad. To some extent the position of Japan and Australia and Taiwan may be explained by their geographical location and, in order to reach other major world destinations, they face long haul trips which will account for a significant proportion of their tourism expenditure.

Another comparison is by ranking countries according to their total tourism expenditure and annual growth rate between 1980 and 1992. The United States, Germany, Japan and the United Kingdom all remain in the top ten places, followed by Italy, France, the Netherlands, Austria and Taiwan.

If the world's tourism destinations are ranked in order of tourist arrivals and share of arrivals, France is clearly the world's number one tourist destination, followed by Spain, the United States, Italy, Austria, Canada and the United Kingdom. (Table 4.6) (WTO 1994).

The contribution of tourism to economic activity is significantly greater than estimates based on direct spending alone. Tourist spending in a region also makes an indirect contribution to the economy as a whole, as receipts for tourism are then in turn spent on other goods or services within the country or region, generating further income as the effects of this initial tourist spending continue to filter throughout the economy. This impact is discussed in greater detail in Chapter 11 which considers the income 'multiplier effect' as the process is known.

Table 4.6: World's Top Tourism Destinations

Rank 1992	Country	Tourist Arrivals (Thousands) 1992	1980	Rank	Av. Annual Growth Rate (%) 1980/92	% Share of Arrivals Worldwide 1992	1980
1	France	59,590	30,100	1	5.86	12.37	10.46
2	United States	44,647	22,500	3	5.88	9.27	7.82
3	Spain	39,638	23.403	2	4.49	8.23	8.13
4	Italy	26,113	22,087	4	1.41	5.42	7.67
5	Hungary	20.188	9,413	10	6.56	4.19	3.27
6	Austria	19,098	13,879	5	2.70	3.97	4.82
7	United Kingdom	18,535	12,420	7	3.39	3.85	4.32
8	Mexico	17,271	11.945	8	3.12	3.59	4.15
9	China	16,512	3,500	17	13.80	3.43	1.22
10	Germany	15,147	11.122	9	2.61	3.15	3.86
11	Canada	14,741	12,876	6	1.13	3.06	4.47
12	Switzerland	12.800	8,873	11	3.10	2.66	3.08
13	Greece	9,331	4,796	16	5.70	1.94	1.67
14	Portugal	8,884	2,730	19	10.33	1.84	0.95
15	Czechosl. (former)	8,000	5,055	15	3.90	1.66	1.76
16	Hong Kong	6,986	1,748	25	12.24	1.45	0.61
17	Turkey	6,549	921	44	17.76	1.36	0.32
18	Romania	6,280	6,742	12	–0.59	1.30	2.34
19	Netherlands	6,049	2,784	18	6.68	1.26	0.97
20	Malaysia	6,016	2,105	22	9.15	1.25	0.73

Source: WTO 1994

Factors Affecting the Development of International Tourism

The growth and development of international tourism can be influenced by direct government intervention in the management of tourist resources, especially in those countries where the tourist sector is an important element in the national development plan. However, the private sector usually has a crucial part to play in the development of tourist facilities. The first stage for any national tourist organisation or regional tourist body is to develop an effective plan to market an area for international tourists. In order to begin this process, several basic questions need to be asked such as:

- What is the existing market for tourism from abroad?

- What tourist products and services do we already have?

- What are the prospects for growth in tourism within this region?

- What features will attract potential tourists to this country/region?

- What are the strengths and weaknesses of our tourist product?

- What alternative destinations (competitors) are there for international tourists?

- Can our infrastructure cope with an increase in tourist numbers?

Clearly a great deal of desk or field research may need to be undertaken in order to provide answers to these questions, and this general area is examined in more detail in Chapter 10.

For those countries with tourism potential where international tourism has not yet developed, the first task is to produce a detailed survey of existing tourist attractions, perhaps classifying them as natural (scenery, climate, wildlife), cultural (museums and galleries, theatres, historic buildings or sites), or entertainments. The process of planning and development of tourism is again discussed in more detail in Chapter 9.

There are three general factors that will influence the development of international tourism, particularly in the developing regions of the world. These are:

- a growth in lower cost long-distance travel;
- the provision of suitable accommodation and tourist facilities in the destination countries, and a properly trained workforce to service them;
- a stable political and financial climate.

The introduction of larger aircraft, such as the Boeing 747, has already had a dramatic impact on long-haul flights. The deregulation of airline fares and the introduction of new types of aircraft with lower unit costs has helped to lower fares. The growth of inclusive tour packages during the 1980s has also helped to reduce the overall cost of international travel, together with creative pricing policies for the off peak season. In 1994 and 1995 the British Airways 'World Offers', which were introduced in the November to January period, are a good example of this new approach to marketing in the off-season period. Boeing forecasts in its *Current Market Outlooks* that annual increases in air travel in the 1990s will be greater than the total size of the market in 1960. One impetus to increased air travel will be or has been the development of more fuel efficient engines and lighter airframes, which have offered much greater operating range for aircraft. Improvements in aircraft technology have also enabled aircraft to fly to long-haul destination on two engines where three or four would have been necessary before. The Boeing 767, the European Airbus and the new Boeing 777 are examples of this technology.

During the 1990s the introduction of the new generation Boeing 747-400 has begun to dominate the long-haul tourism market. Now non-stop flights are available to Hong Kong and San Francisco from the UK and there will be an upward growth in non-stop flights between Europe and the Far East and the United States and Australasia. If the demand for international tourism continues as predicted, and there is little evidence to see any change, the Boeing company plan to launch a further aircraft, the 747-500 model, in the late 1990s with a range of over 8500 miles and over 500 seats. The most dramatic growth in air travel is expected to be in Asia where the region's market share of world traffic is expected to increase from 33 per cent in 1992 to over 40 per cent in the late 1990s.

Having made it easier to travel from Europe to the Seychelles or Bali, it is important that the tourist destination has the infrastructure and trained staff to handle mass tourism. Any new tourist facilities will be competing with much nearer and familiar tourist attractions, and will have to offer amenities and facilities that are of a high standard and at a competitive price. In developing a new market it is essential that the new tourist destination does not simply replicate facilities commonly found across Europe. The aim will be to develop distinctive facilities that relate to and enhance the atmosphere of the country. Many of these new destinations will also have a competitive edge because of lower labour costs and will be able to be much more labour intensive in the newly emerging resorts in the Pacific, Asia region.

However, more than anything else, competitiveness will depend upon training and investment, and there will be a need to develop and train the work force for the newly emerging tourist industry. The quality of service that international tourists receive is at least as important as the standard of tourist facilities provided. Such training will need to take account of new technologies, to include computerised reservation and booking systems and modern production techniques, particularly for food service and preparation. Training will also have to focus on improving the level and quality of personal service provided, because the international tourist is continually seeking the best combination of price and quality.

The importance of a stable political and financial climate is crucial for the future development of international tourism. Three quite different examples help to emphasise this point:

- In April 1986 President Reagan approved a bombing raid on Libya using aircraft based in Britain. One immediate repercussion was an immediate decline in Americans travelling to Europe, fearing terrorist reprisals. In Britain, in May 1986, there were 40 per cent fewer Americans than in the same month in 1985. Overall, in 1986, Britain lost about £300 million in tourist revenue because of the decline in numbers of American visitors. The picture was worse on mainland Europe where US tourists were down by 60 per cent in France and 50 per cent in Italy.
- In Northern Ireland, after 25 years of civil strife and bombings, the international tourist industry which was once thriving, all but collapsed. The recent glimmer of daylight with the cease-fire and discussion of peace talks has helped the tourist traffic to pick up in a small way.
- 1991 began with the Gulf War, which lead to a sudden and marked decline in bookings for overseas holidays, particularly from the UK. The poor trading situation, combined with high interest rates and over supply in the market place, reduced profit margins and lead to a

number of company collapses, the largest of which was the International Leisure Group. Since 1991, additional wars have broken out in the Balkans and the once thriving Yugoslav market has gone. Similarly, in Sri Lanka, a once fast emerging tourist destination, the civil war over the past 20 years has resulted in a dramatic decline in the number of tourists to the country.

A stable financial climate is important for two particular reasons. Firstly, the private sector needs to have confidence in the stability of the national economy before it will invest in tourist development projects; and often loans and other financial concessions will be necessary for the development of tourist facilities in the early years. Secondly, exchange rates can play a major part in international travel, particularly to and from the United States. When the value of the US dollar is high compared to other (European) currencies, this acts as a great incentive for Americans to travel abroad. Conversely, a high value dollar will cause a sharp decline in the inflow of overseas visitors to the United States.

ASSIGNMENTS
1. Using data on international tourist arrivals for 1990, produce maps to show the main tourist flows and identify:

    ● the main tourist generating countries;
    ● the main tourist destinations;
    ● the main links and routes between them.

    Give a brief account of the changes that have taken place over the past decade and suggest reasons for this.

2. Identify what you think will be the major international tourist destinations by the year 2000, and justify the choices that you have made.

Chapter 5

The Retail Travel Sector

Learning Objectives:
After reading this Chapter you should have an understanding of how the retail travel business operates and also:

- The range of services offered by the retail travel agent;
- The place of the retail travel sector in the tourist industry;
- The procedures involved in setting up and managing a travel agency;
- The relationship between travel agents and tour operators;
- Job opportunities, total manpower needs, and the future of this sector of the tourist industry.

Introduction

The retail travel sector is the one activity most clearly recognised and associated by the general public with the tourist industry, and takes the form of offices of individual or multiple branches of travel agents in High Streets throughout most towns in Britain. Travel Agents have been in existence for over 100 years, with Thomas Cook pioneering the business. Although Thomas Cook began as a tour operator, the rapid growth in his business lead him to opening an office in London and acting as a sales agent for several steamship lines and railway companies. By the end of the 19th century, travel agencies had developed in the United States, including American Express which was an offshoot of the Wells Fargo Company, borrowing Cook's idea of traveller's cheques in 1891.

However, it was not until the 1950s and 1960s that the number of travel agencies increased dramatically. This was due to two main developments:

- The large-scale growth of commercial airlines. By the end of the 1930's there were over 50 commercial airlines world-wide flying over 200 million miles and serving over 400,000 passengers. (Lickorish &

Kershaw 1958). These commercial airlines soon discovered the benefits of allowing travel agents to promote their services, and were willing to pay commissions.

- The post-war growth in package tours, which began in the 1950's with early charter flights and foreign holiday packages put together by enterprising tour operators, who then used the retail travel agencies to sell this product. Now the bulk of the retail travel agent's business is package holidays.

In Britain there are now about 7,000 retail travel agents, 5,000 of whom are members of the Association of British Travel Agents (ABTA) and 2,000 who are non-members. In the United States there are about 30,000 retail travel agents.

Services Offered by the Travel Agents
Most tourists are unaware that the travel agent is acting on behalf of a third party. The travel agent is a retailer and, with the exception of a few agents who are also tour operators (for example Thomas Cook), the agent does not put together the tour or package holiday but only promotes or sells it on behalf of the tour operator. Most small towns and every city will have a number of travel agents in their main shopping district and, although there are a number of large national chains, many agencies are small in size, perhaps employing 4 or 5 staff.

What is the Role and Function of the Travel Agent?
The travel agent generally offers a range of services which usually include:

- Selling prepared package tours, including individual itineraries, and offering personally escorted and group tours;
- Arranging transport; selling airline tickets, rail, coach, and cruise trips and arranging car hire abroad;
- Arranging hotels, motels, sightseeing trips, music festivals, and transfers of passengers between terminals and hotels;
- Handling and advising on many details involved in travel, especially foreign travel, such as travel and luggage insurance, medical insurance, travellers cheques and visa requirements;

- Providing information and advice on airline, rail, and coach schedules and fares; hotel rates, details of hotel accommodation. All of this information can take weeks of phone calls and letters;
- Arranging reservations for special interest activities such as business travel, sporting holidays and religious pilgrimages;
- In the case of legitimate complaints from customers writing to the principal (tour operators or airline), to obtain a refund or written statement for apology for any mishaps that may have occurred;
- Interpreting and advising clients on the many complex discounted fares offered by the airlines and to warn clients of 'overbooking'.

The travel agency then represents all the package tour companies, all the airlines and all the coach and rail operators who use their services. A good travel agent would be able to advise the potential traveller on a wide range of matters concerning the journey, accommodation and final destination.

The agent must have a good knowledge of the product and show what he or she is selling. He or she is giving professional advice and will need to be regularly updated within information from trade journals, promotional material and current reports from colleagues familiar with the destination. In other words, the good agent should know where to go for current information on reliable tour operators and tourist destinations and will be keeping abreast of changes in the travel business. Many small travel agencies may rely on tour operators' brochures or on-screen information supplied on-line from tour operators, and thus offer a limited range of advice to their customers based on this information alone. However, there are a wide range of travel and accommodation directories available, primarily for Britain and the United States, which can provide a wealth of ancillary information on travel and accommodation, and which can be used to provide fast and accurate data.

Establishing a Travel Agency
The capital cost of setting up a retail travel agency is much less than for almost any other kind of retail business, because the agent requires relatively little in the form of stock. The agent is buying or leasing office space, viewdata systems with access to airlines and tour operators' booking and information services, as well as telephones and office equipment. The

stock – in the form of brochures, tickets and related material – is supplied by the tour operator (wholesaler) or carrier (airline, rail, or coach company).

In opening a travel agency the most critical step is finding the right location, and this in turn will be influenced by four factors:

- Identifying the market for the travel product and the type of client the agency hopes to attract. The travel agency must be in a neighbourhood that will service clients who are likely to take foreign package holidays, cruises, special interest holidays and so on;
- The location of competitor agencies is important. Although the Association of British Travel Agents does not object to new members on the grounds of a nearby competitor, the tour operators and transport operators may be less inclined to give agency agreements or licences to a competing business in the neighbourhood;
- The agency must be visible and easily accessible to its customers. Most are found as ground floor offices in the main shopping and business district, ideally with ample nearby parking;
- Investment capital is critical in that most airlines, for example, will not give commission on the sale of tickets until the agency receives appointment as an official agent for the International Air Transport Association (IATA) and (in the United States) the Air Traffic Conference (ATC). In Britain the domestic airlines and other transport operators will also issue licences. Approval or licences can take some time to obtain, and an agency should have at least 2 years' operating capital available before it can expect to make a profit from its operations.

Travel Agency Appointments and Commissions
The travel agency obtains the bulk of its income from commissions on the sale of its products and, to collect commissions, must be officially appointed as an agent for the airline and transport companies and the tour operators. In the United States, in order to be appointed as an official travel agent, the firm must meet certain requirements set by 'conferences' representing the domestic and international airlines, shipping companies, railways and bus companies. Each group has its own regulating board or 'conference'. The main conferences in the US are the Air Traffic

Conference (ATC) representing US domestic airlines, the International Air Transport Association (IATA), the International Passenger Ship Association (IPSA) and the Trans Pacific Conference (TPC), which represents the Atlantic and Pacific shipping lines. Appointment by the Air Traffic Conference is the most important pre-requisite for a travel agency in the United States and, once obtained, most of the other agency appointments are relatively straightforward. To obtain an ATC appointment, the travel agency must be open for business, be operated under the direction of a qualified manager, have a good credit rating and (to protect the financial interest of the public and the airlines) have its operations investigated and approved by a bonding company (who will then guarantee responsibility for the agency's commitments up to $15,000), have sufficient funding to operate for 1 year without commission from the principal, and be actively involved in the production of travel tickets.

In Britain, to obtain commission on airline ticket sales, a travel agency must obtain a license from IATA. Since any retail agency obtains much of its income from commission on the sale of airline tickets, it is usually necessary to obtain an IATA appointment. IATA insists on similar requirements for retail travel agents as those sought by the Air Traffic Conference in the USA and, in addition, IATA requires that at least one employee has one year or more experience in international ticketing and reservations. Proof that the travel agency is actively promoting international air travel is also needed.

To obtain commission on package tour holidays offered by the main tour operators, travel agents should be members of the Association of British Travel Agents (ABTA). Respective members of ABTA must provide evidence of financial stability and deposit a bond (of £7,500 if they are a sole trader or £3,500 if a company) in favour of ABTA as financial protection to the association. ABTA travel agents have the sole right to sell inclusive package tours of ABTA tour operators, and they do not sell package tours arranged by non-ABTA companies. This is because ABTA has a retaining fund, paid for by members, which reimburses members of the public with lost money following an ABTA member becoming bankrupt. This ABTA booking arrangement has been in existence since 1965 and is known in the trade as *Operation Stabiliser*.

In Britain there are about 2,000 non ABTA members, mainly located in London and the home counties. The most active and prominent of these are the 'bucket shops', offering discounts on regular and charter flights to the main holiday destinations. Most of these are located in and around London. With the growth in air traffic in the 1970s and the increasing competition between the major carriers, many of the airlines have established a practice in Britain of selling off unsold seats at large discounts through non-appointed travel agents. The spread and success of these 'bucket shops' is unwelcome competition for the IATA appointed travel agencies who, under the terms of their agreement, are not allowed to sell heavily discounted tickets. However, in recent years ABTA/IATA agents have been able to sell consolidated tickets at discount prices.

Other travel services, such as car hire companies and hotels, do not need individual agency appointments, but will pay commissions for any reservations or bookings made by a travel agency that has been appointed as an official agent by the major travel and tourism organisations.

Commissions
Once the retail travel agent has been appointed to represent IATA or ABTA or ATC, the agency immediately becomes eligible to receive commissions on the sale of any travel tickets or tour operator packages that belong to these associations. The amount of money the travel agency earns from the sale of these products will vary according to the supplier and the kind of service provided. In general terms, firms operating in the same sector of the tourist industry tend to offer the same rates of commission for specific similar services. The *rates* of commission tend to be set by the particular association. For example, IATA sets the rates for the international airline industry – at present at about 8 to 10 per cent. In terms of domestic airline fares, de-regulation in Britain and the United States has meant that airlines are free to establish their own rates of commission, although most have kept to de-regulation levels. The cruise lines at present pay 10 per cent commission and often pay higher commission for group bookings. Most tour operators generally pay 10 per cent commission and, depending on the individual operator, this percentage may increase with group booking or a marked increased in sales during the year.

In Britain the limited restrictions on setting up as a retail travel agent lead to a rapid increase in the number of high street outlets during the 1960s and 1970s, although the overall size of the market grew slowly in the 1970s. The pattern that emerged was that a large proportion of the volume of bookings was generated by a small proportion of highly productive retailers.

In the United States airline de-regulation and the growth in the use of computer reservation systems, has had a considerable impact on retail travel agents over the past 10 years. Although there are now about 30,000 travel agents in the USA, just about 7 per cent of them account for 28 per cent of agency sales, and the general trend is one of fewer agents doing more business. In many cases declining profits have lead to amalgamation and many agents have formed or joined chains that are able to offer good national coverage and various kinds of discount on air tickets, hotel rooms and car rentals that generally are associated with volume business.

Travel Agency Operations

Travel agents are acting as retailers selling a wide range of travel products. Their main income comes from commissions which they receive from each sale, whether it is an airline ticket, a hotel booking, a car rental, or an inclusive tour package. The lesson from experience in the industry in Britain over the past 30 years is that, while it is relatively easy to set up in business as a retail travel agent, it is often much more difficult to achieve a worthwhile level of profitability, even after 2 years' of training. Most travel agents are selling basically the same product at much the same prices. Very often it is the travel agent's knowledge, expertise and service which become the major factors in making a sale, rather than the product itself. Indeed, as travel becomes more expensive, in the case of the top of the range packages the consumer will be more influenced by the quality of service provided by the agency.

As well as paying commission, suppliers also provide travel agencies with brochures, posters, window displays and visits from their sales representatives. The cost of servicing a travel agency with these additional sales tools can be quite high. Many tour operators stipulate that agencies reach a minimum production quota over a certain period time in order to receive commission on these materials. With most companies there will be a minimum sales quota to earn commission from tour operators and, often, there is a structure designed to pay a higher rate of commission as the number of bookings increases.

Given that the travel agent is offering a service and selling a product, it is *time* that is the most valuable component in their operation. An analysis of sales performance over the year can help to identify the 'quiet' periods in the operation of the business, when files can be updated, mailing lists reviewed, familiarisation visits organised and business plans for the coming year updated. Having done this, the travel agent needs also to analyse the operation of the office and the book keeping and reservation systems.

An analysis of bankruptcies among small travel agents has shown that there are three key factors in most business failures:

- Poor financial planning is evident, with inadequate records and/or failure to use available financial information.
- There is poor market analysis and management of sales.
- There is failure to offset general administration costs by generating additional revenue.

Good financial control can help to identify where things are going wrong or where things are doing well in the business. There is a need, therefore, to produce a budget showing expenditure and income from commissions on a regular basis, and to link this to an accounting system which shows deviations from the planned budget. This process can be helped by analysing the nature of the firm's business over the past year and dropping those products or clients that are not providing value for money.

Tour Operators
Tour operators plan, price, package and market an inclusive foreign holiday. They are the 'manufacturing' element of the tourist industry. Most tour operators are wholesalers in that they product a package holiday and negotiate with retail travel agents who, then sell on the product. There are three types of tour operator:

1. *Direct sell* tour operators who by-pass the high street travel agent and sell directly to the public. They will put together package holidays and advertise and sell to their own clientele. The operator may be a small agency or a multi-branch organisation that markets thousands of tours.

2. *Wholesale* operators who do not deal directly with the public, and who put together and operate tours exclusively through travel agents. They do not accept direct bookings and have no direct contact with the public.

3. *General Tour Contractors.* These are tour operators who do not package and promote their own tours. Instead reservations are forwarded to local contractors or to wholesalers. Organisations such as British Airways, special affinity groups organising travel to North America or Australasia, or non-profit organisations all come into this category.

Some tour operators, such as Thomas Cook and American Express, are both wholesalers and retailers.

Organising Tour Operations

The tour operator must plan the inclusive holiday package at least one or two years before the first departure date and, for some events, such as the World Cup or the Olympics, plans have to be made years in advance. The first 5 to 6 months will be spent in putting a saleable package together, chartering aircraft, arranging transfers to coaches or ferries, booking hotel rooms, arranging sightseeing tours and so on. The next 4 to 5 months will be spent letting out and printing promotional material, including photographs and displays. The tour operator then spends 4 to 6 months checking out new places, tourist's developments and hotel operations. Tour testing is an important element in designing package tours, and most operators will sample more than once before the package is made available to the public. The three main elements of a tour package are the cost of the transport, the cost of the hotel accommodation, and the cost of the ancillary services.

The Role of Inclusive Tours

In the UK inclusive tours dominate the outbound tourism market. For the last 20 years the largest proportion of UK holiday travel (52 per cent) has been organised through inclusive tours. Often the major tour operators are horizontally integrated, owning charter airlines and maintaining direct links to high street travel agents. For example,the Thomas organisation own Britannia Airways, Owners Abroad owns Air 2000, and Cosmos is linked with Monarch Airlines. Because the tour operators cater for the mass market, their volume sales have given them a bargaining strength to keep prices down, by buying hotel bed spaces or airline seats in bulk. Their traditional appeal to the mass market has been to offer a complete holiday package at the lowest price to a population often lacking the linguistic knowledge or confidence required to organise independent travel.

Seventy five per cent of inclusive tours leave the UK by air, and the Civil Aviation Authority (CAA) controls this market through the Air Travel Organiser's Licences (ATOL's) it issues each year. Although many operators do not use their full ATOL allocation, the licences granted each year give an indication of market share. An analysis of the performance of the top 30 air travel organisers over the past decade shows that, whilst turnover has increased steadily through to 1989, the balance of profits over losses peaked in 1985, declined in the late 1980's, picked up in 1990 and then declined again in 1991, not least because of the collapse of the International Leisure Group.

A more recent factor which can affect inclusive tour operators has been the introduction of the EC Directive on package travel, package holidays and package tours (90/314/EC). Under Article 7 of this Directive, the tour operator as the organiser of the contract has to have sufficient financial protection to repay clients in the event of bankruptcy. The government decided that, rather than set up a separate licensing authority to address this issue, it would rely on the Civil Aviation Authority being assured that bonds were in place when travel operators' licences came up for renewal.

Also, under EC regulations, all air carriers must offer passengers compensation if they are removed from overbooked or cancelled flights. For flights of less than 3,500 miles, minimum compensation of £120 for each passenger is required, and £240 for longer journeys. Many small companies may be unable to find insurance companies willing or able to provide them with the necessary bond, and the industry does not have an infrastructure to cope with this. For example, at the end of March 1993, the CAA published a list of 48 tour operators that had not applied for renewal of their ATOL licences.

Although over 500 operators hold CAA licences, the market is dominated by 30 companies who between them have 79 per cent of seats licensed. The three largest companies, Thompson, Owners Abroad and Airtours account for over 52 per cent of all seats licensed. (See Table 5.1)

Table 5.1: Inclusive Tours Authorised for 1992 by UK Civil Aviation Authority
(year-end to Sep)

Company	Seats licenced	% of total
Thompson group	3,326	24.5
Owners Abroad group	2,275	16.8
Airtours group	1,487	11.0
Cosmos group	822	6.1
Best Travel	392	2.9
Unijet Travel	343	2.5
Aspro Travel	333	2.5
Granada group	231	1.7
Total	9,209	67.8
Total of 30 largest operators	10,777	79.4
All tour operators	13,574	100.0

Source: Civil Aviation Authority

Although Thompson is still the market leader, its overall market share has declined from 39 per cent of the inclusive tour market in 1989 to 24 per cent of the market in 1993. This is due to intense competition from its two main rivals, with the Owners Abroad group increasing its market share four-fold, and Airtours experiencing a three-fold increase in volume over the same period. This competition, together with adverse trading conditions in the 1990's, has generally squeezed profits for all tour operators.

In September 1992, because of its rapidly increasing turnover, Airtours had a net cash balance of £155 million and sought to increase its market share through acquisitions. It acquired Pickfords Travel, and then in January 1993 launched a hostile take-over bid for Owners Abroad. A merger of the two companies would have created a new market leader, with 27 aircraft carrying 3.7 million tour passengers a year, and with 334 retail outlets. The new company would have accounted for over 27 per cent of the market. However, within 24 hours of this announcement, Thompson Holidays carried out a substantial reorganisation of its business to meet this threat, which involved moving all of its holiday marketing operations to London and strengthening its sales division. The market as a whole has been concerned about the take up of package holidays during the summers of 1993 and 1994 and was aware of the experience in 1992 when firms sold only 7.5 million holidays against a projected target of 9 million.

Between January 6th, 1993 (when the hostile bid was announced) and March 1993, the take-over battle saw a further twist when Thomas Cook intervened with a £20 million purchase of 9 per cent of Owners Abroad shares, which effectively prevented the take-over. This intervention by Thomas Cook was possibly influenced by the parent company (Westdeutsche Landesbank) which anticipated a trading alliance between Thomas Cook and Owners Abroad. Westdeutsche Landesbank also owns the German travel company LTU, which is the fourth largest tour operator in Europe. Many business analysts regard this initial share purchase in Owners Abroad as a forerunner to the acquisition of the company by one of the German travel firms seeking a position in the UK market.

Prospects for UK Tour Operations
If the UK domestic economy continues to remain in recession, the indications are that the package tour sector will continue to be squeezed

by supply outstripping demand, and reduced profit margins. Pessimistic forecasts about the economy will depress discretionary spending, which will in turn restrict sales of summer holiday packages. The performance of the market in 1993 and 1994 has not reversed this forecast.

Other factors that will influence the future shape and makeup of the inclusive tour market and its overall market share are:

- The opening of the Channel Tunnel.
- The EC Directive on package travel.
- Airport and airspace congestion, and peak season well-publicised delays.
- The growth in independent travel, especially to long-haul destinations.
- The move away from sun-based holidays.

The probable impact of the EC Directive, which became law in January 1993, will be to increase the cost of foreign holidays by up to 10 per cent to meet the cost of insuring operators against collapse or legal claims. New legislation makes tour operators legally responsible for everything that goes wrong with the holiday package which they sell.

The opening of the Channel Tunnel in 1994 (which is discussed more fully in the next Chapter) has reinforced the predominance of France as the major UK destination, and has added to the growth of independent travel, providing a further advantage for the car-borne holidaymaker. It has also reinforced the move away from hotel accommodation to rented villas and apartments.

Independent travel is likely to continue to grow during the 1990's, both to destinations within Europe and to long-haul destinations such as the Caribbean and Australasia. The de-regulation of Europe's airfares should help the individual traveller, and competition on some routes (such as the North Atlantic) is likely to keep fares at a very competitive level.

Business Travel
Business travel is often the most profitable element of retail travel and has been one of the fastest growing sectors of the market. It has shown a steady growth in volume over the past decade, with average growth of over 7 per cent a year between 1988 and 1994. In contrast, holiday travel

has declined from its 1989 peak. The UK market for business travel is now worth over £17 billion a year and the volume of travel and spending has almost doubled since the early 1980's. The travel and tourism industry has responded to the growth in this sector of the market by providing special incentives for business travellers, with hotels, airlines and car rental companies stressing first class service and competitive price packages.

Figure 5.1: Trips and Spending on Business Travel in UK 1989-94

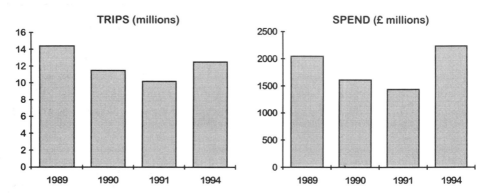

In the United States business travel is now the third largest area of corporate expenditure, after sales and data processing. The world wide boom in business, and the growth of conference and exhibition centres, have all contributed to the expansion in this sector. Globally, business travel is estimated to be in excess of $150 billion. The recent study of over 17,500 passengers on international scheduled airline flights found that 85 per cent of them were flying on business.

The larger, well established multiple retail travel chains are the market leaders in UK business travel. For example, Thomas Cook has 6,000 business clients managed through 80 specialist travel centres. Hogg Robinson Travel handles over £175 million worth of business each year for over 15,000 companies. One measure of the growth in this market segment has been the increasing interest by the financial service sector, with firms such as American Express, Access, Visa and many others offering a wide range of travel support services, ranging from accessories and valet service to world-wide insurance and money supply.

Table 5.2: Growth in Business Travel and Destinations for Business Trips, 1988-91
('000)

	1988	1989	1990	1991	% change 1991/88
EC	2,743	3,202	3,422	3,502	27.7
Other West Europe	444	479	452	441	-0.7
North America	367	410	471	396	7.9
Other areas	403	414	462	432	7.2
Total	3,957	4,505	4,807	4,770	20.5

Source: International Passenger Survey

As Table 5.2 shows, the main growth has been in business travel to EC countries which has increased its share from 63 per cent of the market in 1988 to over 73 per cent in 1991. Business travel to EC countries has grown almost four times as fast as travel to any other major destination during this period.

Figure 5.2: Links in the Retail Travel Sector

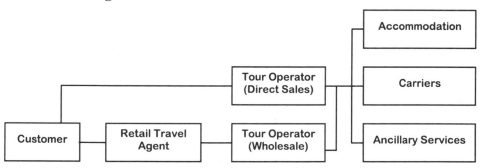

However, the UK recession has had an impact on this sector recently. The Economist Intelligence Unit's *Travel Industry Monitor* (34 January 1993) reported that UK companies travel budgets were continuing to be affected by the downturn in both UK and global economies. According to a 1992 Wagons Lit-Mori business travel survey, over 38 per cent of firms are now undertaking less business travel and 49 per cent have downgraded either the travel class or the hotel class used, to get greater value from business travel budgets. The same report suggested that those corporate travel agencies that may have been high on rebate contracts with corporate clients will be under most pressure as a result of these downgrading measures. This could affect their ability to achieve their override targets associated with airlines.

Table 5.3: Passengers Carried and Revenue Earned Under Air Travel Organisers' Licences, Oct 1988 to Sep 1991

	Return passengers (million)	% change	Turnover (£bn)	% change
Winter 1988/89	4.03		0.96	
Summer 1989	9.12		2.44	
Year to Sep 1989	13.15		3.40	
Winter 1989/90	3.62	-10.2	0.95	-1.0
Summer 1990	8.5	-11.7	2.44	-
Year to Sep 1990	11.67	-11.3	3.39	-0.3
Winter 1990/01	3.06	-15.5	0.87	-8.4
Summer 1991	7.29	-9.4	2.34	-4.1
Year to Sep 1991	10.35	-11.3	3.21	-5.3

Source: Civil Aviation Authority

If retail travel agents are to capture a share of this important market, they need to offer an important and cost effective service for the corporate client. This involves five main stages in business travel planning:

- Setting out the guidelines for executive travel and the way in which travel arrangements will be made.
- Seeking out the most effective and value-for-money travel arrangements and hotel or car rental companies that offer the best corporate rates.
- Flexibility with the trip itself. It is important to be able to change the travel itinerary at short notice, and to have an efficient system for settling expenses.
- There is a need to guarantee corporate clients that company money is being used efficiently and properly, that corporate travel policy is followed and that the system is easy to administer. An effective travel expense system must be able to list specific costs incurred, explain the reasons for these and identify hidden costs that might go unnoticed. Expense reporting, payment, overdue claims and reconciliation all need to be included at this point.

● Finally there is the review and analysis phase of corporate travel which provides the opportunity to review existing company procedures and the development of more cost effective systems, both for the retail travel agent and for the company who is the client.

ASSIGNMENTS

1. Using your local copy of *Yellow Pages*, identify the location and type of travel agencies listed. Selecting, say 10 in one large town, identify their location and plot this on a street plan. What locational characteristics do they show? How many are:

    a. General travel agents?
    b. Specialised travel agents?
    c. Branches of larger chains?
    d. Independent retailers?
    e. Members of ABTA/IATA?

2. You are the manager of a small retail travel agency located in the main central shopping area. Next door is a camera shop and across the road is a bank and a sports shop. Design a joint advertising campaign that will link all of these businesses to the travel agency and increase your turnover in package tour sales.

Chapter 6

The Passenger Transport Sector

Learning Objectives:
After reading this Chapter you should understand:

- The importance to the tourist industry of air, sea, road and rail transport;
- The effects of regulation and de-regulation of transport;
- The impact on tourist resorts since the 1950s of changes in means of travel;
- The changing role of public and private travel in Britain;
- The impact of the Channel Tunnel on cross channel, air and ferry traffic;
- The levels of tourism-related employment in the passenger transport sector.

Introduction
In Chapter 2 and Chapter 4 the growth of mass tourism was seen to be closely linked with improvements in passenger transport. Technological improvements in rail and sea transport during the 19th century enabled the main carriers to transport people in much greater numbers than before. Competition between firms reduced the cost of travel, which opened up the opportunity to travel for a much greater part of the public. The development of air travel in the 20th century continued this process.

Over the past thirty years the speed of travel has increased considerably, so that trains travelling over 125 mph and aircraft flying at over 500 mph are commonplace.

This has considerably shortened journey times and brought more distant destinations within the reach of the average traveller.

When a tour operator puts an inclusive tour together, journey time and reduced unit cost (due to greater utilisation of vehicles), and accessibility are key factors to be considered. The inclusion in mass market brochures of destinations such as the Seychelles or Australia is a result of reducing journey times from Europe to these more distant destinations.

The increasing global spread of mass tourism means that more and more countries have to cope with the impact of mass tourism on the environment, whilst the expansion of transport – in the shape of new airports, motorway networks and railways – also has a dramatic and irreversible environmental impact. These impacts and the issues raised are discussed in more detail in Chapter 12.

Rail Transport

Rail travel grew in popularity during the 19th century and, by the end of the century, most travellers to Britain's resorts arrived by rail. Even today the land use pattern of our seaside resorts reflects their development during the railway age, despite the decline of rail travel over the past forty years. Between 1947 and 1996 rail travel in Britain was managed nationally through British Rail. British Rail divided their railway business into three sectors:

i.   Intercity.
ii.   London and the South East.
iii.   Provincial services.

The Intercity network covers six main routes (see Figure 6.1 on the following page) radiating from London, and it is this network and the provincial services that are mainly used by tourists. The London and South East network is mainly commuter traffic, although it does handle day trippers to Brighton, Southend and the North Kent resorts, as well as a new link between Waterloo and the Channel Tunnel.

Although the railways monopolised the mass travel market during the 19th and early 20th century, they suffered competition from coach and car transport during the 20th century and have most recently lost traffic to the airlines, particularly in the United States. This has been in part due to their failure to recognise the importance of the mass travel market, possibly conditioned by the priority they gave to the freight and

Figure 6.1: The Main BR Inter-City Rail Network

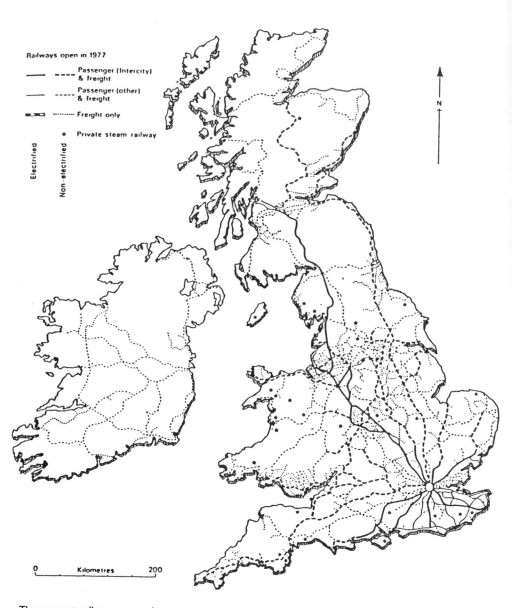

The present railway network.

parcel services. The increasing competition from road freight operations and the decline in revenue during the 1950s lead to a drastic overhaul of British Rail's operations in the early 1960s. The Beeching Report *The Reshaping of British Railways* lead to a drastic reduction in the overall size in geographic extent of the rail network, particularly serving rural areas where many rural lines were axed which had formally served tourist destinations.

It was not until the 1970s that British Rail began to review its marketing policies for passenger transport. To some extent this was due to the threat to its monopoly on internal long distance travel in the UK from the private car and from coach companies who had become much more competitive. British Rail established a Golden Rail subsidiary in 1972 based in York. This organisation began to market Golden Rail holidays where British Rail offered an all-in package including travel and accommodation. The success of the Golden Rail concept can be seen from Table 6.1 which shows that the volume of traffic increased from 166,000 in 1980 to 174,000 in 1986. Encouraged by this development, British Rail began to market short break and mini holiday packages with special discounts for out of season breaks, using rail travel to major tourist resorts, and with tie-ins to the main hotels there. As they had a large control of the rail market, British Rail realised that they had a much greater opportunity to use price discrimination and to target their efforts to particular segments of the market who would be attracted to the benefits of special travel offers. This lead to the introduction of senior citizens' rail cards and student rail cards as part of this policy.

Table 6.1: Mode of Travel to Holiday 1951-1994

Year	Car (%)	Rail (%)	Bus/Coach (%)
1951	28	48	24
1961	49	28	23
1971	63	10	17
1981	72	12	12
1991	76	8	10
1994	75	9	7

Source: BTA UK Tourist Statistics

Table 6.2: Growth of BR Golden Rail Short Stay Holidays 1980-86

	Short Stay 000s	%	Long Stay 000s	%	Total 000s
1980	78	(17)	138	(83)	166
1981	29	(21)	108	(79)	137
1982	35	(31)	78	(69)	113
1983	71	(52)	65	(48)	136
1984	109	(67)	54	(33)	163
1985	130	(77)	39	(23)	169
1986	135	(78)	39	(22)	174

Source: Report of Transport and Tourism Conference 1986 OTTS

Privatisation of British Rail

All this changed when the government's proposals for privatising British Rail became law, when the Railways Act received Royal Assent on the 5th November 1993. The Act enabled the government to take the railways to the market. Between 1993 and 1995 the government's intentions began to take shape, and these took the form of a series of franchises to be offered for companies to operate the trains and for a separate company, known as Railtrack, to operate the network and maintain the network of railway lines and bridges and stations. By the spring of 1996 the first three franchises had been awarded, covering South West Trains, Great Western and London Transport Rail. Stagecoach, the bus operator, obtained the first franchise covering South West Trains operating out of Waterloo.

Early in 1996 Railtrack issued a Network Management Statement, a forty-eight page brochure which outlined its investment plans over the next decade. It remains to be seen whether the privatisation of the railways and their dismemberment will benefit travellers in the long run and whether, in particular, it will reverse the continuing decline in the use of rail travel over the past decade.

Preserved Railway Lines

There has been a resurgence of interest in 'private' railway lines over the past two decades, as many local preservation societies and steam rail enthusiasts have rescued local branch lines after their closure by British Rail. Some of these are standard gauge lines, such as the Nene Valley

Railway near Peterborough, The Watercress Line in Hampshire, The Bluebell Line in Sussex or the Severn Valley Railway. Others are narrow gauge lines, such as the Romney, Hythe and Dibchurch Railway in Kent, the Ravenglass and Eskdale railway in Cumbria or 'The Great Little Trains of Wales'. These are now all mainly tourist attractions which rely on income during the season as well as donations from the public and the unpaid services of enthusiasts to maintain the trains, track and rolling stock and to man the stations.

Road Transport: 1. The Private Car
The growth of tourism across Europe in the 1970s and 1980s has been dominated by the use of the private car as the preferred mode of transport for holiday travel. As Table 6.3, shows the market share of rail and bus/coach travel continued to decline, whilst the use of private cars increased from 69 per cent to 75 per cent. The growth in private car ownership, with most families either arriving or having access to at least one car, is a relatively recent phenomenon. But it has had a dramatic impact on the types of holiday that people take as well as on the environment of the resorts and holiday regions. In 1951 only 28 per cent of holidaymakers travelled by car to the main UK holiday destinations. In 1994 over three-quarters travelled by car. In 1960 there were 5.7 million private cars in Britain. Today there are 16 million. As the number of car-owning households increases, and as more households acquire a second car, the private car will continue to dominate the domestic tourist scene in Britain, the United States and most European countries. In the peak summer period a considerable proportion of the road traffic travelling to the south of France or through Germany and Switzerland to Italy, is generated by tourists in private cars.

Table 6.3: Main Method of Transport Used to Reach the Destination on Holidays of 4+ Nights in Great Britain 1981 to 1994

Base	All holidays [%]									
	'81	'82	'83	'84	'85	'86	'87	'88	'89	'94
Car	69	68	72	69	71	72	73	74	74	78
Bus/Coach	12	15	12	15	14	15	14	13	13	9
Train	13	12	10	11	10	8	8	8	8	7
Other	5	3	5	4	4	4	5	4	4	5

Source: BNTS/BTSY

Note: Figures may not add up to 100% because of rounding and because of a proportion of people who could not recall method of transport used.

The growth of tourism across Europe in the 1970s and 1980s has been dominated by the use of the private car as the preferred mode of transport for holiday travel. Between 1980 and 1990 the market share of rail and bus/coach travel continued to decline, whilst the use of private cars increased from 84 per cent to 88 per cent.

Assuming a reasonable road system, the private car provides an unrivalled degree of mobility for the tourist and it provides a degree of convenience not offered by any other form of transport. It enables the tourist to travel from his home to his destination with all his family and luggage, with the minimum amount of transfer, and without having a rigid timetable. Once at the tourist resort, the car enables the tourist to gain access to the surrounding tourist region.

In addition, use of the private car for holiday travel is perceived by the tourist as being cheaper than other modes of travel. Although it is expensive to acquire a car, once bought the cost of journeys is relatively small, particularly if several passengers are carried, and most drivers just calculate the cost of oil and petrol when considering using the car for holiday travel.

The growth in car ownership has also led to a growing preference for touring holidays where resorts are now seen as a base from which to visit a much wider hinterland. Resorts have to face competition from a wide range of attractions in the surrounding region and, indeed, many now market these attractions as part of the overall 'appeal' of the resort.

In Britain and Europe there has been a corresponding growth in the ownership of touring caravans and campers and this trend has affected the tourist resorts and holiday regions in two ways. Firstly, the traditional forms of holiday accommodation have lost some of their market share as caravanning and camping has increased. Secondly, the proliferation of caravans and tents has spread from the fringes of the traditional seaside resort into the formerly less accessible parts of tourist regions, creating significant planning problems. This issue is discussed in more detail in Chapter 12.

In the United States there has been corresponding growth in recreational vehicles (RVs), from 80,300 in 1962 to over 7.5 million in 1986. The growth of camping in the United States has encouraged the creation of a nationwide consortium of campgrounds (Camp Coast to Coast) representing over 400 campground owners. Most of the users of these campgrounds arrive in recreational vehicles. One in ten Americans own a recreational vehicle. (*USA Today* 1986).

Road Transport: 2. Coach Transport

Most resort towns will have a variety of outlets selling coach excursions to the surrounding area, particular beauty spots or evening concerts. Nearly 90 per cent of the excursions and tours business is run by private operators, and this proportion has increased as de-regulation of the coach business came into effect. Most of these firms are small in size, often having less than 6 vehicles (Transport Statistics HMSO 1981).

Coach travel was in its heyday in the 1920s and 1930s and, as early as 1920, British coaches ran six-day tours of the battlefields of France and Flanders (Taylor 1956). By 1939 37 million passengers were carried on regular long distance services and tours, and of these over 10,000 were taken on continental tours by British coaches. By 1955 there were 100 million passenger journeys on long distance services and tours (Lickorish 1958). However, the growth in car ownership since the 1950s, has led to a gradual decline in the numbers travelling by coach, although it is still a significant element of passenger transport and has increased again since 1980.

Coach transport has several functions. It can provide:

- Express services between major cities and major tourist resorts;
- Group travel for special interest groups, associations and so on;
- Transfers between airport or ferry terminals and hotels;
- Tours and excursions.

Express Services

Following the introduction of the Transport Act 1980, the coach transport business was de-regulated, and a price war broke out between National Express and a consortium of private coach companies (British

Coachways). This finally led to the demise of British Coachways and an increase in business for National Express. Coach traffic grew by 67 per cent between 1980 and 1985, from 9.2 million to 15.4 million passengers, and the company accounted for 80 per cent of Express coach services.

In 1989 a management buyout saw the formation of National Express Holdings. In 1991 the company was sold to the Drawlane Transport Group (now British Bus) and in 1992 National Express plc was floated on the stock exchange. Three holding companies have emerged as major bus groupings: Badger Line, British Bus and Stagecoach. Badger Line, based in Weston-Super-Mare, has concentrated its operations in the South West. Drawlane Transport Group/British Bus Group is based in Salisbury and operates mainly, but not exclusively, in the Midlands and North West. Stagecoach Holdings, based in Perth, is organised into three subsidiaries covering Scotland, the North West and the South, and also operates internationally. Indeed Stagecoach, in January 1996, won one of the first passenger rail franchises between London and Bournemouth. Despite the prospect of greater competition following privatisation, express passenger services continue to decline in the recession of the early 1990s.

The de-regulation of express services in the 1980s has produced cheaper, faster and more luxurious coaches and, although larger independent operators continue to dominate the express market, there will be scope for smaller firms with lower overheads to compete for excursion traffic and feeder routes. Coach companies wishing to develop their tourist trade will rely increasingly on entrepreneurial senior managers to develop and maintain the market share.

In the United States President Reagan signed a Bill in 1982 which de-regulated the coach industry, opening it up for competition. Since then about 1,700 new bus companies have received Inter-State Commerce Commission operating authority and there are now 3,500 operating bus companies in the United States (US Travel Data Centre). Many of these new companies, just like their counterparts in Britain, are small but aggressive. The result is that a number of the old established bus companies, perhaps 45 to 50, have gone out of business faced with a strong downward pressure on prices for charters and tours. The average fare paid by a charter or tour passenger dropped from $10.57 in 1982 to $8.80 in 1984. Although fares went down, ridership went up and there was an increase of four million passengers on charters and tours. However, since de-regulation profitability has declined steadily in the face of cuts in fares. In Britain this will effect the larger carriers more since they have a higher cost structure with high overheads.

Tours and Excursions
Tours and excursions come under two categories. The first are local, based on individual resorts and providing a variety of day and half day excursions to tourists attractions in the surrounding hinterland. The second are long distance tours, for example through Scotland, or to countries in Europe, and are usually of 8 to 14 days duration. These are packaged to include couriers, overnight stops and local tours from the main resorts on the itinerary. These tours appeal to the elderly and retired in that they offer a local pick-up service, a courier to deal with any day-to-day problems and language difficulties, and the transport of heavy luggage right to the hotel. Often the spirit of 'camaraderie' built up between the coach passengers, driver and courier, and companies in this field means that they have a high level of repeat business. Information on sales of coach excursions over the last decade shows that the volume of business has grown steadily and now equals the express coach sector in size.

The two leading companies in the UK coach tour market are Shearings and Wallace Arnold, and focus their efforts largely on the over 55's. Shearings also serves the growing youth educational tours market, which is now recovering following the collapse of the International Leisure Group in 1991. Shearings has a fleet of 400 coaches under 4 years old and a network of 800 pick-up points across the country. Wallace Arnold has 250 joining points using a similar feeder service. The domestic market is the core business for each operator, although continental holidays are organised in most European countries and a growing number of Eastern European destinations. Table 6.4 also shows that a large number of independent operators serve the domestic coach market with Shearings/Wallace Arnold accounting for about one fifth of the market.

The continental coach market is dominated by P&O European Ferries who have a 58 per cent market share.

Many of the smaller coach operators have not been able to compete with large organisations, such as National Express, as the industry has undergone dramatic changes following de-regulation. More professional organisations, such as Drawlane/British Bus and Shearings, have turned coach travel into a major business venture. However, these new private monopolies in bus and coach operations do not increase customer choice.

Table 6.4: Coach Holidays Taken by the British Population, 1991-92

	1991 (m)	1992 (m)	Wallace Arnold/Shearings market share (%)
All GB holidays (4 nights +) [a]	34.00	32.00	14.8
Inclusive coach holidays	2.89	8.19	21.4
Coach tour holidays	2.06	5.22	20.9
Other inclusive GB coach holidays	0.83	2.67	22.4
All foreign holidays by sea & coach [a]	20.00	21.75	6.7
Foreign inclusive coach holidays	4.30	5.56	2.5
Foreign coach tour holidays	n/a	1.24	11.3
Fly-coach holidyas	n/a	0.39	2.6
GB short breaks [b]	26.70	26.10	3.3
Foreign short breaks	1.20	1.50	3.3

[a] Based on British National Travel Survey
[b] Based on the UK Tourism Survey

Source: Shearings, 1993

Coach travel remains a low priced means of travel within Europe, and price remains the single most important selling point, followed by image, quality of service and time cost.

Recent research has shown that, if the coach industry in Europe is to consider its future development, it needs to take account of an improved image for coach travel, more market research to understand customers' needs and changing preferences, and the development of market brands which are clearly identifiable.

Maritime Transport
This can be divided into three categories, two of which are strictly maritime:

i. Cruises and ocean-going ships
ii. Ferries
iii. Services on Lakes, inland waters and canals.

The main shipping lines who organise cruises or ocean-going passenger routes have established two conferences to represent their interests in the tourist industry. These are the International Passenger Ship Associates (IPSA) and the Trans Pacific Passenger Conference (TPPC), which represent the Pacific and Atlantic shipping companies.

Cruise Ships
Until the 1930s steamships provided the only means of long distance transport between the major continents, and the growth of air travel, especially of inclusive air tours, has had a severe impact on the shipping lines. In the post-war years they were faced with increasing competition from the airlines, rising operating costs and growing obsolescence in their shipping fleets and very high rebuilding/refitting costs. Most companies chose to diversify into other areas of activity and, now, those that remain have turned increasingly to the cruise line business. This is the luxury end of the tourist market. For example, only 4 per cent of the population of the United States has taken a cruise, but the majority of that 4 per cent is repeat business. The tourists on a cruise ship are not just buying a trip from A to B, they are buying a stay on a floating resort, with a level of service and accommodation comparable to the best resorts and hotels. The appeal of the cruise is that it is an all-inclusive package, with accommodation, meals and entertainment all included in the price of a ticket.

In the past 10 years the cruise lines have introduced innovations and special interest packages to appeal to a wider clientele. Most cruise lines offer a fly-cruise deal, for example, where passengers fly out to the Caribbean before joining the cruise ship in the West Indies. The most prestigious is probably the Cunard package which involves flying out of

Britain to the United States on Concorde and returning on the QE2. The appeal to passengers of these fly-cruise packages is that in the past when cruises started at Southampton or New York, it took several days of sailing through cold waters and possibly rough seas before warmer waters were reached. Now tropical sunshine and warm waters are just several hours travel away.

In order to appeal to a younger clientele, many cruise ships now offer full spa and fitness facilities as well as a wide range of sporting activities. For example, the Norwegian Caribbean Lines offer snorkelling and scuba diving lessons on board by qualified instructors; golf and tennis clinics are available on many ships. Some companies offer unique cruises, for example, the Sun Line have an Amazon River Cruise that includes a performance at the Opera House Manaus and their Trans Atlantic Grand Cruise begins in Athens and ends in Fort Lauderdale, with stops in the eastern and western Mediterranean and the Caribbean. The three main centres for cruise trips are the Caribbean, the Mediterranean and the Far East. The cruise market is dominated by United States tourists, who account for 80 per cent of all cruise passengers, although the headquarters of the main cruise line companies are based in Europe. For Caribbean sailings many lines now fly passengers to San Juan, Puerto Rico or Jamaica or Barbados, or cruises begin at the Florida Ports. The west coast cities of Los Angeles, San Francisco and San Diego are attracting more cruise lines and are beginning to rival the Florida based lines, especially for Mexico and Panama Canal cruises.

In the Pacific more cruise lines are offering seven day cruises from Hong Kong and the ships of the Holland America, Cunard, Royal Viking and P&O Lines offer larger cruises calling in at Hawaii, Tahiti, New Zealand, Australia and Japan.

In Europe, DFDS Danish Seaways took over Tor Line and the West German Prinsferries in the early 1980s and built up a separate inclusive tour operation of short cruises outbound from UK ports to Scandinavia. These now account for 100,000 passengers a year out of a total of 1.2 million carried. About 30,000 of these are from the USA (Travel and Tourism Analyst 1987) and 45,000 from the UK.

Cruise ships are very labour intensive and average about one crew member for every two passengers. In other words, a ship carrying 800 passengers should have about 400 crew members. Cruise ships vary in size from the relatively small ship, carrying 100 passengers, to the luxury liner carrying 900 to 1,000 passengers, with cinemas, swimming pools and a wide range of onboard entertainment facilities.

The best data source is the *OAG Worldwide Cruise and Shipline Guide* which is published every two months. This provides information on shipping companies, ship profiles of individual ships, port terminal diagrams, cruise listings and itineraries and a wide range of ancillary information.

In the 1990s the cruise industry embarked on the most expansive stage of its development. In the Spring of 1995 the delivery of new ships to P&O Cruises and Royal Caribbean Cruise Line marked the beginning of an investment of nearly US $9 billion in new ships. However, the market has been increasingly dominated by just three companies – Carnival, Royal Caribbean, and P&O. One emerging problem is that many of the newer ships are so large, with an average passenger capacity of around 2,000, that their area of operation would be limited to the Caribbean and possibly Alaska.

Table 6.5: US Cruise Passenger Growth, 1989-94

	1989	1990	1991	1992	1993	1994
No of passengers (m)	3.3	3.6	4.0	4.1	4.5	4.6
Annual average growth rate				1980-94: 9.2%		1989-94: 7.0%

Source: Cruise Lines International Association (CLIA)

The growth in the number of US cruise passengers has been on a steadier upward curve since 1980 (see Table 6.5). It has also been consistently greater than the overall growth of US overseas tourism, which increased by 3.5 per cent annually between 1985 and 1994, according to World Tourism Organisation figures. Market research has shown that there is a growing demand for cruise passenger potential and, as Table 6.6 shows, there is significant scope for growth during the 1990s. The key elements in Table 6.6 are in the age and income sections, which show that the potential cruise passengers are younger and less wealthy than the current passenger profile. Half are over forty and just one in ten are over sixty instead of more than one in three, as at present. It is also significant that nearly half of the potential cruise passengers have children and almost a third would holiday with children. This clearly will have an impact on the nature of the industry in the future. A younger, low income clientele with family commitments would have more appeal to the mass or middle market cruise lines.

Table 6.6: Characteristics of Past and Potential Cruise Passengers from North America, 1994

	Cruise passenger of past five years	"Hot prospect" [a]
Sex (%)		
Male	54	53
Female	46	47
Age (%)		
25-39	29	50
40-59	36	39
60 & over	35	11
Mean	50	42
Annual Income (US$)		
20,000-39,900	31	36
40,000-59,900	30	40
60,000-99,900	28	20
100,000 & over	11	4
Mean	63	51
Marital status (%)		
Married	76	70
Single	24	30
Type of household (%)		
Children in household	27	46
Vacation with children	15	29
Vacation without children	12	17
No children in household	72	54

[a] "Hot prospect": never cruised client who will – according to market research – definetely/probably take a cruise within next two years

Source: Cruise Lines Industry Association

Two thirds of the twenty nine ships currently on order are for lines owned by the top three cruise companies, the Carnival Corporation, Royal Caribbean, and the P&O Cruises Division. Of the twenty nine ships on order, only three will not be marketed in North America, and it is likely that at least twenty will spend all or part of the year at sea. The Caribbean now accounts for more than half of the North American cruise market (see Table 6.7). The introduction of these new ships will also increase the gap between the top three companies and the rest of the cruise lines.

Table 6.7: Share of North American Cruise Market by Destination (Based on Capacity), 1994

	(%)
Caribbean (including Bahamas)	52.0
Mediterranean	9.2
Alaska	7.8
Trans-canal	5.9
Mexican Riviera	5.3
Northern Europe	3.8
Bermuda	3.0
South Pacific	2.2
Other	10.8

Source: CLIA

The Carnival Corporation has had a series of very profitable years in the 1990s with net profits of over $350 million in 1994 and increased revenues in 1993 and 1994. It is estimated that the Corporation will have profits of over $500 million per year in forthcoming years, which will mean that Carnival will produce enough through its earnings to pay for the $2.5 billion it has committed to new ships, without borrowing. A second important market is emerging to serve the fast growing economies of South East Asia. In 1993 the Star Cruise Line was established by the Lim family and operates out of Singapore. They now have five cruise ships which are aimed at first time cruisers from local markets and also wealthier passengers which are marketed in the USA and Europe. All cruise out of Singapore and some also use Hong Kong. There was a rapid increase in the number of cruise passengers using Singapore from 165,000 in 1993 to over 700,000 in 1994. During 1995 at least twenty two ships will be based in Singapore, and the port authorities are expecting a 15 per cent increase in cruise passengers.

It is clear that, by the end of the 1990s, cruise ships will be firmly established as one of the world's major tourism developments, with significant markets in North America, the UK, Europe and Asia. The total number of annual passengers will exceed 8 million and the industry has all signs that it will continue to expand in the next century.

Passenger Ferries
The first steam passage of the Channel was in 1816 and the first regular steamer service in 1820. By the 1830s about 100,000 passengers were using the cross-Channel Ferries and by 1882 this had increased to 500,000. The present-day cross channel traffic carries 2.3 million passengers a year between seven different English ports and France, and on the East coast three ports operate ferry services across the North Sea (See Figure 6.2).

In the United States, with the exception of the Mississippi river cruise lines and the Great Lakes cruise ships, there has not been a similar massive development in ferries linking different parts of the country. The American seamen's unions and restrictions by intracoastal transportation laws which prohibit traffic between USA ports, have prevented any development of shipping links.

The other main concentration of ferry routes is in the Mediterranean, particularly the links between mainland Spain, France, Italy and Greece and the islands that form part of their jurisdiction, where there is an extensive network of ferry links. Greece is a good example. There are over 20 main islands in the Aegean and Ionean seas and dozens of smaller ones. All of them rely on ferry services to bring in supplies and essential goods and of course, tourists. The ferry may be a car ferry of several thousand tons or an ultra modern hydrofoil, providing a link between an airport and surrounding islands.

There are several key factors that determine the viability of ferry services:

i. They need to be equipped to deal with large numbers of passengers and their cars;
ii. They need to be equipped for a fast turn-round at their destination port at either end of the ferry link, so as to increase the number of sailings during the peak season;

iii. They require a roughly equal flow of traffic in both directions so that they have no 'dead' journeys;

iv. They need to be on routes that provide a good year-round flow of traffic.

The cross channel routes are all operated by roll-on-roll-off (RoRo) ferry services which minimise the time spent in port and provide a fast efficient service for car travellers. Over 3 million Britons take cars abroad each year and the only threat to the cross channel ferry services is the opening of the Channel Tunnel. In addition to the conventional ferry services, jet foil, hydrofoil, and hovercraft services offer high-speed water-borne links between Britain and the Continent.

Great improvements in the efficiency of ferry operations have occurred over the past 25 years. In 1953 it took up to 2½ hours for a small drive-on drive-off ship with a stern door to unload and re-load in port. By 1962 a drive through ship with 120 cars and 180 passengers took 1½ hours. Today a ferry taking 350 cars and 1,350 passengers can be turned around in 1 hour.

The English Channel and North Sea crossings from the UK to the continent carried an estimated 23 million passengers in 1985. Most of these were car-based holidaymakers. In the late 1950s there were just four car ferries operating. There are now over 200 ferry services around North West Europe, most of them serving the UK. In the 1970s there was a steady growth in passenger traffic through UK ports and the number of passengers almost doubled between 1975 and 1985 (Table 6.8). The Channel ferries, which account for about 75 per cent of total crossings from the UK, are dominated by two companies, Sealink and P&O European ferries (formerly Townsend Thoresen). In recent years both companies have been engaged in fierce competition to protect and increase their market share in the face of the forthcoming threat of the channel tunnel.

Table 6.8: Growth of Channel/North Sea Ferry Traffic 1975-1985
(millions)

Year	1975	1976	1977	1978	1979	1980	1981	1982	1983	1984	1985
Passengers	13.89	14.78	16.09	17.4	18.73	20.89	22.6	23.62	23.86	23.17	23.24

Figure 6.2: Sealink Route Map

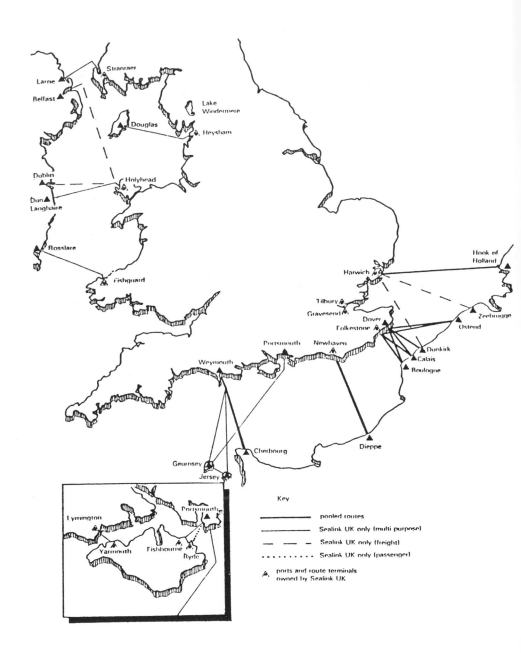

The ferry business between the UK and Europe is worth over £500 million a year. During the 1990s demand has seen a rapid growth and new investment in ferries, despite the challenge from the Channel Tunnel. In 1990 the Swedish shipping group Stena acquired Sea Containers and thus the bulk of the ferry operations of Sea Containers, Sealink, British Ferries' subsidiary. This was followed with a substantial level of investment of over £200 million in new ships, refurbished ships, improved terminal and port facilities, reservation systems and staff training.

The market is now dominated by three main companies: Brittany Ferries, covering the western channel routes, and P&O European Ferries and Stena Sealink, covering the mid and other channel routes. During the 1990s the fastest traffic has been car traffic, with a growth of passengers with cars travelling to both France and Spain. Overall there has been an annual growth of around 8 per cent in car carryings. Much of this growth has been based on the ferry companies rapidly developing inclusive tour programmes with a demand for ferry based holidays, but very flexible options. There has been a greater European presence on the ferry routes, with the emergence of Olau Line, which began as a freight operation transporting new cars on the Sheerness-Vlissingen route. In the 1990s it invested over 120 million on new passenger, port facilities and ferries. Olau has a West German sister company the TT Line which is competitive in the Scandinavian market. The fall in the value of the pound since 1993 against strong European countries makes all of these ferry routes attractive for increasing the inbound UK traffic from continental Europe.

Impact of the Channel Tunnel
The Channel Tunnel transport system linking the UK and France has now been in operation since 1994. It consists of three main elements – Eurotunnel, which owns and operates the physical infrastructure; the Shuttle rail service moving passengers, cars and freight between the terminals of Folkestone and Calais; and the direct passenger (Eurostar) service running between London and Paris and Brussels.

Eurotunnel's 'Le Shuttle' service is for road vehicles linking the M20 motorway in Kent with the A16 and A26 auto routes in France. Three types of service are provided:

- Freight shuttles
- Double deck tourist shuttles
- Single deck tourist shuttles

Through rail services linking the Channel Tunnel terminal at Ashford and the French side are operated by the national railways of UK, France and Belgium.

In addition, Eurostar trains offer a passenger service between London, Paris and Brussels which has been operating since the autumn of 1994. There are now six trains a day from London to Paris and three a day from London to and from Brussels. The planned service is essentially hourly to each destination, with additional trains at peak times and, since January 1996, an additional stop at Ashford in Kent.

Since the early days of its development Eurotunnel has been beset with financial problems, which have arisen mainly due to cost over-runs and delays. At the time of the public flotation in November 1987 the total financing cost was estimated at £4.8 billion and the £6 billion of debt on equity raised a reasonable margin. By November 1990 the total financing cost had risen to £7.7 billion, which in turn led to further re-financing, raising an additional £2.7 billion. However, by May 1994, the estimated total financing cost had risen again to £8.9 billion, requiring a further debt and equity injection to bring the re-finance up to £10 billion. As the project's debt continues to rise, until traffic revenues build up sufficiently to cover operating costs and financial charges, the available finance will again need to be raised. The securities markets have had major problems in handling the equity for such a project and the stock has shown enormous swings in price.

Many of the increased costs were due to delays and arguments over the division of risk between the various contracting parties, including the British and French governments, Eurotunnel, the contractors and the respective national railways. The UK government's prevarication on railway investment has slowed down the delivery of Eurostar trains and also created problems in terms of the quality of the track and infrastructure between the terminal at Folkestone and central London.

Clearly the project is dependent on future revenue growth to rescue it from its current financial difficulties. This depends on the growth of Channel Tunnel traffic and of competition from cross channel ferry traffic. Eurotunnel's Traffic and Revenue Consultants have produced forecasts of the growth of traffic between 1986 and the year 2000. Eurotunnel forecasts growth in traffic from 71.4 million passengers in 1993 to over 100 million passengers in the year 2000. It is likely that there will be a substantial reduction in cross channel prices in real terms because of the substantial increase in capacity in the market since the tunnel's entry into service in 1994.

As the cross channel ferry companies geared up for this competition, they have increased the size of their ships and have brought in more modern and faster ships. These have brought typical crossing times on the Dover-Calais route down to 75 to 90 minutes. Increased frequency of ferries, faster loading times and shorter turnarounds have all helped to reduce the critical motorway auto route time for passengers.

What may be of greater importance is not the competition *per se* between the ferries and Eurotunnel on the short sea crossings, but the impact of this competition and a general reduction in prices on short sea crossings of the North Sea or western channel routes. A general reduction on prices for the Dover-Calais crossings, compared with the longer crossings, may cause a switch in traffic (of up to 10 per cent of market share to the shorter routes via Kent). A reduction of this kind could lead to Eurotunnel taking a higher share of the total market. This, in turn, may reduce the number of ferry operators focusing on the Dover-Calais service.

Air Transport

This has been the most rapidly expanding transport sector over the past 30 years and is now the main form of long distance travel. The great increase in inclusive package tours abroad has been largely due to advances in aircraft design and performance, with the long-haul market now dominated by wide-bodied jets carrying over 500 passengers at speeds averaging 600 mph for several thousand miles, and smaller capacity jets for the short-haul routes.

Between 1974 and 1984 the number of airline passengers carried world-wide increased by 66 per cent, with the main increase occurring between 1974 and 1979. During the same period, the number of passenger/ kilometres almost doubled. The market share was redistributed over this period, with a decline in the North American and European share and a rapid increase in the airlines of East Asia and the Pacific.

Table 6.9: World Scheduled Domestic and International Air Traffic 1974-1984

Year	Number of passengers (millions)	% Change	Passenger/kilometres (millions)	% Change	Load Factor
1974	515	..	407,000	..	59
1975	534	3.6	433,000	6.4	59
1976	576	7.8	475,000	9.7	60
1977	610	5.9	508,000	6.9	61
1978	697	14.2	582,000	14.5	65
1979	754	8.1	659,000	13.2	66
1980	748	–0.8	677,000	2.7	63
1981	752	0.5	695,000	2.6	64
1982	764	1.6	710,000	2.1	64
1983	796	4.1	738,000	3.9	64
1984*	860	8.1	780,000	5.7	65

* Estimates

Source: ICAO

During the 1950s and 1960s, air passenger traffic increased in volume by 15 per cent a year, encouraged by increasing market demand and technological developments in aircraft design which increased the speed, range and passenger capacity of aircraft. Table 6.10 summarises these developments since 1940.

Table 6.10: Aircraft Operational Characteristics 1940 – 2000

Year	Type	Range (miles)	Speed (mph)	Capacity (seats)	Engine (type)
1940	DC-3	1,510	210	28	Piston
1950	DC-6	3,000	316	108	Piston
1960	B707	6,110	600	189	Turbofan
1970	B747	7,090	608	350	Turbofan
1980	Concorde	3,970	1,400	144	Turbojet
1990	B747-400	8,000	620	414	Turbofan
2000	B747-500	8,500	620	500	Turbofan

Source: Travel and Tourism Analyst

In the 1980s, the impact of de-regulation on the US market and moves to liberalise air fares in the European and transatlantic markets, have meant that airlines need to be much more flexible in the face of changing consumer demand. However, current forecasts indicate that the passenger travel market will rise by about 5 per cent per annum up to the year 2000, when annual passenger movements will be rapidly approaching the 2 billion level.

There are over 7,000 aircraft currently in service in the world's airline fleets, and about 40 per cent of these are short to medium range aircraft with less than 125 seats, many of which, such as the BAC 1-11, are no longer in production. Twenty-five per cent of the world's aircraft are short to medium haul types carrying up to 185 passengers. The long-haul market, epitomised by the Boeing 747, accounts for 20 per cent.

Figure 6.3: Growth in International Air Traffic 1974-92

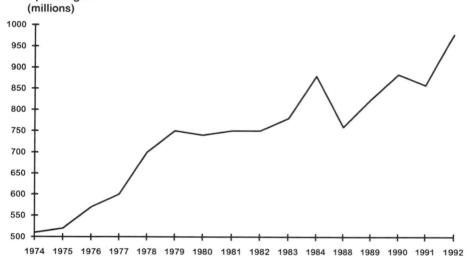

Source: WTO Statistics

However, nearly 50 per cent of the world's fleet is over 12 years old and some 2,000 aircraft (i.e. 28 per cent of those in use) are approaching the end of their working life. Renewal of aircraft is now a major issue with many fleets, especially those in the less developed countries of Africa, South America and Asia. The following table outlines estimates of expected aircraft requirements up to 1995.

Aircraft Manufacturer	Boeing	Airbus	McDonnell Douglas
Type			
Narrow bodies			
Short range	-	1,134	815
Short/medium range	-	1,719	1,347
Total	**2,560**	**2,853**	**2,162**
Wide bodies			
Short/medium range	-	2,509	1,150
Long range	-	894	703
Total	**1,179**	**3,403**	**1,853**
Overall Total	**3,739**	**6,256**	**4,015**

Assumed RPM growth (% per year)

Source: *Flight International* March 15th, 1986

The growth in traffic led to a growth in competition between airlines and they had to adapt fares and products to market needs to achieve better capacity levels in their aircraft. As Table 6.9 shows, load factors rose from 59 per cent in 1974 to 65 per cent in 1984 (seats sold as a percentage of seats available). One of the main means of increasing capacity levels has been to offer discounts in air fares for advance bookings (APEX, Advance Purchase Excursion or Super-APEX), seasonal discounts, and very competitive fly-drive packages with substantial discounts for car hire. All of these variations in pricing relate to scheduled services, and they have been very successful. However, the greatest increase in air traffic over this period has been in the air charter business, with the growth in inclusive air tours since the 1960s.

The tour operator prepares sample brochures for specific tours and then forwards this to one of the IATA member carriers (normally the one that will be used for the charter) for approval. The carrier then assigns an IT (Inclusive Tour) code number, which must appear on the air ticket in order to qualify for the tour commission. Tour operators take advantage of the unsold capacity in existing aircraft owned by the airlines, who in turn wish to fill as many seats as possible and to avoid 'dead' legs on an airline route where few passengers may be travelling.

Charter Flights

The early charter flights in the 1960s took several forms because of existing regulations which limited the operations of charter carriers in Britain and the United States. There were the 'one stop inclusive tour charter' (OTC) the 'inclusive tour charter' (ITC) and the advance booking charter (ABC), as well as special interest 'affinity' groups which were set up simply as a means of obtaining low-cost air fares. The rules for these charters were constantly abused and ignored (especially for the affinity groups) since the government agencies regulating the operations of air carriers lacked the manpower to police them effectively. In 1994 over 31 million passengers took outbound charter flights from the UK.

There are now seven main airlines flying charter package holidays, mainly to the mass market destinations around the Mediterranean, although in recent years flights have been extended to cover North America and Africa and more distant destinations. These airlines are:

- Britannia
- Monarch
- Air 2000
- Air Tours International
- Caledonian
- Air UK Leisure
- Excalibur

These airlines normally fly from Gatwick and the main regional airports such as Manchester or East Midlands.

The European charter airline business has weathered the recession of the early 1990s. In the 1990s in the UK saw the high profile failure of Air Europe and the takeover of Dan Air. However it was recognised that these owed more to strategic and financial mis-calculations and over-ambitious planning, rather than any fundamental decline in the traditional charter markets. In the period between 1990 and 1995 the charter airlines of the International Air Carrier Association (IACA) averaged almost 15 per cent growth, as economic recovery was re-established in most European markets, particularly in the UK. The charter airlines have been much more able to adapt to the cost and market stringency of the early 1990s than their scheduled counterparts. Airlines such as Britannia, Monarch and Air 2000 have remained constantly profitable over the last five years. The charter sector share of traffic within Europe has continued to rise and, in terms of passenger-kilometres, has exceeded scheduled services since the mid 1990s.

As they operate outside of the scheduled services, tour operators must obtain a licence to operate inclusive air tours as a safeguard for passengers who would be stranded abroad if a company collapsed during the holiday season. The collapse of the aviation division of Court Line in August 1974, when 50,000 British holiday makers where stranded abroad, prompted a change in earlier arrangements. (Department of Trade HMSO 1975) Package tour organisers must apply to the Civil Aviation Authority for an Air Travel Organiser's Licence (ATOL) and the tour operator must provide evidence of financial viability, as well as depositing a bond to meet the costs of repatriating passengers should the need arise.

Since 1945 the air transport industry has been regulated in three ways:

● At international level, with IATA and the International Civil Aviation Organisation (a UN body).
● At national level, by state control over fares and cargo rates offered to the public.
● Bilateral agreements between governments covering specific routes and the number of flights on these routes, and the airlines who can fly them.

Although concern over safety standards and the financial viability of airlines is as strong as ever, there was a move during the later part of the 1980s to relax controls over fares, capacity, markets and the frequency of flights, in an effort to increase competition, This was based on the belief that market forces would create the best environment for air travellers. This move is referred to as 'de-regulation'.

De-regulation
In the United States cargo de-regulation was introduced in December 1977 followed by passenger de-regulation in November 1978. Although this only affected internal domestic flights, the US began to negotiate de-

regulated bilateral agreements for international services, coming into direct conflict with IATA which opposed complete de-regulation. Within the United States, the whole regulatory system was further relaxed when the Civil Aeronautics Board was abolished in 1984. It is too early to predict the long-term impact of de-regulation in the United States, but it already appears to be having the following impacts on domestic air services:

- an expansion in small and medium sized regional and local airlines;
- more airline bankruptcies as competition intensifies;
- a growth in commuter services;
- fare wars;
- mergers between airlines in the face of increased competition;
- accelerated development of hub-and-spoke interchanges;*
- commuter lines sharing code designations with larger lines;
- consumer services strained;
- higher proportion of all passengers flying on discounted tickets;
- one airline may dominate traffic into and out of one city.

In 1978 ten major carriers dominated US domestic traffic, accounting for 88 per cent of the market share. By 1984, this group had shrunk to nine and their market share to 75 per cent. Fifteen new airlines were started up, although they accounted for less than 5 per cent of all traffic (Pryke 1987). Most of the newly certified carriers were located at secondary airports such as Midway, Chicago or Newark, New Jersey and many offered limited amenities, preferring to compete with low fares. *One structural development that has emerged with de-regulation is the appearance of hub-and-spoke networks, with airlines increasingly basing their activities at a limited number of major airports.

The long-term effect may well be that, although fares may drop in the short-term, mergers will mean that much domestic traffic will be in the hands of a few large companies who will squeeze out the smaller operators. In Britain there has been increasing emphasis on competition between airlines and, since 1983, talks have taken place within the European Economic Community to liberalise air fares throughout Europe, although this has met strong opposition from several national carriers and it will be a slow and gradual process.

At the international level the first moves to de-regulate air fares were initiated by the United States in the late 1970s early 1980s. Unfortunately, this was a period of rising costs and declining profits for all international airlines and this led to concerted opposition to wholesale de-regulation, as airline financial losses were growing. The main problem with applying de-regulation internationally is that it affects national airlines of countries in different stages of development. Some countries may provide services as a means of generating foreign exchange, providing tourist access, as a national flag carrier, or to generate foreign trade and may not operate at a commercially viable level. Some of the developing countries come into this category and they may feel that they are unable to compete with the larger, well-established international carriers based in Britain or the US.

However, overall efforts to increase de-regulation on international routes are likely to continue, albeit slowly. One benefit of the increased competition created by de-regulation is that it forces airlines to be more efficient by scaling down their operations, increasing productivity, aircraft load factors and their attractiveness to the traveller, particularly the business traveller.

De-regulation came about in Europe in 1993. With it came consistent forecasts that the charter sector and its airlines would come to an end with general impact similar to that which occurred in the United States. This has not happened and is unlikely to happen due to a number of factors.

Unlike the USA, the European charter market has forty years of business behind it and, for the last twenty years, charter services have been the dominant sector within the airline industry. Many charter carriers are very closely linked to the overall tour operator sector and are either owned by, or in strong contact with, major national holiday companies. This vertical integration with the leisure market leaders has provided a sound foundation for the major charter airlines.

In addition, these tour operators have proved extremely flexible and responsive to market conditions, and have developed a range and quality of inclusive tour holiday products to match changing expectations and increasing prosperity of customers. The charter airlines have themselves maintained a strong cost gap between them and the major scheduled official carriers within Europe.

Finally, European de-regulation has strengthened rather than weakened the position of the charter airlines. The removal of the legal and licensing distinction between charter and schedule services has given them an equal status which has increased the charter airlines' power to ensure airport and airway access, and has offered them equal protection under European competition laws.

During the 1990s there has been increasing vertical integration between the charter airlines and major tour operators and travel agency chains which has consolidated the major companies and paralleled consolidations which have occurred in Europe's scheduled airline industry. This has seen the emergence of a small number of very secure charter companies with strong ties with holiday tour operators, and a second tier of non-aligned carriers which sell their inventory when and where they can.

It was also felt that de-regulation in Europe would most seriously affect the charter airlines' traditional holiday routes from Northern Europe to the Mediterranean. It was felt that increasing competition from scheduled flights would see a reduction in this share of the mass tour market. However, this has not proved to be the case and, between 1993 and 1994/5, there has been an overall growth of charter flights of over 18 per cent in this market. Part of this growth has been due to the abilities of the tour operators, many of whom owned charter airlines, in upgrading and refining resort standards and increasing the choice of holidays and destinations, whilst keeping cost levels reasonable.

A more recent development has been the growth of the long-haul holiday market. This has followed considerable investment by the tour operators in finding more distant destinations and facilities and by the airlines in acquiring larger longhaul aircraft and enhancing in-flight service levels to match the expectations of the more affluent clientele. Since the early 1990s major UK outbound growth areas have included Central America, the Caribbean, Indian Ocean islands and Australasia.

Figure 6.4: Charter Versus Scheduled Airline Productivity, 1993/94
(revenue ton-km per employee ['000])

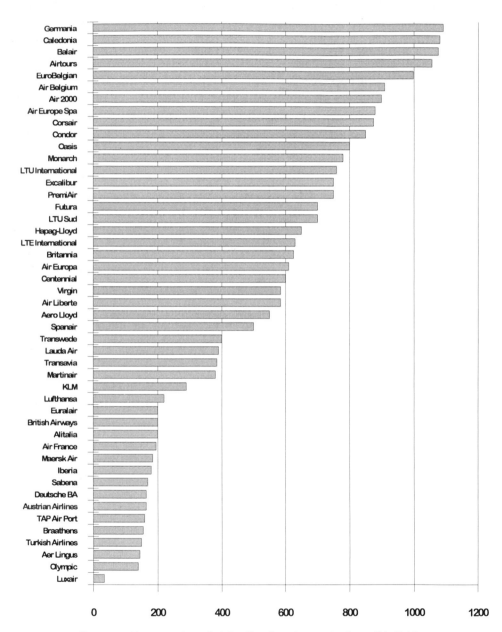

Source: International Air Carrier Association (IACA)

A further prediction was that there would be an increase in intra-European alliances and merger activities within the charter sector, as there has been within the European scheduled airlines sector. However, apart from the Air Tours acquisition of SAS Leisure in 1994 and the early investment in SPAN Air by SAS, there has only been one cross border development of any significance. In March, 1993 the UK tour operators Owners Abroad, owners of Air 2000, reached a broad-ranging strategic alliance with Germany's LTU. LTU, part owner of West Deutsche Landesbank, had taken a stake in Owners Abroad through acquiring the UK travel agency chain Thomas Cook, and in so doing had obtained access in the UK to Thomas Cook's 340 travel agency outlets. In 1995 the flag carrier British Airways sold its Caledonian charter operation to the tour operator Inspirations, which did not have its own airline. This sale indicated that the flag carriers did not see the charter market as an area for further expansion. It also reflected BA's recognition that the close ties in the UK between the big charter airlines and the tour operator/ travel agency chains would make it hard for a carrier like Caledonian to compete.

The charter fleets have also been transformed by heavy investment in modern aircraft during the late 1980s and early 1990s. The original fleet largely consisted of twin jets, such as the early Boeing 737s and McDonall Douglas DC9s, BAe111s, and have now been replaced by aircraft such as the Airbus A320, the Boeing 757 and Boeing 767s for longer haul or medium haul markets. This re-equipment programme has been encouraged by the need to maintain operating cost efficiency. The charter airlines have preserved their historic cost advantages over the scheduled airlines and, in terms of revenue passenger-kilometres per employee, they are much more cost efficient than any of the scheduled airlines. On the basis of present evidence, it would appear that inclusive tour holiday air charter flights will continue in the UK for many years to come.

Future Developments in International Air Travel
The major factors likely to influence international air transport are in the areas of aircraft technology, operations and distribution systems. Improvements in the operating efficiency of engines will help reduce fuel

consumption as will the greater use of composite materials in airframe construction, together with more sophisticated flight systems which will make aircraft easier to fly. Estimates of operating costs vary, but the new generation of engines in use in the 1990s are likely to have cost savings 10 per cent lower than existing versions. The main body of the Boeing 767 has only 3 per cent composite materials, but this gives it a weight saving of 630 kg, equal to the weight of 8 passengers. By 1992, composites, such as carbon fibre thermoplastics, could cover up to 30 per cent of the surface area of new aircraft, with corresponding savings in the payload cost. Improvements in on-board computers and display technology are likely to give volume savings of 60 per cent and weight savings of 70 per cent in the flight decks of the 1990s aircraft. Miniaturisation will also bring in small personal video screens for in-flight movies and individual passenger entertainment systems.

These technological advances will bring very real cost savings to those airlines who invest in the new aircraft types and, assuming that de-regulation produces a more liberal air transport environment worldwide, the airlines will be able to pass on these savings to their customers in the form of reduced fares, in order to maintain their market share. For example, Northwest Orient which has purchased up to 100 Airbus 320-200 aircraft, estimated that their fuel consumption will be 50 per cent lower per seat than the existing fleet. This will enable the company to operate more effectively in a very competitive US market.

The steady growth in air travel during the 1980s and 1990s has once again caused concern that the air transport industry's infrastructure may soon be inadequate to meet growth of demand. The latest airport data (Table 6.12) show that the two world regions that which are giving most concern on their airport capacity are Europe and the Pacific. These regions are growing the fastest, while the overall growth rate was depressed only by low growth in the North American market. In Europe the major airport hubs are already constrained for growth and this has reflected the trend of high growth in traffic, with much lower movement growth at London/ Heathrow. In the Asia-Pacific airports passenger growth at Hong Kong, Singapore and Bangkok has again raised concerns about the ability of the airports to meet the growth of passenger and freight traffic.

Table 6.12: World Airport Traffic Growth, Jan-Sep 1995

	Passengers (m)	% Change on Previous Year
Africa	18.4	– 1.9
Asia	45.8	3.9
Europe	535.1	6.6
Latin America/Caribbean	82.9	1.3
North America	754.5	3.3
Pacif	269.5	7.6
Total	1,706.1	4.9

With the real cost of air travel continuing to fall each year, and airline fleet re-equipment cycles regaining momentum after the slow down in the early 1990s, both demand and the airborne capacity to meet that demand are expanding at a rate which the major airports are struggling to match.

At the end of 1995 there were only eleven all-new airports in firm planning or under construction in the world's three leading air transport regions – three in Europe at Oslo, Athens and Berlin; eight in Asia-Pacific at Sydney, Hong Kong, Seoul, Bangkok and Kuala Lumpur; and three sites in China at Shanghai, Guangzhou and Zhuhai. There were non in the Americas.

In Europe and in the United States major infrastructure projects are very slow to go through the process of approval and planning and construction. This is affecting further airport developments, for example, at Heathrow and in Germany. Increased lobbying on behalf of environmental concerns is also affecting the debate on airport expansion.

Asia-Pacific is seen as the leading world area for the growth of passenger travel for the next ten years, and passenger growth is forecast at an average annual rate of 8.6 per cent, until the year 2000 and 7.2 per cent between 2000 and 2010, according to figures supplied by the Air Transport Action Group (ATAG). By the year 2010 the Asia-Pacific region is expected to account for more than half of the world's total air passenger traffic.

However, despite investing more in new airports and infrastructure in other regions of the world, there is still a risk that the planned growth for the Asia-Pacific region will not be accommodated, and that congestion caused by this growth may be severe enough to slow down airport expansion.

Within Europe, although there have been considerable improvements in air traffic control systems and other related efficiencies within the infrastructure, the existing runway capacity constraints are still cause for concern. The European Commission is aware of this problem and has included airport developments in policy directives. However the EU preferred solution which is to direct growth and demand into regional airports rather than pushing development at key central hubs, is seen increasingly as unrealistic and unworkable.

The Association of European Airlines (AEA), the representative body for Europe's major carriers, put forward proposals in 1995 for more action to tackle airport congestion, both now and in the future, at the key airports across Europe. The AEA report warned that problems will continue to develop at the major hub airports which offer a comprehensive world-wide coverage of destinations. These are: London/Gatwick and Heathrow, Frankfurt, Paris/Charles de Gaul, Amsterdam, Rome, Madrid and Zurich. At present only Amsterdam has firm plans for a fifth runway, while Madrid is in the early stages of planning its third runway. All of these airports, except Gatwick, have plans for significant terminal capacity enhancement.

No new airport of any significance is planned anywhere in the Americas. Indeed in the USA, the world's largest air transport market, four new airports are in various states of progress, but these will not greatly enhance capacity. Growth of air transport within the USA will be lowest at just 3.8 per cent a year to 2014 in the domestic market (according to Boeing).

Throughout Central and South America and Africa there are no plans for new airport developments and, unless air transport changes to grow faster than forecasts suggest, the first part of the 21st century will see real problems in airport capacity for the first time since civil aviation began. Either airport development will have to be speeded up, against the wishes of environmental campaigners, or the real costs of air travel will start to rise, because there will be no alternative but to ration demand for access to airports by price, a process which is normally left to market forces.

ASSIGNMENT

1. Outline what you consider to be the impact of de-regulation on:

    a. Domestic coach operations;
    b. Domestic air travel;
    c. International air travel.

2. Describe the impact of changing travel preferences on the traditional holiday resort.

Chapter 7

The Accommodation Sector

Learning Objectives:
After reading this Chapter you should have an understanding of:

- The main components of the accommodation sector;
- How these components operate;
- Changes in accommodation preferences since 1970;
- The main companies in this sector;
- The distribution of accommodation in the UK;
- Recent trends in this sector.

Introduction

In terms of jobs provided the accommodation sector is the major element of the tourist industry in Britain. Out of 1.5 million people employed in the tourist industry, 900,000 work in the hotel and catering sector. The growth in jobs in tourism between 1975 and 1985 was most evident in this sector with 270,000 out of the 325,000 new jobs created during that period. (English Tourist Board/Institute for Manpower Studies 1985). Between 1982 and 1985, while employment levels in the leisure and related services sector remained ·fairly static, over 92,000 jobs were created in the hotel and catering sector. So, the accommodation sector has also demonstrated its resilience in times of economic recession and its ability to recover more quickly than many other tourism-related activities. Although these figures refer to the commercial accommodation sector, it is important to have an understanding of all types of accommodation used and their importance to the tourist industry or the economy of a tourist region.

During the eighteenth and nineteenth centuries accommodation mainly consisted of coaching inns, boarding houses, and houses let for the 'season', with the emergence of 'grand hotels' following the development of the railways, when few major resorts were without at least one luxury hotel. The growth of mass tourism and the spread of holidays with pay saw the emergence of smaller hotels and boarding houses catering for the summer trade and, in the 1930s, the development of new types of accommodation including camping, caravanning, youth hostelling and holiday camps. Post 1945 developments have included a mix of commercial activities such as villa holidays abroad, time-share holidays, consortia marketing country cottage or farm-house holidays; and non commercial activities such as visiting friends and relatives (VFR) and house exchange schemes, as well as the growth in the ownership of second homes.

Structure of the Accommodation Sector
The accommodation sector can be divided into two categories – commercial and non-commercial. In turn each of these has two components, the first is serviced accommodation; the second is self-catering accommodation.

Commercial serviced accommodation is dominated by the hotel sector, and this accounts for 25 per cent of the tourist market in the UK. The types of companies operating in this sector cover the whole range from multi-national companies to franchises, co-operatives or sole owners. The Catering Intelligence Unit (CIU) of the Consumer Industries Press estimates that there are now 145 hotel groups in the UK operating 2,000 hotels with a total of 146,000 bedrooms. Table 7.1 outlines the share of the British hotel market, and emphasises the importance of the international hotel chains. Two of the top three companies are US based, and have developed the system of *franchising* where the person operating the hotel pays a fee and royalties for using the brand name and marketing back-up of the parent company. Trusthouse Forte, Crest Hotels (owned by Bass PLC) Thistle Hotels (owned by Scottish and Newcastle), Holiday Inns and Ladbroke Hotels are the main companies with overseas interests. The Hotel Development Incentive Scheme (1969-73) which arose from the Development of Tourism Act 1969, encouraged several companies with broad interests in leisure activities to invest in the tourist industry. Bass PLC acquired the Crest Hotel group; Scottish and Newcastle, the Thistle Hotels, and Ladbrokes have established their own hotel chains. Since the end of this scheme in 1973 few new hotels have been built.

Table 7.1: Largest UK Hotel Groups and Branded Chains, 1995

Parent group	Hotels	Rooms	Av. rooms per hotel	Main branded chains
Forte (Granada Group)*	359	30,959	86	Posthouse, Travelodge, White Hart, Meridien, Crest
Mount Charlotte Thistle	93	13,556	146	Thistle, Mount Charlotte
Ladbroke	42	8,763	209	Hilton, Hilton National
Queens Moat Houses	81	8,500	105	Moat House, Country Hotels
Whitbread	165	10,643	65	Country Club, Travel Inn, Marriott
Bass	79	7,200	91	Toby, Holiday Inn
Stakis	40	4,900	123	Stakis
Jarvis Hotels	60	4,549	76	Jarvis
Rank Organisation	39	4,500	115	Shearings, Butlin's Warner
Total for major chains	964	91,927	54	

* branding and ownership at January 1996, subject to change following Granada takeover

Source: Mintel

Table 7.2: Marketing Consortia Operating in Great Britain

	World Rank*	Total Rooms	Great Britain Hotels	Rooms
Best Western	1	216,640	170	8,000
Leading Hotels of the World	7	44,000		
World Hotels	10	18,500		
Minotels	13	12,972		
Consort Hotels	20	5,000		
Exec Hotels	33	1,900		
Prestige Hotels	34	1,712	22	1,712
Guestacom	37	863		
Inter Hotels			103	n.a.

* According to the Top 37 International Consortia prepared by Hotels and Restaurants International.

However, the UK hotel market has remained fairly unchanged during the 1980s and 1990s and, faced with increasing competition for a share of this market, a number of new companies have emerged as well as consortia of independent hotels who have combined their marketing operations. Examples of new companies include the Queens Moat Hotels (55 hotels) and the Virani Group (19 hotels). The independent hotels who have formed marketing consortia have gained access to national and international markets through joint promotions. Table 7.2 shows the main hotel marketing consortia operating in Britain.

In the 1995 annual survey from Horwath International, average world-wide hotel occupancy increased only marginally from 62.3 per cent from 61.6 per cent in 1992, whilst the average room rate dropped by about 5 per cent between 1993 and 1992. The decline in the average room rate was largely due to a decline in rates achieved in Europe, although European hotels in general performed better than their counterparts in North America. Poor business conditions in Europe and the UK during the early 1990s had a significant impact on total revenues and on demand for hotel accommodation.

However, according to the latest business confidence survey from BDO Consulting, in 1995 UK hoteliers were much more confident about their business prospects. The state of the UK economy and low inflation were seen to be positive factors which would boost the industry. Nearly 80 per cent of UK hotels reported increases in average daily room rates and room occupancies. The business travel market has shown the biggest improvement, although conference business has also assisted in this growth. The increase in revenue also saw an increase in expenditure on marketing and training which was greater than advertising expenditure.

The *self-catering sector* has grown in importance over the past 30 years at the expense of the unlicensed hotel and guest house sector. This includes rented accommodation, caravans, and tented camp sites. In 1957 15 per cent of British holidaymakers used self-catering accommodation and 31 per cent stayed in unlicensed hotels and boarding houses. By 1971 these proportions were reversed and by 1991 over 36 per cent of Britons used self-catering accommodation on holidays in Britain.

Self-catering accommodation can take several forms. It can be:

- rented holiday flats, cottages or houses
- rented caravans
- rented tents
- holiday camps

Most of this self-catering accommodation is located on or close to Britain's coast, reflecting in part the long-standing preference for seaside holidays by most domestic tourists. The rapid growth and spread of coastal caravan and camping sites during the 1960s and 1970s gave rise to a range of conflicts and these are discussed in more detail in Chapter 12.

A recent study by the author of the *Bournemouth and South East Dorset Holiday Region* showed that there had been relatively little change in the proportion of serviced and self-catering provision between 1974 and 1984. Most of the self-catering accommodation is along a coastal strip within about half a mile of the sea. (Brown and Lavery 1987).

Farm-based accommodation has grown in importance over recent years as farmers have turned to other activities to supplement their income, and development grants have been made available through the tourist boards, notably the West Country Tourist Board and the Wales Tourist Board. This accommodation may be serviced or self-catering. Accommodation in farm premises consists of rooms let, either in the main building where the farmer and her/his family live, or in another structure that has been converted from agricultural use to holiday accommodation. Letting of farm cottages is also popular, as is the development of small touring caravans or camping sites.

Although comprehensive and reliable statistics on farm tourism are not yet available, what is clear from the data that does exist is that in most EEC countries it has already established itself as an important element in the rural economy. Most of the information outlined below has been drawn from papers presented at the Marienhamn Symposium.

- *France* There is a long tradition of farm tourism in France dating back to 1955 when the policy of *gîtes ruraux* was established. The amount of rural farm accommodation has almost trebled between 1973 and 1981 from 9,978 units to over 25,000. About 150,000 beds are provided in this sector with an estimated 7.5 million overnight stays.
- *West Germany* Farm Tourism has a 15 year history in West Germany with almost 25,000 farms now offering tourist accommodation. Recent surveys by the University of Munich have shown that about 3 million West Germans are interested in spending their holidays on farms.

- *Ireland* Farm tourism was developed in the early 1960s and the first listings contained only a few farm premises. The 1988 guide contains over 500 farm-houses offering tourist accommodation and a further 500 farm cottages.
- *United Kingdom* A conservative estimate suggests that 10,000 farms offer farmhouse accommodation and a further 10,000 offer self-catering accommodation. A further 5,000 farms provide camping and caravanning facilities.
- *Denmark* The marketing of farm tourism is heavily subsidised by the Danish Tourist Board, who are also involved with the promotional literature.

No information is available on the extent of and growth in farm tourism among the other Member States of the European Economic Community. The summary report of the Marienhamn Symposium concludes that most of the farms depending on non-agricultural income are interested in farm tourism (i.e. 40 to 60 per cent of all farms) and some regions, particularly in Scandinavia, show a very high growth rate in this activity. Farm tourism has not yet developed in Italy or Greece.

In the non-commercial accommodation sector, visiting friends and relatives (VFR) is taking a growing share of the accommodation market. In 1961 VFR accounted for 32 per cent of accommodation used. By 1994 this had increased to 47 per cent of accommodation used by British tourists. In the past the VFR market has been neglected as a segment of the total market, but it is important also when marketing Britain to overseas tourists. In 1994 40 per cent of overseas visitors to Britain stayed with friends and relatives.

The growth in the ownership of private caravans and large trailer-tents has made self-catering mobile holidays available to a growing number of British holiday-makers. Membership of the Caravan Club of Great Britain increased by 40 per cent between 1950-1960 and by 80 per cent for individual and 221 per cent for family members from 1960-1990.

More recent trends include national and international home exchange schemes where, for a small annual fee, individuals can exchange houses for the holiday period, and time-share developments where purchasers can buy exclusive use of a property for a specific period of the year. This development is discussed in more detail in Chapter 13.

Classification of Accommodation

There is no statutory registration system for hotels in the UK, although from January 1987 the National Tourist Boards for England, Scotland and Wales introduced a new Crown Classification System. It covers serviced accommodation and includes all types of serviced establishments from listed for simple accommodation, to five crowns for top class accommodation. Previous attempts at voluntary classification were unsatisfactory because they relied on facts supplied by the owners/ managers themselves without any checking. The new Crown System is an attempt to ensure that no classification will be granted until a verification check has been carried out. Subsequent checks will be made on an annual basis. From 1987 onwards only those premises classified by the tourist boards will be included in their accommodation guides. The tourist boards hope that, by introducing one scheme common to all serviced accommodation in Britain, it will help the industry to market itself more effectively at home and overseas. By the end of 1986 over 10,000 establishments had been classified under this scheme.

The AA and RAC also operate their own classification schemes. Until the introduction of the Crown scheme, the star rating awarded by the AA has been one measure of the quality of the serviced accommodation sector. Nearly 80 per cent of the entries in the AA guide are in the 2 and 3 star categories – 6 per cent are 4 star and under 1 per cent are 5 star.

However, these systems of classifying or grading serviced accommodation are all voluntary, unlike many European countries who have compulsory classification systems. With any voluntary system there will be many premises that, for whatever reason, choose not to apply for registration.

Accommodation classification and grading schemes are only one basis on which customers make a choice of hotels. Hotel choice is also influenced by location and price and neither of these can be encompassed in a classification grade. A classification scheme therefore needs to reflect the different types and standards of accommodation to enable the tourist to make a more informed choice. Therefore, there needs to be a simple, consistent and reliable system of descriptive information such as crowns and stars. There is now growing pressure for the government to enact a statutory requirement for the registration and basic categorisation of all types of tourist accommodation the UK. This statutory scheme would not extend to classification of grading for which there is no strong support within the industry. There is a need to establish inspection standards, criteria, training and monitoring consistency of operation. Inspections could be carried out by the Tourist Boards, the AA or RAC, or any other licensed body so far as common core criteria are concerned.

Problems Affecting the Accommodation Sector

The owner or manager in the accommodation sector is working in a highly competitive commercial environment, and has to deal with several issues that can affect the success of her/his operation.
These include:

- the seasonality of hotel occupancy rates
- the cost and availability of manpower
- the supply of raw materials
- the availability of new technology
- interest rates and taxation policy

The domestic holiday market is still heavily concentrated in the period between June and August, and the accommodation sector faces the dilemma of gearing up to meet peak-season demand and then having under-used resources for the rest of the year.

To offset this seasonal peaking the British Tourist Authority introduced 'Operation Off-Peak' in 1972, with the aim of encouraging operators to put together development packages that would promote overseas visitor numbers during the trough periods – particularly the autumn and winter months.

During the 1970s organisations such as British Rail (see Chapter 6) and hotel consortia began to market short-break holidays outside of the peak period, and the growth in these has helped to improve hotel occupancy rates. Between 1977 and 1982 short holidays in serviced accommodation increased by 24 per cent (BTA 1984).

In 1983 the Education and Training Advisory Council (ETAC) of the Hotel and Catering Industrial Board (HCTB) published a five-volume report on *Hotel and Catering Skills – Now and in the Future* (HCTB 1983).

This report suggested that about 8 per cent of the workforce leave the hotel and catering industry each year and that, with the growth in the accommodation sector, there would be an overall shortfall of about 50,000 people by 1990.

New technology is playing an increasingly important role in the accommodation sector. A Gallup survey for the *Caterer and Hotelkeeper* in 1983 found that more than a third of hotels with 3 stars or more, regardless of size, possess computers. These are used for a wide range of functions including:

- Front office activities – reservations, accounting, ledgers, credit control;
- General office activities – financial control, day-to-day accounts, purchases, invoices, credit control;
- Room service accounting;
- Restaurant/meals and drink accounting;
- Telephone accounts.

Hotels that form part of a chain may have their activities linked by computer networks and the General Management/Boards of Directors can receive up to date information on the performance of individual hotels and consortia of hotels. Clearly staff working the front office or finance and accounting divisions of an hotel will have to have training in computer applications and usage, particularly database packages, viewdata systems and spreadsheets.

There is still a view in financial circles that hotels are a high-risk investment and this hampers the industry's attempts to raise sufficient quantities of capital, particularly long-term capital. The Government in their report *Action for Jobs in Tourism* (HMSO 1986) considered that it was largely for the private sector to finance new hotel development (in London) and asked the English Tourist Board to take the lead in discussing with financial institutions ways of improving the industry's access to private sources of capital. At that time the Regional Tourist Boards, under the Section 4 scheme, could assist hotel developments which would otherwise not go ahead. In 1983/4 the English Tourist Board, the Regional Tourist Boards and local authorities approved £6.4 million in grants for hotel development/improvement schemes. Outside of London, the Urban Development Grant Scheme was available to assist hotel schemes, provided they met the criteria for economic regeneration of deprived areas and provided a net increase in jobs and investment. The smaller hotel groups could also take advantage of the Business Extension Scheme which has been widened to cover existing businesses.

The Distribution of Accommodation in Britain
Serviced accommodation is concentrated in London and the main resort towns, although there has been a growth of new hotels around Heathrow and the major provincial cities. During the period 1971 to 1987 there was a significant decline in the number of hotels with less than 15 rooms, but little change in the overall number of hotel bedrooms available, because of the trend towards large hotels with over 100 bedrooms.

London has the greatest concentration of hotel accommodation, accounting for over 17 per cent of all rooms available in Britain. This reflects its pre-eminence as a tourist destination especially for overseas visitors. (In 1990 hotel occupancy in London was 69 per cent compared with a national average of 57 per cent.) (BTA).

In the regions, the South West including the resorts of Torbay and North Cornwall, the South East (including Brighton, Eastbourne and Thanet, and Scotland) have the main concentrations of hotel rooms.

In terms of the domestic tourist market, the main concentrations of accommodation are associated with the large resort towns, although the growth of business trade and the development of purpose-built conference and exhibition centres has led to a growth of new hotels in cities like Birmingham and Manchester which are not normally considered 'resorts'. Indeed Manchester now has the largest stock of accommodation, in terms of bed spaces, outside of London.

Some hotel groups have moved into national prominence by buying up established hotels rather than seeking to build new ones. For example, the Swallow Hotel Group, the North-East hotel chain owned by Sunderland brewers Vaux, bought a large London hotel in order to gain access to the London market. A recent trend has been for the independent hoteliers to form marketing consortia in order to achieve a market 'presence' at the national or international level. There are now at least 10 hotel marketing consortia operating in this way in Britain (Table 7.2).

Recent Trends in the UK Accommodation Sector
The hotel sector has withstood the recession years quite well, by adapting to changing trends, identifying new markets, better market segmentation and more efficient management. The growth in the numbers of foreign tourists during the 1970s and 1980s has clearly helped the hotel sector, and the numbers of foreign visitors to the UK has grown steadily during the 1980s. Hotels have begun to cater for the short break domestic market and most major chains offer special short break packages aimed at increasing occupancy levels during the shoulder and winter months. This pattern has increased dramatically during the 1980s.

Figure 7.1 shows the types of accommodation used by British residents on short-break holidays (1 to 3 nights) and longer holidays (4 or more nights). It shows the three main types of accommodation used, distinguishing between trips staying in hotels, other commercial accommodation, and staying with friends and relatives or using own caravan/second home. VFR now dominates the short break market, accounting for over two thirds of accommodation used 1982-1994. The hotel sector share is fairly static at 13 per cent to 14 per cent, but other commercial accommodation (42 per cent) is more important for longer holidays.

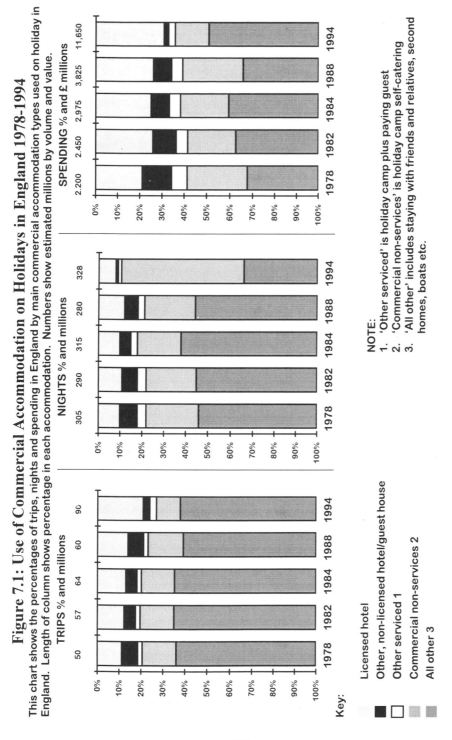

Figure 7.1: Use of Commercial Accommodation on Holidays in England 1978-1994

This chart shows the percentages of trips, nights and spending in England by main commercial accommodation types used on holiday in England. Length of column shows percentage in each accommodation. Numbers show estimated millions by volume and value.

TRIPS % and millions

| 50 | 57 | 64 | 60 | 90 |
| 1978 | 1982 | 1984 | 1988 | 1994 |

NIGHTS % and millions

| 305 | 290 | 315 | 280 | 328 |
| 1978 | 1982 | 1984 | 1988 | 1994 |

SPENDING % and £ millions

| 2,200 | 2,450 | 2,975 | 3,825 | 11,650 |
| 1978 | 1982 | 1984 | 1988 | 1994 |

Key:

■ Licensed hotel
□ Other, non-licensed hotel/guest house
▨ Other serviced 1
▨ Commercial non-services 2
▨ All other 3

NOTE:
1. 'Other serviced' is holiday camp plus paying guest
2. 'Commercial non-services' is holiday camp self-catering
3. 'All other' includes staying with friends and relatives, second homes, boats etc.

Source: British Tourism Survey. All holidays by adults and children accompanying them

121

Spending on accommodation on holidays in England increased from £2,200 million in 1978 to £11,650 million in 1994 (English Tourist Board). As Figure 7.1 shows, this increase in spending has mainly benefitted the hotel sector, (an increase from £484 million in 1978 to £3,611 million in 1994) at the expense of the great house and holiday apartment sectors.

Holiday Camps

Another trend is for more people to go on holidays which do not need serviced accommodation. This was pioneered in the 1980s by entrepreneurs such as Billy Butlin and Fred Pontin, and by 1939 there were about 200 permanent camps scattered around the coast of Britain. During the 1950s and 1960s these holiday camps came to be concentrated into about 150 main centres. The majority are controlled by four major companies – Rank, Bass, Ladbrokes and Grand Metropolitan (now owned by Mecca Leisure).

Table 7.3: Main Holiday Camp Operators

Holiday Camp Operators	Number of centres	Beds
Butlins (Rank)	31	92,00
Pontins (Bass)	24	44,100
Ladbroke	18	31,000
Warner (Mecca)	14	10,500
	87	177,600

Source: *Euromonitor*

In the 1950s these holiday camps tended to attract a largely regional and working class clientele and their canteen-style catering and range of entertainments reflected this client group. The growth of cheap inclusive tours in the 1960s was aimed at this same market segment and the numbers of visitors to the holiday camps began to decline or fall off during this period. In response to this, they have changed their mode of operation, improved their range of amenities and aimed for a greater marketing mix. The emphasis is much more on self-catering based on small blocks of chalets or bungalows, with an image that is quite different to the traditional holiday camp of seaside chalets, bars and dance halls.

Table 7.4: Trends in the Financial Turnover of the British Hotel Industry 1974/1982

Year	Hotels and Guest Houses	
	Current Prices £ million	Constant Prices 1980 = 100
1974	935	85.5
1975	1132	88.0
1976	1404	92.3
1977	1760	99.1
1978	2164	105.4
1979	2493	102.0
1980	2888	100.0
1981	3173	96.8
1982 estimate		95.2

Source: Catering Inquiry, DTI

On the continent, a Dutch company pioneered a new concept in holiday villages. The company is called Center Parcs (formerly Sportshuis Centrum) who started in the early 1970s as a chain of shops selling camping and caravan equipment. They developed the concept of bungalow parks, usually set in a landscape of trees and lakes and focused on a large central complex of covered all-weather tropical pools. Water temperatures are around 25°C and they have wave machines, water shutes, saunas, solariums, bars and crèches which are all part of the main pool complex. There are also a whole range of indoor and outdoor sports activities. There are now 8 sites in Holland and one in Belgium (Figure 7.2) and they are planning 6 developments in Britain by the mid 1990s. The company was acquired by Scottish and Newcastle in the early 1990s. Two have now opened, the first at Sherwood Forest in 1988 and the second at Thetford in 1989. They are open all year round and have occupancy levels of over 95 per cent over a 52 week period.

How do they do it? Well, clearly they have got the product right. The pool complex is the major attraction, particularly for families with children. They have gone for particular market segments for particular times in the year. So, outside of the main school vacation times they aim to attract families with pre-school children and older people who no longer have children. In Holland over 70 per cent of bookings are repeat visits.

Figure 7.2: Distribution of Center Parcs in Europe

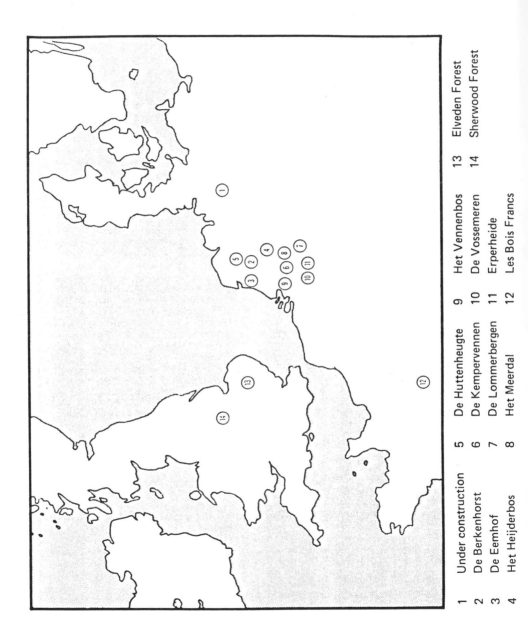

1	Under construction	5	De Huttenheugte	9	Het Vennenbos	13	Elveden Forest
2	De Berkenhorst	6	De Kempervennen	10	De Vossemeren	14	Sherwood Forest
3	De Eemhof	7	De Lommerbergen	11	Erperheide		
4	Het Heijderbos	8	Het Meerdal	12	Les Bois Francs		

They also carry out regular surveys of their visitors to determine their likes and dislikes, and they have a special staff training programme for hospitality. In addition they advertise widely in newspapers, magazines and on the TV and radio. Another mark of a successful product is a large number of repeat visits; and nearly half of their visitors are on repeat visits.

The concept of all-weather tropical environments with de luxe accommodation and a wide range of water-based recreation facilities, appeals to several market segments and appears to be attracting new people to the bungalow park in considerable numbers. The additional appeal of these leisure complexes is that they can be enjoyed in all weathers and all seasons.

Not content with their success in Holland, they have now invested £40 million in developing their first holiday park in England. Sherwood Forest, about 100 miles north of London, was chosen as their first site and was opened in 1988. They have now identified 2 further sites for bungalow parks. The second UK site to be developed was Thetford, in East Anglia which opened in 1989. The Sherwood Forest bungalow park is focused on an all-weather dome complex containing swimming pools, waterfalls, whirlpools and waterslides. The holiday village has 600 stone-built villas in small clusters, set in 450 acres of trees, streams and a man-made lake. The luxury holiday village has a peak-season capacity of 3,000 and the first season operated at near full capacity.

In the face of this competition, and the evident success of Center Parcs, the Rank Organisation are spending over £40 million to redesign their Butlins holiday camps. Butlins at Minehead has been re-named Somerset World and £10 million was spent in 1985 to develop a water-leisure complex with enclosed water slides, new deluxe accommodation and a themed showbar. Bookings in 1986 were 30 per cent up on 1985 and 60 per cent up in 1987. The company plan to spend a total of £100 million over the next five years. Butlins at Skegness has been remodelled on similar lines and re-named Funcoast World, and the camp at Bognor Regis has become Southcoast World.

One further development is the selling of resort accommodation in Britain in the same way as overseas holidays, with brochures and computerised booking systems. Five British resorts co-operated in a computerised central booking system known as WAVES. This is accessible through the Tourist Information Centres, and provides a comprehensive computerised reservations and booking system that is available to all hoteliers. The recent hot summers, especially 1995, have seen a resurgence of interest in holidays in many of our traditional seaside resorts.

In the face of increased competition, some hotels are broadening their range of functions to provide leisure or sports facilities, whilst others are developing conference business. The English Tourist Board has identified over 200 sites in Britain with development potential and is encouraging many of the traditional seaside resorts to invest in modern facilities. Tourism is now an international activity and, if our accommodation stock is not modernised and comparable to standards in the best resorts overseas and marketed imaginatively, it will lose its market share to new types of accommodation being developed.

Recent Trends in the USA Accommodation Sector
This sector in the United States is generally referred to as the lodging industry. The forerunners of today's major hotel chains were developed by Conrad Hilton and Ernest Henderson (Sheraton), followed in the post war period by Marriott (which developed in 1957 from a fast food operation) and Ramada, founded by Marianne Isbell in the late 1950s. Each of these major hotel chains was based on land ownership and managing the hotel was just part of a wider portfolio of real estate.

During the 1970s and 1980s companies such as Hilton, Holiday Inn, Marriott and Sheraton expanded by selling off their real estate but retaining management contracts of the hotels. This enabled them to develop larger up-market hotels charging premium rates. In the 1980s around 7000 hotels with 900,000 rooms were constructed in the United States. Development was encouraged by the ease of access to capital and by favourable tax laws. However, in the later part of the 1980s, changing tax laws and the savings and loan crisis began to see a rapid reduction in development capital. As funds for new hotels began to dry-up, funds for refurbishment of increasingly ageing hotels also became scarce. A downturn in the economy and then the Gulf War in the early 1990s also saw a further decline in new hotel construction.

Because of the deteriorating conditions in the USA, several major US-based chains began to look to the global market place for capital and growth. At the same time many foreign firms began to acquire hotel assets in the United States. For example, Holiday Inn was acquired by Bass and Westin was acquired by Aoki in 1988. As the economy begins to strengthen in the United States, it can be expected that North American firms will begin to undertake more aggressive expansion in overseas markets.

Conclusions

As the global economy emerges from the recession of the early 1990s, major hotel firms will be looking for growth strategies. Growth and quality production services, with a strong base supported by technology, are the most likely preferred strategy. Growth will be based on franchising and management service contracts, with a limited number of firms acquiring assets and real estates. Some companies will also grow through acquisition of smaller chains.

Increasingly major hotel chains are investing in technology in order to remain competitive. This will shape their marketing programmes, their product design and their corporate strategy. Again, during a period when large amounts of investment capital may be scarce, the main competitive method will be to franchise services such as reservation systems, advanced technology and sales and marketing. Facilities management and management contracts may also emerge as a major approach to growth.

ASSIGNMENT

Produce a proposal (for a major multi-national company with a wide range of business interests) setting out:

a. the optimum locations for accommodation development in Britain;
b. the types of development.

Justify the reasons for your decisions.

Chapter 8

Public Sector Tourism

Learning Objectives:
After reading this Chapter you should have a clear understanding of:

- The main aspects of public sector tourism;
- The role of the Tourist Boards;
- The development and future of public sector tourism;

Tourism is the mixed economy in action, and nowhere is this more evident than in the promotion of tourism where the public sector plays a major role. An important part of the promotion and marketing of individual resort towns, and indeed of the UK as a tourist destination generally, is done by public sector bodies such as the National, Regional or Local Tourist Boards – yet the product being sold is largely run and owned by the private sector. Why is this? How has this come about?

There are at least five sound reasons why public sector bodies promote tourism:

  i. it can make a significant contribution to the overall economic activity of a country, region or town;
 ii. it can create new jobs;
iii. it can make a significant contribution to the balance of income over expenditure – for a city, region or country.
 iv. synergy, i.e. the working together of corporate organisations and regional/national bodies to produce an effect greater than the sum of their individual efforts.
  v. they can control the development of tourism by sponsoring projects in areas of high unemployment and by directing new developments away from environmentally sensitive areas.

The origins of public sector tourism in Britain can be traced back to the

'Come to Britain' movement which was founded in 1926 by Sir Francis Toule (British Tourist Authority 1975). Following a series of meetings in 1927 and 1928 between representatives of the Department of Overseas Trade, Members of Parliament and other prominent public figures, an organisation known as the Travel Association of Great Britain and Ireland was formed in April 1929 with a £5,000 grant from HM Government. The Association had two principal aims:

a. to increase the numbers of visitors from overseas to Great Britain and Ireland;
b. to stimulate the demand for British goods and services and to promote international understanding.

Within 12 months a 'Come to Britain' folder had been produced, giving information on tourist attractions, and coming events in Britain. In 1930 the Scottish Travel Association was established and it was agreed that they would supply the Travel Association of Great Britain and Ireland with information about Scotland and they would receive a grant from the parent body to promote tourism.

The public sector became more involved with promoting tourism following the Local Authorities (Publicity) Act 1931 which enabled local authorities 'to contribute towards the cost of collecting and collating information in regard to the amenities and advantages of the British Isles or any part thereof, whether commercial, historic, scenic, recreational, curative or climatic, and of disseminating that information outside the British Isles provided that the expenditure did not exceed the amount which would be produced by the rate of one halfpenny in the pound levied at the rateable value of the area of authority'.

The Travel and Industrial Development Association faced the problems common to many industrial associations during the Great Depression of the 1930s, but by 1939 it had over 1,000 members drawn from the hotels and restaurants sector, the main rail and shipping companies and air and road transport firms. In 1938 over 720,000 overseas visitors had been attracted to Britain, spending almost £29 million – a figure which compared with the revenue from coal exports.

The most significant development in the years immediately after World War 2 was the decision to discontinue its industrial activities and concentrate on promoting travel to the UK, and in 1946 the Board of Trade proposed the creation of a non-governmental organisation to develop tourism, catering and home holiday services.

In 1947 the government set up the British Tourist and Holidays Board (incorporating the Travel Association). This new body was the pre-runner of the present-day British Tourist Authority. The Board had three main objectives – to rebuild an effective tourist promotion organisation; to carry out market research and related studies; and to establish links with other national tourist organisations overseas. In 1948/9 the Board of Trade gave a grant of £326,500 to the Board and this marked an ongoing commitment to the involvement of the public sector in the tourist industry – a commitment that remained constant over the intervening 30 years. The essential role of this organisation was summed up in 1950 when the British Tourist and Holidays Board and the Travel Association divisions were integrated to form the British Travel and Holidays Association. The Association was seen to have two main functions – bringing visitors from overseas to this country (the UK) and ensuring that they, as well as home holidaymakers, are well received and accommodated and have the best facilities that can be provided.

By 1960 the British Travel Association had offices in fifteen countries throughout the world and there were over 1.6 million visitors to Britain. During the 1960s several regional tourist associations were established with local authority support, including the London Tourist Board and the Lakes Counties Travel Association. However, these associations arose out of a voluntary approach towards developing tourism and it became increasingly clear that, if a major expansion in tourism promotion was to come about, central government must play a greater role.

Development of Tourism Act
The growth in the numbers of overseas visitors – over 5.8 million in 1969, spending £359 million – highlighted the potential of tourism as a creator of wealth and jobs. In 1969 the government issued the Development of Tourism Act which contained three main sets of proposals.

Part I established a statutory British Tourist Authority and Tourist Boards for England, Scotland and Wales with responsibility for promoting the development of tourism to and within Great Britain, and to encourage the provision and improvement of tourist amenities and facilities in Great Britain. The English, Welsh and Scottish Boards had similar functions. In addition each National Tourist Board was given the authority to:

a.   promote or undertake publicity in any form; and

b.   to provide advisory and information services

c.   to promote or undertake research.

The Act also enables the British Tourist Authority, after consultation with the English, Scottish and Wales Tourist Boards, to prepare schemes giving grant aid or loans to tourism development projects which, in the opinion of the Board, would provide or improve tourist amenities or facilities.

The British Tourist Authority and, likewise, the English, Scottish and Wales Tourist Boards had the duty to advise any Minister or public body on any matters relating to tourism.

These Tourist Boards received their funding through the Board of Trade and the Chairman and members were appointed by the Board of Trade. So, for the first time, after over 40 years of tourism promotion in Britain, the government established a national organisation with a statutory responsibility for the development and promotion of tourism in Britain.

Part II of the Act, which followed from an earlier White Paper on *Hotel Development Incentives*, provided financial assistance for hotel development schemes. This assistance took two forms – grants and loans. Hotel Development Grants were available from the National Tourist Boards – but the hotel had to have at least 10 bedrooms (in Greater London 25 bedrooms) and the grant could only be claimed *after* the completion of the hotel. However, this provision meant that all small hotels were excluded from the scheme. Grants were also available for the extension or alteration of existing hotels, provided at least 5 additional bedrooms were added. The grants would meet 20 per cent of the expenditure or £1,000 per bedroom, whichever were the less. In development areas this grant was increased to 25 per cent of total expenditure.

The National Tourist Boards could make loans of up to £500,000 to provide new hotels or to extend or improve existing hotels. They would generally lend up to 30 per cent for new hotels and 50 per cent for improvements to existing ones. These grants or loans were directed to the private sector, and were not available to local authorities.

At the time this Act was passed, three-quarters of hotel rooms in Britain were over 50 years old and many lacked modern amenities. Before 1969 new investment in hotel development was very limited and confined to a few larger companies. In 1969 new hotel building was producing about 2,000 rooms a year for an annual investment of £15 million. Section I of the Development of Tourism Act led to a rapid growth in the hotel industry and, by 1973, over 70,000 additional hotel bedrooms and had been provided at a total cost of over £300 million, almost doubling the capacity of hotel accommodation. However, the bulk of these were in London and many of the old traditional resorts still lacked modern hotels. In 1973 the Hotel Development Grants Scheme was terminated and the Section 4 system of grants and loans has largely replaced it. The next section of this chapter discusses the Section 4 scheme in more detail.

Part III of the Development of Tourism Act enabled the respective Tourist Boards to maintain registers of accommodation and to introduce classification and grading of accommodation.

In the intervening years since 1969 there has been a massive increase in both international and domestic tourism. In 1969 Britain received over £350 million from spending by overseas visitors. By 1994 this had increased to over £12,000 million, and domestic tourism produced a further £14,000 million. A large measure of this growth is due to the efforts of the National Tourist Boards promoting Britain as a tourist destination and encouraging the development of tourism facilities and amenities throughout Britain.

ROLE OF THE TOURIST BOARDS

The British Tourist Authority
The main role of the British Tourist Authority is to promote incoming tourism to Britain. In order to do this it has established a world-wide network of 21 overseas offices and employs over 200 staff overseas. It has three primary objectives:

i. to increase visitor spending in Britain;
ii. to increase and spread the overall level of travel beyond London to the regions of England, Scotland and Wales;
iii. to extend the tourist season by promoting travel in the autumn and winter months.

The BTA works in partnership with the trade and other tourist interests and encourages support from the trade for their promotional work overseas. The BTA overseas offices work closely with all tourist interests in the territories for which they are responsible who wish to market or commission travel products and holiday packages in overseas countries. This may include familiarisation trips and educational tours for overseas travel agents, tour operators and their sales staffs. They also run British Travel Workshops which bring together British producers with tourist services and products to sell and overseas buyers – travel agents and tour operators – who are keen to develop their business to Britain.

The English, Welsh and Scottish Tourist Boards
The three National Tourist Boards were all established in 1969 and each was given a remit to encourage tourists to visit and take holidays in their respective countries, and to encourage the provision and improvement of tourist amenities and facilities. Like the BTA, all are financed by a grant-in-aid from central government. The Act also gave powers to the National Boards to establish committees to advise them in the performance of their functions and, in the light of this, the English Tourist Board created twelve Regional Tourist Boards to ensure effective co-ordination and co-operation on tourism matters at regional and local levels with local authorities and commercial operators. Figure 8.1 outlines the Tourist Board framework, and Figure 8.2 shows the distribution of Regional Tourist Boards in England.

Figure 8.1: Tourist Board Structure in Britain

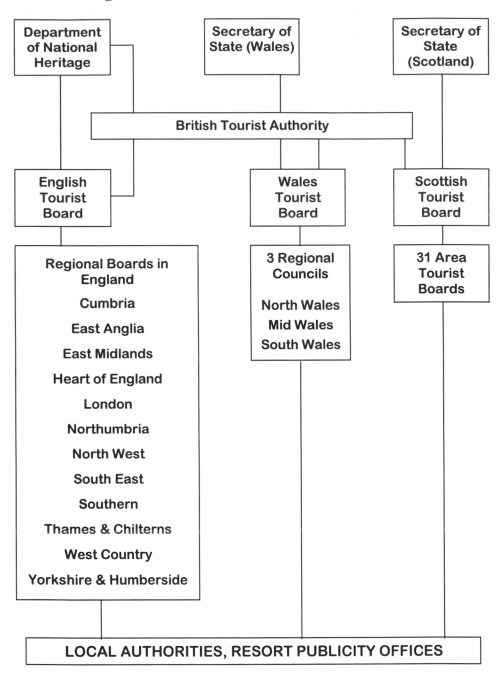

The English Tourist Board undertakes a wide range of marketing and promotional activities and one of its main campaigns is 'operation off-peak' aimed at extending the holiday season by promoting spring and autumn holidays. The ETB was empowered under section 4 of the 1969 Development of Tourism Act to give financial assistance for tourism development projects and, in the financial year 1987/8, over £14.8 million was provided by the Board for tourism development projects. (ETB *Tourism in Action* July, 1988). A very wide range of projects have been assisted by the Board, ranging from hotel extension schemes to support for museum and theatres and countryside recreation projects. The Section 4 system funded two main categories of project. There was an *Innovation Fund* for projects costing over £100,000. The maximum grant was 20 per cent of capital cost, given that the project had a significant tourism impact, was clearly viable, and clearly needed financial assistance. For projects costing over £100,000 ETB often inserted a clause making the grant repayable after a certain period of years, provided that the business was sufficiently profitable. The major function of Section 4 funds was to act as seedcorn to encourage innovations and business expansion schemes that will benefit tourism generally.

On January 30th 1989 the Secretary of State for Employment, who had ultimate responsibility for funding the English Tourist Board's operations, announced that the 'Section 4' scheme of financial assistance for tourism projects was to be suspended in England, pending completion of a major review of tourism policy which began in 1988. In answer to a Parliamentary Question, the Secretary of State pointed to the high levels of private sector investment where in England over £2 billion was invested by the private sector in major tourism and leisure projects during the first half of 1988, compared with £10 million in assistance through the Section 4 scheme in 1988/9. Clearly the Government felt that, in the late 1980s, the continuing high level of investment and confidence of the private sector in the tourism industry made it unnecessary to continue incentives through grants and loans.

In 1993 the Government changed the overall responsibility for management of the ETB/BTA and it now reports to the Department of

National Heritage. This was also followed by a reduction of £2.6 million in grant-in-aid to the English Tourist Board, from £13.9 million in 1993/4 to £11.3 million in 1994/5, with also direction from the Security of State to devolve more responsibility to regional tourist boards. Under the new structure, the English Tourist Board's own direct marketing role has reduced and a newly created Tourism Fund, managed by the English Tourist Board and the regional tourist boards working with BTA, has been established. It has the aim of improving the international appeal of England as a tourist destination, and enhancing the quality of the tourism product.   The eleven regional tourist boards will assume greater responsibility for delivering domestic marketing, development and quality standards programmes.

At the same time, the British Tourist Authority has restructured and streamlined its operations in London in order to find up to £1 million more for overseas activities. BTA grant in aid was increased slightly from £32 million in 1993/4 to £33.2 million in 1994/5. The changes in BTA operations overseas included increasing resources for Far East operations and in markets which offer great potential. In North America a New York information service has been strengthened and a new office in Miami has been opened.

The Wales Tourist Board, which is based at Cardiff has a similar range of services to the ETB, although there are just three Regional Boards for Wales.

The Scottish Tourist Board originally established nine Regional Tourist Boards but, by the early 1980s, it was clear that such large Boards were too unwieldy, given the distribution of population in Scotland and the distances between settlements in the North and West of Scotland. By 1983 the nine Regional Tourist Boards in Scotland had been replaced by 32 Area Tourist Boards, almost completely covering the country. (Figure 8.3 on page 138).

Figure 8.2: England's Regional Tourist Boards

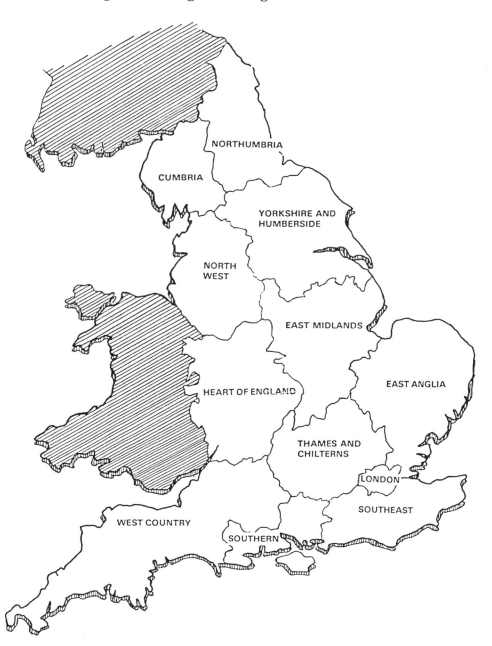

Note: Southern Tourist Board took over responsibilities for Thames and Chilterns after regional board went into liquidation in early 1990s.

Figure 8.3: Scotland's Area Tourist Boards

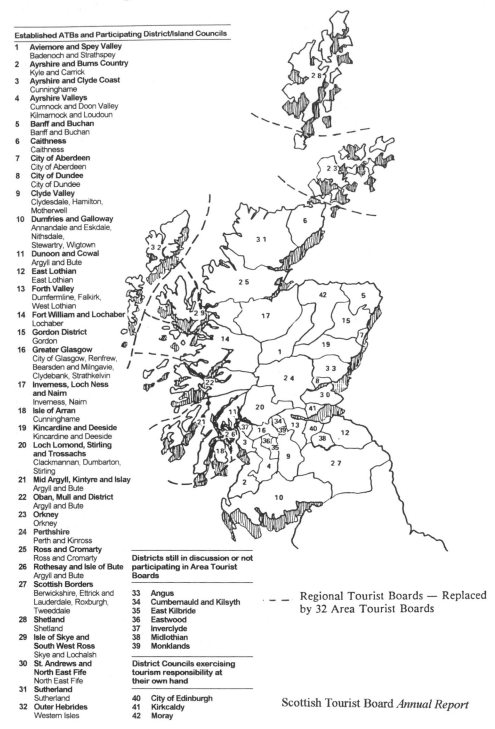

Established ATBs and Participating District/Island Councils

1 **Aviemore and Spey Valley**
  Badenoch and Strathspey
2 **Ayrshire and Burns Country**
  Kyle and Carrick
3 **Ayrshire and Clyde Coast**
  Cunninghame
4 **Ayrshire Valleys**
  Cumnock and Doon Valley
  Kilmarnock and Loudoun
5 **Banff and Buchan**
  Banff and Buchan
6 **Caithness**
  Caithness
7 **City of Aberdeen**
  City of Aberdeen
8 **City of Dundee**
  City of Dundee
9 **Clyde Valley**
  Clydesdale, Hamilton,
  Motherwell
10 **Dumfries and Galloway**
  Annandale and Eskdale,
  Nithsdale,
  Stewartry, Wigtown
11 **Dunoon and Cowal**
  Argyll and Bute
12 **East Lothian**
  East Lothian
13 **Forth Valley**
  Dumfermline, Falkirk,
  West Lothian
14 **Fort William and Lochaber**
  Lochaber
15 **Gordon District**
  Gordon
16 **Greater Glasgow**
  City of Glasgow, Renfrew,
  Bearsden and Milngavie,
  Clydebank, Strathkelvin
17 **Inverness, Loch Ness
  and Nairn**
  Inverness, Nairn
18 **Isle of Arran**
  Cunninghame
19 **Kincardine and Deeside**
  Kincardine and Deeside
20 **Loch Lomond, Stirling
  and Trossachs**
  Clackmannan, Dumbarton,
  Stirling
21 **Mid Argyll, Kintyre and Islay**
  Argyll and Bute
22 **Oban, Mull and District**
  Argyll and Bute
23 **Orkney**
  Orkney
24 **Perthshire**
  Perth and Kinross
25 **Ross and Cromarty**
  Ross and Cromarty
26 **Rothesay and Isle of Bute**
  Argyll and Bute
27 **Scottish Borders**
  Berwickshire, Ettrick and
  Lauderdale, Roxburgh,
  Tweeddale
28 **Shetland**
  Shetland
29 **Isle of Skye and
  South West Ross**
  Skye and Lochalsh
30 **St. Andrews and
  North East Fife**
  North East Fife
31 **Sutherland**
  Sutherland
32 **Outer Hebrides**
  Western Isles

Districts still in discussion or not participating in Area Tourist Boards

33 Angus
34 Cumbernauld and Kilsyth
35 East Kilbride
36 Eastwood
37 Inverclyde
38 Midlothian
39 Monklands

District Councils exercising tourism responsibility at their own hand

40 City of Edinburgh
41 Kirkcaldy
42 Moray

– – Regional Tourist Boards — Replaced by 32 Area Tourist Boards

Scottish Tourist Board *Annual Report*

The Regional Tourist Boards

The Regional Tourist Boards are autonomous bodies and draw their funding and membership from local authorities and commercial tourist operations within their areas, as well as funding from central government via the English or appropriate National Tourist Board. They are autonomous, commercial companies limited by guarantee. The constitution and internal organisation varies from Board to Board, as do the staff and financial resources. Many of the functions and operations of the Regional Tourist Boards are similar in kind, if not in scale, to the National Tourist Board. A major part, therefore, of the Regional Tourist Boards' activity is focused on the marketing and promotion of their own region. Activities will include the production of regional accommodation/facilities guides, advertising campaigns, exhibitions and workshops. Most Regional Boards receive their main source of funding from commercial revenue-earning activities, such as selling space and consultancy activities. Table 8.1 shows the percentage of income from such activities compared with their subvention from the National Board.

Table 8.1: Regional Tourist Boards Sources of Income

	English Tourist Board Subvention	Local Authority %	Commercial Membership	Other*	Total
Cumbria	23	14	13	50	100
East Anglia	22	12	7	59	100
East Midlands	30	15	6	49	100
Heart of England	22	20	14	44	100
London Visitor & Convention Bureau	19	-	44	37	100
Northumbria	23	48	5	24	100
North West	17	15	4	64	100
South East	26	19	12	43	100
Southern	15	9	6	70	100
West Country	18	13	11	58	100
Yorkshire & Humberside	21	25	8	46	100

*("Other" includes selling, space, advertising revenue, consultancy, etc.)

Source: English Tourist Board Annual Reports

The Regional Tourist Boards are closely concerned with the network of Tourist Information Centres throughout Britain (TICs) and generally provide the local contact and distribution for the Boards. In some instances, particularly the more important tourist destinations, the Regional Tourist Boards also provide and staff limited number of centres to complement those provided by the local authority.

The Regional Tourist Boards were also responsible for the local administration of the Section 4 grant aid scheme for capital projects. Initial applications for assistance were made to the Regional Tourist Board, who advise the ETB on particular applications. The Regional Boards had the delegated authority to recommend for approval grants of up to £100,000 for tourism development projects, although the actual decision-making authority still rests with the English Tourist Board.

A major role of the Regional Tourist Boards is the provision of development advice to commercial operators within their area, and liaison and advice on tourism planning and management matters with local authorities. As well as disseminating information about surveys undertaken by the National Tourist Boards, the Regional Tourist Boards also undertake their own surveys and research to provide more detailed local information.

Each Regional Board is also responsible for the preparation and development of tourism strategies for their regions. These will be generally co-ordinated with strategies prepared by other bodies concerned with tourism and recreation, such as the Countryside Commission, the Sports Council and the Association of District Councils.

The Regional Tourist Boards have the advantage of both local authority support and backing from commercial tourism operators, and are, therefore, in a strong position to help individual local authorities in preparing inputs to local structure plans, expressing comment on applications for tourism developments, and providing advice and information during the consultation and submission stages of major plans which affect the Travel and Tourism Industry.

Local Authorities and Tourism

At the most local level, many local authorities are directly involved with the tourism industry in a variety of ways. Often they own and manage facilities that are major tourist attractions, such as museums, theatres, country parks or historic monuments. They often have their own tourism officers, or recreation and leisure officers who include tourism in their remit. All the major resort towns have their own publicity and promotion units, either in the Town Hall or in the borough's tourism department. They often set up and run the tourist information centres and they manage camping and caravan sites, the beaches and the seafront areas. Some local authorities, such as Bournemouth, Brighton and Harrogate, have built large conference centres to promote and encourage business tourism. Often these facilities – such as the Bournemouth International Centre – are also designed as venues for major sporting events and festivals.

The first priority of local authorities is to provide a range of leisure and cultural facilities for local residents. These will vary from outdoor facilities, such as playing fields, parks and gardens, golf courses, country parks and picnic sites, to indoor facilities, such as sports centres, leisure pools, museums, art galleries, theatres and concert halls. All of these facilities and their related infrastructure of car parks and amenities, will also attract tourists and will be used by them.

Local authorities also often provide indirectly for tourism by contributing to the income and work of the Regional Tourist Boards, and by giving planning permission or grants-in-aid to tourism development projects. No two local authorities are exactly alike in the way tourism is developed or promoted, and the importance of tourism in the local authority's policy plan will vary, depending on whether tourism is perceived as being of value to the local economy. In the early 1980s it was estimated that local authorities were responsible for over 500 art galleries and museums, 700 indoor swimming pools, 600 indoor sports centres and 200 golf courses.

The local authorities provide and resource these facilities in a variety of ways. The public has free access to beaches, picnic sites, country parks, nature trails and so on and, whilst the public doesn't pay directly for these facilities, it does so indirectly through the community charge. Local authorities also provide other facilities, such as leisure pools, marinas and golf courses where there is a direct payment by the user, although this is often highly subsidised.

That tourism is the mixed economy in action is best demonstrated by the major British seaside resorts. Much of the advertising, marketing and general promotional activity is done directly by the local authority, although it is the private sector in the form of hotels, guest houses, coach operators and tourist attractions that benefit from this.

Local authorities spend a considerable amount of money – in excess of £500 million on sport and recreation facilities and about £80 million on cultural activities, shared equally between museums, galleries and theatres. Much of this spending goes on staffing existing resources, although some of it is used for a wide range of grants to voluntary bodies working in the tourism and recreation sector.

As planning authorities, they can assist tourism development projects by making land and/or resources available. They can also give planning approval to private sector tourism developments where they are seen to be for the general benefit of the town or region. Local authorities have very wide discretionary powers and, by channelling resources to tourism and recreation, they can have a major role to play in developing a town or region as a tourist destination.

Between 1984 and 1987, district councils spent over £521 million on tourism-related projects and over 10,000 new jobs were created, both directly and indirectly, as a result of this investment. Over the past decade many local authorities, in association with Tourist Boards and various other agencies, have developed tourist facilities based on their cultural, industrial or historic heritage. For example, Torfaen Borough Council in association with the Welsh Development Agency, the Wales Tourist Boards and the National Coal Board, developed the Big Pit Mining Museum. Portsmouth has developed a range of attractions based on the theme of maritime heritage with HMS *Victory*, HMS *Warrior* and the Tudor warship *Mary Rose*, as the centrepieces of a former Royal

Naval Dockyard. The city is now embarking in a major development programme with a £5 million water recreation centre; a £100 million marina; and a £100 million indoor shopping centre.

Local authorities play a key role in tourism development in three ways:

A.   Agents For Growth
- They promote business confidence.
- They encourage private investment.
- They are often partners in commercial projects.
- They will draw up local forward plans and co-ordinate local publicity.
- They will help to rejuvenate declining areas.

B.   Agents For Change
- Creating marketable identity.
- Assisting with new developments.
- Promoting and funding schemes.

C.   Agents For Continuity
- Local authorities provide long term stability.
- They maintain the tourist infrastructure.
- They can influence architecture, townscapes and landscape through planning legislation.
- They can provide local co-ordination for all parties involved in tourism.

Local authorities have also begun to realise the advantages of coming together to establish marketing consortia with the common aim of increasing their region's share in the domestic and international tourist market. For example, Devon, Torbay, Exeter and Plymouth have formed a consortium to attract more US visitors to the south west of England. Several local authorities combined to promote nationally the "Great English City Break" campaign.

The Future of Public Sector Tourism
In the mid 1980s the Government adopted a higher profile in tourism policy and, with the report *Pleasure, Leisure and Jobs – The Business of Tourism* (HMSO 1985), it outlined the growing importance of tourism to

the UK economy, and suggested ways in which obstacles to the industry's faster growth may be removed. In September 1985 responsibility for tourism policy in England and for Great Britain as a whole was transferred from the Department of Trade and Industry to the Department of Employment, which was a much larger ministry, thus giving tourism policy makers access to more finance and resources.

Both BTA and ETB were asked to give particular attention in both marketing and development programmes to encourage tourism in those areas of the country with untapped tourism potential and higher than average levels of unemployment, and to seek ways to extend the tourist season. The Government provided a 20 per cent increase in grants-in-aid and Section 4 support, giving a combined total of £40 million for 1986/7. Much of this funding was directed at newish initiatives, such as highlighting the tourism potential of inner city areas (*Action for Jobs in Tourism*) (HMSO 1986).

As a means of encouraging greater local authority commitment to the development of tourism in the area, as well as better links with the private sector, the English Tourist Board introduced a series of *Tourism Development Action Programmes*. A Tourism Development Action Programme consisted of a package of development, marketing and research initiatives which could be implemented rapidly, and was usually a partnership between the local authority, the English Tourist Board, the Rural Development Commission and other agencies. They concentrated on initiatives that could be achieved in the short-term and usually operated for a limited duration for up to 2 to 3 years. By 1990, over 20 TDAP's were in operation.

By 1990, most of the areas of England with tourism potential had taken advantage of Tourism Development Action Programmes, from the Isle of Wight to Shropshire, Lancaster, Carlisle and Kilder.

By the late 1980s, the English Tourist Board had given over £15 million in tourism development grants to over 600 projects. These cash injections generated £117.5 million of further investment and created almost 3000 full-time jobs (Tourism in Action, July 1988). A further

£3.8 million in grants was given to 481 small business projects costing under £100,000 from the Business Development Fund. In addition, the English Tourist Board gave an unprecedented £1.5 million grant towards the construction of the first Center Parc at Sherwood Forest.

However, this public sector intervention into tourism development was scaled down markedly following the review of the English Tourist Board's functions, which was completed in 1989. The Section 4 grants scheme was abandoned. Much of ETB's activities were scaled down or devolved to the regional tourist boards and other functions were privatised or phased out. Among the key functions privatised or contracted out were the promotion of trade events and the production and publication of accommodation guides.

The main consequence of the Fowler Review of 1989 has been devolution of much of ETB's activities to the regions. At the same time the British Tourist Authority was required to devolve more of its activities and initiatives to its overseas offices. The process also saw the transfer of some overseas marketing responsibility to the Scottish Tourist Board and the Welsh Tourist Board. Finally, in 1992, responsibility for tourism was given to the newly formed Department of National Heritage.

The effect of these changes has been to reduce the English Tourist Board's staff complement by over one third, and the loss of so many experienced and qualified staff is likely to have a detrimental impact on public sector tourism at national level in the 1990s. The abandonment of the Section 4 grant scheme has been particularly felt by many small tourism businesses in the region, who relied on ETB grants and loans to upgrade and improve their facilities to meet the challenge from destinations abroad.

ASSIGNMENTS

1. The South coast resort of Seamouth has a tourism infrastructure that dates back to its Victorian heyday. Since 1945 it has had a gradual decline in visitor numbers and has become better known as a retirement area than as a tourist resort. There has been little investment in its tourist industry over the past 40 years.

You have been appointed as a consultant to undertake a feasibility study into the prospects for reviving the tourism industry in order to attract jobs and investment into the local economy. Show how this can be done, taking advantage of the Regional and National Tourist Board network, and suggest what changes are needed to improve the management of the resort at a local authority level.

2. You are a Senior Civil Servant and have been asked to produce a memorandum for the Minister with special responsibility for Tourism, setting out how public sector tourism should be re-organised and developed in Great Britain.

Using *NO MORE THAN* 3 sides of A4, outline and justify your proposals.

Chapter 9

Planning and Development of Tourism

Learning Objectives:
After reading this Chapter and the references contained in it, you should have a clear understanding of:

● The role of both the public and private sector in planning for tourism;
● The stages involved in preparing a feasibility study of new tourism developments;
● The financing of tourism developments;
● The main elements in the tourism planning process.

Introduction

Historically, many interests – both public and private – have played a part in the development and provision of facilities for tourism over the past 150 years, from the parks, promenades and piers of the Victorian period, to the hotels, leisure complexes and conference centres of the present-day. This planning and development was generally influenced by speculative developers and entrepreneurs up to the 1930s but, after the 1947 Town and Country Planning Act, local authorities for the first time were given wide powers to control the development of public and private land and facilities in towns and countryside.

As tourism grew in scale during the 1930s, and increased rapidly with the growth of mass tourism in the post-war years, this brought with it the recognition that the tourist resources of the community and the region needed to be managed. The main aim was to recognise conflict over the use of land, to meet future needs, and to create an environment within which tourists could enjoy both natural and man-made resources without damaging or destroying the very features that attracted them to the destination in the first place.

Any organisation or firm planning for tourism development has to compare the supply of tourist resources (both natural and man-made) with the *demand* for them, in order to identify any shortfall in provision. A public or commercial organisation will require an inventory of the supply and distribution of tourist facilities, and the use of these facilities, in order to identify potential for tourism development.

Demand can be identified in three forms:

● The people who take part in tourist activities now make up the *effective demand*.
● In addition, there is *deferred demand*, which consists of those people who could take part in domestic or overseas tourism, but do not, either through lack of knowledge or lack of facilities, or both.
● Finally, there is *potential demand* which consists of those people who cannot at present take part in tourist activities and require an improvement in their social and economic circumstances to do so.

Planning for Tourism
In this context, what does 'Planning' mean? It means several things, and attempts to be an amalgam of the best of them. For the public sector it means reconciling conflicts over the use of land. In the case of both private and public sector organisations, it means managing resources effectively (both natural and man-made) so that the best use is made of scarce resources. It means identifying features or sites with tourism potential and preparing proposals to develop them to meet an actual or predicted demand. Planning is concerned with relating the supply of tourist facilities to the demand for them, so that public needs are met without under or over-provision. Planning can be pro-active in initiating tourism projects, and should not be seen as a negative approach associated with controls, regulations and restrictions. Planning has increasingly been seen as a means of safeguarding the environment from excessive or ill-thought-out tourism development, and there are now several public and quasi-public bodies with an interest in, and responsibility for, land management. Planning should be a partnership between the public and private sector and, in recent years, there has been a trend towards more public-private partnerships. These are epitomised

in the Tourism Development Action Plans which assemble large parcels of land and complex financial packages, and creating opportunities for large-scale private investment in tourism projects.

These projects are not only focused on urban areas, but also in the countryside. The 10 national parks and stretches of heritage coast around Britain represent major tourist resources identified over the past 40 years. During the 1960s and 1970s it was recognised that the network of national parks was not sufficient and many country parks were developed around all the major towns and cities, with the aim of encouraging more people to enjoy and use the countryside on their doorstep.

Planning for tourism raises issues related to *resources* and *management*. Resources can be natural (forests, lakes, beaches, scenery) or man-made (theatres or visitor centres), or the financial investment needed to translate plans into reality. Management covers management policy and management action, both in the provision of tourist facilities and their day-to-day operation. In other words, the provision of facilities is not enough. They must be managed efficiently so as to maximise the public's use and enjoyment of them, whilst ensuring that the public organisation or private business covers its operating costs.

Both the public and private sector have a common approach towards managing tourist facilities. Both are concerned about value for money, effective control of budgets and looking at ways of maximising their income over expenditure. The growth of public and private sector partnerships suggests that each sector needs to understand how the other operates and to share management skills. Usually the major professional bodies, such as the HCIMA or the Tourism Society, draw their members from both sectors.

The public and private sector should have similar, if not identical, approaches towards preparing proposals for new tourism developments. Five main factors need to be considered when preparing a feasibility study for new tourism facilities:

   i. the market for the facility;
   ii. the optimum location;

iii. the site;

iv. the management structure of the facility;

v. the financial appraisal.

The Market

The principles and practice of tourism marketing are discussed in more detail in Chapter 10, but in planning any tourism project several questions need to be asked:

- who is/are the target market?
- what facilities/features will attract them?
- is it a growing or declining market?
- how much will people pay to use the facilities?
- how can this market be reached?
- what competing facilities exist and what are their objectives and weaknesses?
- what is the planned capacity?
- what is the planned season?

The answers to these questions can be found by undertaking detailed market research and this is discussed in the next chapter.

The Location

What is the best location for a new tourism development? Clearly this depends on the type of facility being provided and whether or not it needs to be adjacent to a lake, a river or the sea. Should it be near a major concentration of population, or in a quiet country area? Accessibility is usually a key factor because, unlike other products, the tourist product has to be consumed on the spot and potential customers need to be able to travel to the facility quickly and inexpensively. Is there good road, rail and air access? Does it need to be located adjacent to other tourist resources?

Having identified a location, the next step is to select a site for the development. Is it an established tourist area, or is it a new area with tourism potential? What is the local authority or government policy towards this kind of tourist development?

The Site
At this stage planning issues need to be carefully considered. Does the site have planning permission for the land use proposed? If not, can this permission be obtained or will there be planning constraints on the site? Are there mains services available or, if not, can they be provided? Is the site accessible from the main road? Will the development require extensive landscaping works? Is there sufficient land to provide adequate car parking? Is there room for expansion on the site should the development be very successful? All of these factors need to be considered when the developer applies for outline planning permission, which is the first stage in getting a project approved. This work would lead to an outline site plan, building elevations and sketches showing the main land use layout, with details of the function of buildings and range of services to be provided.

The Management Structure
This is a critical element in deciding how a business is to be run and what it will cost to operate. How many permanent and how many seasonal staff will be needed? What tasks will each staff member do? What specialist skills will be needed? Will they have to be recruited nationally or locally? Will a staff training programme need to be developed? A typical management chart for a public sector and commercial sector organisation would probably have a senior management group above the facility manager and, in turn, the senior managers responsible to chief executives and council committees or boards of directors. At the facility level, the main management activities will be planning and forecasting, budgetary control, dealing with the public, organising work, recruitment, selection and staff training, working computerised systems and industrial relations.

Financial Appraisal
This follows from decisions about the type of tourist facility to be provided and the range of markets to be served. Very often financial appraisal will include several forecasts, based on a range of assumptions about the management of the project and changes in the financial climate. The assumptions must be based on accurate estimates of the capital cost of the project, the potential operating cost and the potential revenue. A

further factor is the degree of 'risk', if the project is providing a new form of tourist facility, related to the level of capital investment required and the rate of return on capital that can be earned. The element of 'risk' operates at two levels. Firstly, the break even point below which the business will not survive. Secondly, the break even point beyond which investors will get a return on their investment. Potential guarantors will need to have this information. This will need to be set against a time scale which allows for the facility to come into full operation, to build up a 'market' and to produce actual, as against forecasted, accounts.

Tourism Development (Project Appraisal)
Having identified a market, chosen a site, obtained clearance for building and funding for the project, there is a need for the national, regional or local government to assess the impact of tourism developments. Tourism projects cannot be planned independently, because they have a wide range of impacts on the cultural, physical and economic environments of the locality. Physical planning (i.e., land use planning) is important as a means of organising the distribution of facilities, the conservation of natural resources and integration with other sectors of the economy. The scale of tourism developments is a critical factor and one that will have the most immediate impact on the environment. This issue is discussed in more detail in Chapter 12.

At national or regional level the first strategic decision is whether to concentrate developments in those regions or localities which are accessible and most likely to attract tourists, or to disperse facilities so as to ensure that as many areas as possible benefit from tourism developments. Concentrating development projects provides economies of scale, but raises problems of environmental impact.

There is a need to study the effects of new facilities on usage rates from within their catchment area. Supply of new facilities may transform latent demand into effective demand; and bring changes within the pattern of effective demand. The degree of substitution between one kind of facility and another should be measured, and depends on the inherent attraction of different tourist resources in relation to centres of demand. The 'drawing power' of tourist resources is linked to individual perception of tourist facilities or landscape resources and the motivation of tourists.

It is essential to have a tourism development plan in the following situations:

   i. in regions that cater for mass tourism;
  ii. in regions with a fragile natural environment;
 iii. in newly-developing tourist regions.

One of the paradoxes of mass tourism is that, in particular cases, tourists, by arriving in large numbers, may cause overcrowding and congestion which can destroy the very thing they come to see. In any tourist region there is likely to be a range of development opportunities and a series of thresholds for development. Thus, for areas that have fragile environments which make them highly sensitive to visitor numbers, access has to be discouraged. Areas that are scenically attractive, which are wild and relatively remote, should have limited vehicular access. Areas suitable for intensive tourist use should be identified and developed so as to absorb visitors. Development Planning operates at three different levels – national, regional and local. At the national level the National Tourist Board produces strategic plans (usually on a four to five year basis) which set out the broad framework within which all the agencies involved in tourism can co-ordinate their activities. This document usually outlines investment plans and policy decisions in tourism development. For example, in its document *Strategy for Growth 1984–1988* (BTA 1984) the British Tourist Authority reviews the trends in tourism to Britain 1972–1982 and identifies the main strengths and weaknesses of the British market. It then identifies economic and social factors and government policies likely to affect tourism over the plan period. The document concludes by identifying, in the light of BTAs objectives, the target markets and new product development required to translate this strategy into action.

At the regional level, the Regional Tourist Board will produce a co-ordinated strategy for tourism. This is usually implemented through a Development Panel, consisting of both local authority and private sector interests, who are members of the Tourist Board. The final part of this chapter outlines two case studies which demonstrate the planning and development process.

Financing Tourism Projects

(a) Public Sector Finance
In the public sector finance for tourism projects can be classified under two main headings. *Capital* finance and *revenue* finance. Capital spending is generally financed through borrowing approved by central government and is divided into two categories – key sector and non-key sector projects. The key sector developments reflect national policy or, for example, maintain maximum standards for roads and hospitals and are controlled by agreement with central government departments. Tourism projects are non-key sector and here the local authority has a block allocation each year to spend as it wishes. Many local authority services, such as housing, education and the social services, will be competing for this money. In addition, local authority capital expenditure can be funded in several ways:

- direct government grant (e.g. Countryside Commission, or English Tourist Board grants from the regional or national tourist board);
- revenue contributions to capital spending (i.e. from the community charge);
- capital receipts from the sale of local authority land;
- loans from commercial concerns;
- income from other sources, such as lotteries.

Revenue finance comes from four main sources:

    i. from the users of facilities (income from membership fees, admission charges, hire of facilities, catering);
    ii. grant aid from central government or quasi-public bodies, such as the Tourist Boards, Sports Council, or Countryside Commission;
    iii. from the rates paid by local residents;
    iv. from central government Rate Support Grant.

(b) Private Sector Finance
The scale and type of private sector finance will depend on the scale of the project and the resources of the organisation planning the development. If it is a large organisation, it may have sufficient capital

reserves to finance new projects without borrowing, or can raise new capital through a share issue. If capital has to be borrowed, there are two types of finance which relate to the timescale of the project. There is *fixed* capital to develop the land and buildings, plant and amenities, and *short-term* capital to provide cash flow when the project is in its early stages of operation.

All tourism businesses, particularly small businesses will need short term finance for one to three years until the business becomes established. The most common source is overdraft facilities provided by the commercial clearing banks. An alternative source is using Hire Purchase Agreements to obtain fixed-term interest to meet the cost of plant and equipment.

Medium-term finance (four to eight years) is provided by the clearing banks, the Industrial and Commercial Finance Corporation (ICFC), the merchant banks, and the finance houses. Usually medium-term finance is at a variable rate of interest and this has the benefit of fixing the cost of money for the future and, where operating profits are high, paying for the capital loan out of net operating profit. This type of financing is particularly attractive if inflation increases and general interest rates rise.

Large scale projects involving say, capital investment of over £100,000, will require long-term finance (over 10 years) if the loan repayments are to be of a manageable size. These loans are mainly provided by insurance companies and building societies and by some of the clearing banks.

Another source of finance is through sale and leaseback, which can realise 100 per cent of the valuation of a property. A case in point is the sea front development at Great Yarmouth, where a £5.7 million indoor leisure development was financed by a 25 year leaseback agreement between the Council and CIN Industrial Investments Ltd (a company wholly owned by the British Coal Pension Fund) for the sum of £4.5 million. The balance was funded by Lloyds Industrial Leasing Ltd.

Other sources of finance are through venture capital provided by the leading merchant banks, or funds obtained through the government's Business Expansion Scheme.

Case Studies in Planning and Development

(a) Tourism Development of Languedoc – Roussillon

This development was carried out between 1966 and 1980 by the French Government in close co-operation with local authorities and private interests. Its objective was the overall development of a 100 mile length of coastal strip in order to stimulate the stagnant local economy in the Languedoc-Roussillon area. The impetus behind the project was the growing pressure on the Cote d'Azur and the need to protect the undeveloped stretches of the Mediterranean coast from unplanned development. This region formed an almost uninterrupted stretch of large beaches often separated from the inland area by a series of lakes and salt marshes. Access was limited and roads were of poor quality.

The Languedoc-Roussillon development plans had three main objectives:

- To relieve pressure on the Cote d'Azur and meet the growing demand for mass tourism facilities on the Mediterranean coast.
- To raise the level of incomes in the region and to attract both French and foreign visitors help France's international balance of payments.
- To diversify a predominantly agricultural economy, provide employment for young people and stem the depopulation of the region.

In 1963 a government agency (Le Mission Interministerielle) was established to co-ordinate the activities of the State Ministries and to implement and supervise the development decisions. Joint public and private development companies were established, with the state providing the infrastructure needed for mass tourism, local development companies responsible for providing the ancillary infrastructure, and the private sector responsible for construction and marketing.

Six new resort areas were developed (Figure 9.1) with a total capacity of over 700,000 beds, capable of accommodating up to three million tourists a year. Each resort area has been zoned into areas for villas, apartments, hotels, holiday villages and camp-sites. The whole development has provided moorings for 20,000 boats and 80,000 new jobs. The construction of the new resorts involved the acquisition of 4,000 hectares of land at a cost (1970 prices) of £10 million. By 1980 the Development Commission, the mixed Development Boards, Local Authorities and the Private Sector had invested an estimated £600 million in the whole scheme.

A network of express motorways was created, linking the six new tourist resorts. Seven main marinas and thirteen smaller marinas were developed.

Figure 9.1: Resort Development in the Languedoc-Roussillon Region

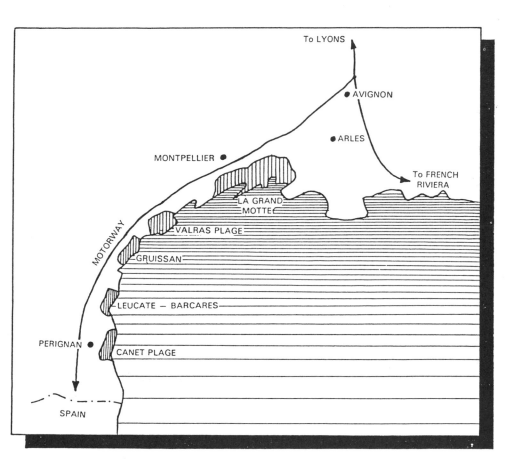

In addition a large-scale re-afforestation programme was implemented in what was a largely treeless region, and about 12,000 hectares has been planted.

Finance for the development companies was provided in the form of low interest loans from the Caisse des Depots and the Fund National d'Amenagement Foncier et d'Urbanisme. They developed and improved the plots transferred to them by the State and then offered the improved land to private builders. The development costs were high, ranging from 50 francs to 2,000 francs per square metre. (*The Economist*, 1970).

This project achieved four main aims:

- it created a new tourist region, and provided important employment opportunities in a stagnant regional economy;
- it relieved pressure on the Cote d'Azur by opening up a 100 mile stretch of beaches;
- it controlled the type and location of development on a stretch of coast that had previously been developed in a piecemeal fashion;
- by a substantial programme of tree planting, it reversed the extensive deforestation that had taken place since the nineteenth century.

One further by-product has been the rapid growth of new industry in the region, attracted by the massive infrastructure developments and the attractive location.

Following these 20 years of development, Languedoc-Roussillon has developed to become one of the major tourist destination areas in the Mediterranean and, in 1994, attracted 13 million visitors. However, by the early 1990s, it was clear that there was an imbalance in terms of prosperity and job creation with the economic benefits concentrated in the coastal area and the major inland areas remaining depressed. Moreover, by the early 1990s, changing tourism trends prompted the need to re-develop coastal resorts built initially in the late 1960s/early 1970s. Over half the accommodation in the region was located on the coast mainly in the form of fairly basic self-catering apartments. By the early 1990s the demand for this kind of accommodation was beginning to decline and there was an increasing preference for rural gîtes. However, tourism accommodation was limited in the rural areas and standards were very variable. In response, in 1993, the regional government put forward a strategy to redevelop the coastal resorts and to introduce new products in the historic towns, the countryside and mountain areas of the region which had been previously neglected.

One problem on the coast is that a large percentage of tourist visitors have second homes in the area, and that much of the coastal resorts are relatively deserted in the out of season periods. This absence of a year-round population and a lack of entertainment and sporting facilities was identified by the regional government as a major challenge for the redevelopment of the coastal resorts. For the coastal areas the new plan had three main strands:

- An improvement in the quality of the resort infrastructure.
- The intervention by local councils to restore the character of local, traditional seaside resorts and introduce more sporting and cultural activities.
- A focus on the unspoilt and protected coastal areas by better signing and improvements to the infrastructure.

Inland from the coast, and west of the A9 motorway, there is a huge rural area with very attractive scenery and under-exploited tourism attractions, including small historic towns and numerous monuments. However, this huge rural area has only half of the accommodation capacity of the coasts. In order to improve the attraction of this area and to develop a tourist infrastructure, the regional government has concentrated on:

- The provision of grounds to support the development of rural tourism around major attractions which have potential for accommodation development.
- Support for the development of the day visitor market, and sporting and cultural facilities, including the development of footpaths, cycle paths and information on local heritage.
- The social tourism theme, which was part of the original mission for the region, is included within the new strategy, with funding available

for projects to help disadvantaged or handicapped people to develop leisure pursuits in the countryside.

The mountain areas of the region, which include the Pyrennees, have great potential for both summer and winter tourism. However, the winter sports infrastructure is quite limited and there are plans for investment in improving lift systems in the existing ski resorts and the provision of more trails and facilities. Again, a focus on the development of accommodation, with improved services and sign posting, will help this area to attract more staying tourists.

One of the challenges facing the official bodies responsible for planning and development in Languedoc-Roussillon is that there are five *departements* and, within these, a large number of *cantons* and *communes*. At four of these levels there is a tourism promotion organisation, and most communes have at least one tourist office and staff preparing promotional material. The regional committee for tourism co-ordinates activities for the region, but there is a deal of local rivalry, particularly between towns with strong local Mayors. It is more difficult to develop a coherent planning strategy with so many different interests at ground level.

(b) Development of a Strategy for Hadrian's Wall
Hadrian's Wall is one of the finest archaeological and historic features in Britain and is unique in Western Europe. It is over 70 miles long and its chain of outer earthworks, milecastles and forts encompasses an area managed by three County Councils and six District Councils. Part of it lies within a National Park: two Regional Tourist Boards are responsible for promoting it and several national agencies have functions within this area. In addition there are many private interests concerned with the land on which the major remains are located.

From the early 1960s through to the 1970s there was a gradual but steady increase in the numbers of visitors to the Roman Wall, particularly to the well known and accessible sites. This, in turn, led to problems of visitor pressure at specific locations along the Wall, causing erosion of the monument and the main footpaths leading to it, and creating problems of congestion, access and lack of suitable services.

In 1974 the Countryside Commission appointed as consultants the Dartington Amenity Research Trust with the brief to 'appraise the existing and likely pressures on the Wall and its setting, give guidance on the broad planning strategy for their conservation, and to advise on traffic and visitor management and on interpretation and publicity related to the Wall'. In that year an officer working party was established, consisting of representatives of local authorities, the Countryside Commission, DoE Ancient Monuments branch, and the Regional and National Tourist Boards. Their brief was to consider the DART report and review comments on it, to prepare a strategy for the Wall and to seek its implementation.

In preparing the strategy, it was clear that a wide range of interests had to be accommodated including landowners, farmers and local residents, local and County planning policies, archaeological and environmental issues, and the many other bodies with an interest in the land covered by the Wall.

Aims of the Strategy
The broad aims of the strategy were:

a) to safeguard the splendid heritage of Roman monuments and all associated remains so that they are not lost or spoilt for future generations;
b) to protect, and, where possible, enhance, the quality of landscape setting of the Wall sites;
c) to encourage appropriate public visiting of the Wall area, with convenient access and high-quality experience and (for those who seek it) understanding of the Roman monuments and way of life.
d) to ensure that local people derive the best possible benefits from tourism by way of income and employment, whilst ensuring that all appropriate steps are taken to minimise the adverse effects of tourism, particularly on agriculture.

Clearly, these aims may appear to conflict with one another. How can one safeguard the Roman heritage and protect the landscape quality of its setting whilst, at the same time, improving public access and encouraging the public to visit the Wall? With this in mind, it was clear that any final strategy had to be realistic and practical if it was to be acceptable and capable of implementation.

Preparing a Strategy
The first step in the preparation of a strategy was to make a comprehensive assessment of all the relevant forts and earthworks and visible parts of the monument in the light of four criteria. These were:

● existing and projected number of visitors;
● environmental constraints;
● the appropriate timescale for proposed developments;
● land ownership.

i. Assessment of future visitor numbers to the Wall sites
Any plan for the Wall had to take account of growth or change in the numbers of visitors to the monument. As Figure 9.2 shows, the numbers of visitors to the major sites grew rapidly between 1965 and 1973, when this upward trend was reversed after the sharp increase in petrol prices following the 1973 Arab-Israeli conflict. After 1973, numbers declined but began to increase again, albeit slowly, in the 1980s. The Northumberland Structure Plan assumes a general growth in the numbers of visitors to the countryside of the order of two to three per cent a year, and other indicators suggest that this may be an underestimate. However, even with a growth rate of two to three per cent a year, this would bring back visitor numbers at Chesters and Vindolanda to previous peak levels by the early 1990s. Other factors that may influence this growth are the development of Keilder Water as a major tourist attraction and the designation of the North Pennines as an area of outstanding natural beauty. In addition to forecasts on the long-term growth in visitor numbers, an assessment was made of potential peak usage at the nine major sites along the Wall, taking into account development proposals, development of visitor services and increased car parking (Table 9.1).

ii. Environmental constraints
These estimates were then related to the ability of the major sites to accommodate visitors. Four environmental criteria were used to determine the acceptable number of visitors:

162

Figure 9.2: Growth in Tourists to the Roman Wall

Annual totals of visitors to four major sites 1965 to 1975

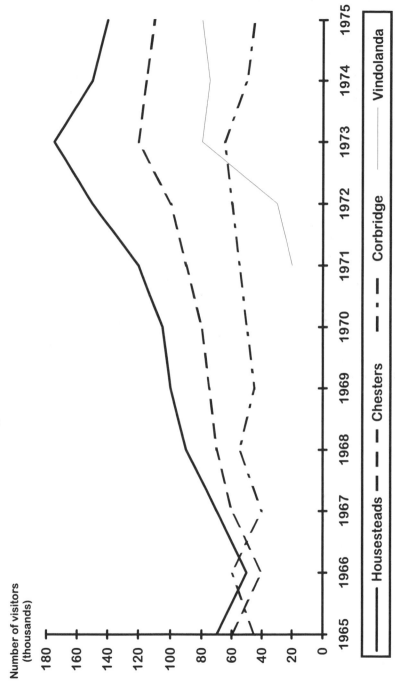

Number of visitors
(thousands)

Housesteads ——— Chesters — — — Corbridge — · — · — Vindolanda ———

a) the capacity of the landscape in the Wall corridor to absorb the infrastructure which visitors need, e.g., car parks, access roads, toilet blocks, picnic sites;
b) the effect of visitor pressures on farming and the capacity of existing and proposed footpaths, including that along the Wall and other factors;
c) the implications for nature conservation (a subject of particular concern in the consultation exercise);
d) the protection of the archaeological fabric itself, particularly from the effects of increased visiting.

Table 9.1: Forecasts of Peak Capacity at Main Sites on the Roman Wall

Site	Annual No. of Visitors	Forecast Peak Capacity at any one Time
Birdoswald	NA	250-400
Carvoran	NA	480
Vindolanda	80,000	600-650
Housesteads	113,000	450
Carrawbrough	NA	40
Chesters	101,000	1,000
Rudchester	NA	200
South Shields	40,000	450

The Strategy for Major Sites

After reviewing the Dartington Amenity Research Trust's recommendations for each site and making a site-by-site assessment on the lines set out above, four categories of site were identified.

i. Sites where no development is envisaged

These are sites which either are not of strategic importance or where there are particular considerations which would restrict development in the foreseeable future. There are three such sites: Great Chesters, Housesteads and Carrawbrough (Brocolitia). At Great Chesters visitor numbers are small and there is a well established working farm. At Housesteads the site already receives over 100,000 visitors a year and it was felt that any major increase in visitor numbers would lead to unacceptable wear and tear on the monument and the access routes to it, and would greatly diminish the quality of the visitor's experience. At Carrawbrough (Brocolitia) visitors are attracted because of the Mithraic temple which has been excavated. The present site capacity is low and the existing car park is already intrusive. Any further car parking provision should be discouraged.

ii. Sites where limited development would be acceptable

These are sites where limited improvements in car parking, access and visitor facilities could occur, but which would not be able to absorb large-scale developments. There are two sites, Birdoswold and Vindolanda. Birdoswold is the most westerly fort in the central section of the Wall and is in a very fine landscape setting. The difficulties of access via narrow roads from Gilsland or Lanercost, and the impact of any large car parks on the site, are major constraints. However, because of the great archaeological potential of the site, the willingness of the Department of the Environment to support some excavation, its location well to the West of the central section, and its acquisition by Cumbria County Council, it was felt that limited development should be a priority. Vindolanda is a major civilian settlement excavated in the 1970s, with a new museum. It currently receives around 80,000 visitors a year. However, road access is difficult and the existing car and coach parks are very obtrusive and it will be some time before planting around them provides an effective screen. At peak times in the visitor season overcrowding and congestion are very evident.

iii. Sites with major development potential

These are sites that have the space to accommodate increased visitor numbers and facilities without damaging the monument or the landscape setting, where the intrinsic interest is very great, and where existing accessibility is good. There are four such sites – Carvoran, Chesters, Corbridge and South Shields.

iv. Sites with long-term potential

These are sites with a high intrinsic interest but, because of existing circumstances, there is no opportunity for development in the immediate future. However, they were considered to have important potential for development in the long-term. There are five sites Maryport, Portgate, Halton-Chesters, Rudchester and Wallsend.

165

Since Victorian times the Roman Wall has been recognised as a major archaeological monument and tourist attraction. By the 1970s wear and tear caused soil erosion and, in parts, the foundations of the Wall itself began to erode as the soil was washed away. Visitors found the main sites crowded at peak times, there was a lack of visitor services and interpretative facilities were limited. The DART report highlighted these problems but it was clear that no single organisation could provide a solution because the Wall extends over such a large area, with a great number of different landowners, and cuts across several local authority boundaries. For the first time 32 public and private organisations came together to prepare a single policy framework for decisions affecting the whole length of the Wall.

(c) Portsmouth Harbour Tourism Development Action Programme

This programme was one of over 14 tourism development action programmes initiated by the English Tourist Board during the 1980s. It was a joint venture, undertaken on a partnership basis by Portsmouth City Council, Gosport Borough Council, the English Tourist Board, Hampshire County Council and the Southern Tourist Board, between 1985 and 1989. The aim of the TDAP was to stimulate and develop tourism in Portsmouth and Gosport. The primary focus of this action programme was the immediate surroundings of Portsmouth Harbour, although it did include initiatives elsewhere in Portsmouth and Gosport. It was designed to complement and strengthen existing tourism development initiatives, such as the Portsmouth Naval Heritage Project and the Hampshire Defence Heritage Project, and other schemes undertaken by both the public and private sector. The overall objective was to use tourism as a central factor in enhancing the economic prospect for the area by stimulating economic development and creating new jobs. This latter point was particularly important with local unemployment levels at over 12 per cent. An Economic Impact Study commissioned in 1985 estimated that in Portsmouth 10,000 jobs in accommodation, catering, transport, retailing and related services were directly supported by tourism.

The plan area (Figure 9.3, on page 170) contains a wide range of attractions and underlines the potential for the harbour area to attract

166

more tourists and more repeat visits. The key to the action programme was the Portsmouth Naval Heritage Project which formed part of the Portsmouth Naval Base. It contains:

- the *Mary Rose* Ship Hall and Exhibition. This is a Tudor Warship built in 1510, sunk in 1545, and recovered (with many relics of the period) in 1982.
  HMS *Victory*, Admiral Lord Nelson's flagship at the Battle of Trafalgar, which has been on display since 1922.
  HMS *Warrior*, built in 1860 as the first British iron-hulled warship, fully restored and returned to the harbour in 1988.
- Royal Naval Museum. This has artefacts and memorabilia from over 500 years of naval history.

The town also contains numerous other tourist attractions including the D-Day Museum, the Submarine Museum, Gosport, Southsea Castle and Dicken's Birthplace Museum, as well as traditional seaside resort facilities.

There were several factors which suggested that Portsmouth was a good choice for a TDAP. These included:

the unique nature of the Maritime Heritage project and its appeal to both domestic and overseas tourists.
- a strong marketing and development team already in place.
accessibility to an extensive hinterland and the existence of strong links with France through a ferry route.
- local authorities favourably disposed towards tourism and a commitment to local authority investment in the tourism infrastructure.

However, there were existing weaknesses. The area in 1985 suffered badly from a shortage of modern good quality hotel accommodation and had limited self-catering facilities. City centre shopping facilities were poor. The area had no purpose-built Conference or Exhibition facilities. On-site information and interpretative facilities were very limited. Signposting was poor, both in the city and in the surrounding area. Car and coach parking were inadequate, especially in the Naval dockyard area.

Portsmouth had a poor image as a tourist destination. Many saw it simply as a dockyard city and people confused it with Plymouth, unaware of its exact location.

Key Tourism Issues in the TDAP
The Tourism Development Action Programme focused on six key issues:

i. Raising the tourism profile;
ii. Identifying and developing the potential of the Heritage Attractions;
iii. Improving the visitor's experience of the area;
iv. Developing other attractions, events and activities;
v. Increasing the amount and improving the quality of the area's accommodation, both serviced and self-catering;
vi. Conducting specific marketing campaigns at the major sectors of tourist demand.

Within the plan area, tourism priority areas were identified where priority was given to improving the facilities and environment for tourism through planning policies and development programmes. The scheme brought together three local authorities, the English Tourist Board and the Southern Tourist Board.

Public sector involvement was mainly designed to provide a climate where tourism developments would be encouraged to take place, provided they met the broad aims of the development programme. The different levels of investment between the public and private sector highlight this point. At the initiation of the TDAP the public sector had allocated £50,000 to £60,000, whereas private sector tourism related development in Portsmouth amounted to over £50 million. (Portsmouth Harbour TDAP report Appendix 2).

By the 1990s the main attraction for visitors from Britain and abroad was the Maritime Heritage Centre, based on the historic naval dockyard, with HMS *Victory*, a Tudor warship *Mary Rose*, and the associated museum facilities, and HMS *Warrior*. The former Royal Naval Dockyard, the military buildings and the museums all reinforce Portsmouth's links with the Defence of the Realm. In addition, other facilities have been developed including a leisure centre, a D-Day Museum, a Sea Life Centre, and a new £100 million marina at Port Solent. A professional marketing team has been in existence for over 12 years and has been a key feature in promoting the City as a major tourist attraction on the south coast.

ASSIGNMENTS

1. You are a farmer with 400 acres of good quality farmland on the South Devon coast. 10 acres are partly wooded, gently sloping land that you wish to develop as a small holiday village. The site is served by a 'B' road. Put together a proposal setting out:
    a) the main aims of the project including the market to be served and the level of use envisaged;
    b) the proposed sources of financing and phasing of expenditure;
    c) a case for the local planning authority setting out why this site should be developed for tourism.

2. You are a director of a regional Tourist Board. Prepare a paper setting out your regional plan for tourism development over the next five years. In this paper you should consider existing provision of facilities, distribution of resources, existing and planned infrastructure and proposals for new tourism developments over the plan period.

Figure 9.3: Portsmouth Harbour Tourist Development Action Programme Area

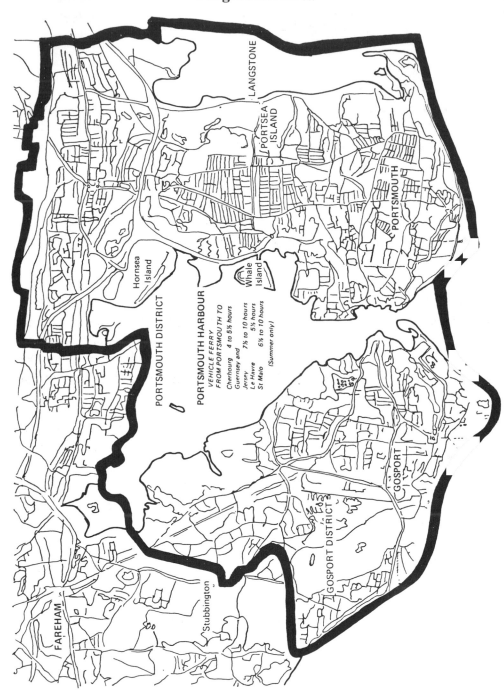

Chapter 10

Tourism Marketing

Learning Objectives:
After reading this Chapter you should have a clear understanding of:

- The difference between selling and marketing;
- Identifying the tourist product;
- The elements of market research;
- Market segmentation;
- Advertising, publicity and promotion as marketing tools;
- The main elements of a marketing plan.

Introduction

Marketing covers a wide range of activities including promoting, selling and developing a product. Marketing is a process which involves persuading a potential buyer that a particular product or service is the most suitable for his or her needs. This is relatively straightforward if the product is a motor car or detergent. It is less so if the product is a tourist one. The demand for tourism is entirely discretionary.

It is not essential and is influenced by people's tastes, perceptions and preferences and other intangible factors. The tourism product is often seasonal and if 'unsold' by a particular date, it is lost. Unlike a manufactured article which can be reduced in price or sold at a later date, an airline seat or hotel bedroom has to be sold by a set date, otherwise it has no value/earning potential. In order to overcome these problems, a tourism marketing plan needs to be developed which includes the following stages:

- identifying the existing tourism product;
- undertaking market research to identify the psychology of the tourist, the market segments, the strengths and weaknesses of the tourism product;

- modifying the tourism product in response to the market research (product strategy);
- identifying the marketing mix;
- promotion, including advertising and publicity;
- selling the tourism product;
- analysing the results of the marketing strategy and modifying it, if necessary.

Each of these elements may be thought of as tourism marketing – but in isolation they are not. Together they make up marketing. It is a cyclical process, with periodic reviews of the product-market mix and the promotional strategy, in order to measure their effectiveness and to decide whether new strategies are needed.

The Tourist Product
In Chapter 3 the tourism product is defined as the resort or historic town, the beaches, scenery, mountains, historic sites, theme parks, museums and other tourist attractions, as well as the accommodation stock. The difference between this and almost any other product is that the consumer (i.e. the market for the product) travels to the place of production and consumes the product on the spot. So tourism marketing must take account of the psychology of the traveller as well as the consumer.

The travel element of the tourism product may simply be a means of getting from home to resort as quickly and as cheaply as possible. Or, it may be an end in itself as with cruising, or the Orient Express, where the journey *is* the product. Again a distinction must be made between discretionary travel (tourist travel) and non-discretionary travel (business travel). The marketing approach is quite different in each case.

A less tangible element of the tourism product, but in many ways the most important, is the quality of service provided to the tourist (the consumer). It is not enough to identify who the customers are and what their needs are. It is important to remember that customer satisfaction depends on the standards of quality and service meeting the expectations of customers. If a charter flight is cancelled or a hotel room is over-booked, it can affect the whole holiday experience. Similarly, poor service cannot be retrieved and can lead to adverse publicity and a decline in trade. An emphasis on quality control and staff training in customer relations are essential elements of a good tourism product.

Seasonality may be a key influence on the tourism product. Sales may be concentrated into four or five months, and the level of sales during that period must be sufficient to make the business financially viable.

Good marketing can help to extend the season, to identify new client groups, to develop new pricing strategies, and to improve the profitability of a tourism business.

As the tourist industry has developed, certain elements, such as international hotels or major airlines, have evolved a broadly similar product. One jumbo jet is very similar to another, regardless of the logo; a 4-star hotel should have similar facilities, regardless of its location. This raises the question, how do companies offering a very similar product succeed in persuading the public to choose them in preference to their competitors? The answer is found in their marketing strategy. In order to develop a marketing strategy, you need to know as much as possible about the market. In order to obtain this information, it is necessary to undertake market research. The following section outlines the principles and practice of market research.

Market Research
This should provide answers to the following questions:

- what is the total size of the tourist market?
- who are the existing customers?
- where are they from?
- what are the existing customers seeking?
- what level of pricing (in relation to facilities), will the customers accept?
- what are the past and existing trends in the tourist market?
- what factors influence these trends?
- who are the potential future customers?
- what are the strengths and weaknesses of the product compared with competitors?

Market research uses two types of data – primary and secondary.

Primary data can be obtained from two sources, from in-house data and from field surveys. *In-house data* can provide information about the performance of the business, measured by daily, weekly, monthly figures on:

- occupancy rates
- visitor spending
- sources of business
- profit margins
- revenue costs

This can be analysed for an individual business or group of businesses, or for a region – if the data is available.

Field surveys
These can take several forms, but the most frequent means of collecting primary data is by using questionnaires. These can be either self completed or filled in by trained researchers during personal interviews. Self completed questionnaires are commonly used by hotels and airlines, but they suffer from two main drawbacks which seriously limit their value for market research. They allow no control over the 'sample' of tourists completing and returning the questionnaires. It is not a representative sample and often consists of people who were dissatisfied with some aspect of the facility/service provided.

In carrying out field surveys the most valuable results are generally obtained by taking a random sample and using a trained interviewer to complete a structured questionnaire during personal interviews. A *random* sample assumes that it is un-biased and representative of the population being studied. Using random number tables and names drawn from the Electoral Register, it is possible to produce a general random sample. However, in doing field surveys with interviews at airports or harbours or hotels, it is more difficult to produce a genuine random sample, and it may be more practical to produce a *stratified sample* where the data and the sample are related to particular groups weighted according to the proportion in each group as part of the total population.

The questionnaire generally provides two types of data. First, there is the demographic and socio-economic profile of the tourist, that is, the age, family composition, income, occupation and place of residence of the tourist, and their spending patterns on holiday. The second set of data relate to the opinions, perceptions and motivations of the tourist – in relation to a particular tourist product and/or competing tourist products. The way in which these more subjective questions are put and the order in which they are asked is a critical aspect of questionnaire design.

Secondary-data can be obtained by undertaking Desk Research using census returns, company reports, local, regional, national or international tourist surveys, general household surveys, studies of leisure trends, and reports from trade associations and professional bodies. This can provide information on tourism trends and changing public preferences over time. In Britain the National and Regional Tourist Boards regularly publish a wide range of statistics on tourism trends.

In the United States the US Travel Data Centre, based in Washington DC, publishes frequent reports on many aspects of travel and tourism. Most of this information is readily available, either in public libraries or at a cost.

The Marketing Mix
Having undertaken the market research, using either desk surveys, or field surveys, or a combination of both, the resort or tourist company should have acquired a mass of information about the elements of their tourist product that attract or deter tourists, the preferences and attitudes of the tourist, and an extensive profile of the different types of tourist that together make up the 'market'. One of the first questions requiring an answer is 'What factors influence the tourist to buy my product?' or 'How did s/he hear of my product?' These and related questions enable businesses within the tourist industry to design or modify a product that will improve their competitiveness and, ultimately, their profitability. The consumer, in this case, the tourist, is rarely buying a single product. He or she is buying a set of 'products' that appeal to him or her and the choice of product may be influenced by income, education, age and life-style. The preference may be for exclusive, exotic, cultural tours or low

175

cost self-catering beach holidays with guaranteed sunshine. Between the high cost low volume trade and the low cost mass market there are a wide range of possible products. Ideally, a tourist region, or resort or individual business, aims to develop a range of tourism products that will appeal to the widest possible market. This is known as the *product mix*. So a resort will offer a wide range of types of accommodation and a variety of forms of entertainment. Special pricing packages for hotels or airlines within a range of prices/fares are also examples of product mix.

After the market research is complete, a profile of the tourist can be constructed and the product can be improved or modified to make it more competitive in the marketplace. The next step must be to examine the ways in which the consumer is made aware of the product. Unless and until the customer knows of the existence of a product, he or she will not be able to consider buying it. The product is made known to the tourist by a method known as the *communications mix*. This is done in a variety of ways including:

● direct marketing (mailshots, telephone canvassing, etc.);
● media displays (TV ads, newspapers, magazines etc.);
● special events/promotions;
● exhibitions, (trade shows, displays etc.).

The tourism 'product' is often a combination of elements, including transport, accommodation, amenities and entertainments. The way in which these products are sold to the consumer is known as the *distribution mix*. This mix can include inclusive tours bought through travel agents, or direct sell holidays or special promotions carried out by the airlines or selected hotels. There is a great variety of possible distribution channels, and the aim of a marketing strategy should be to use these as cost-effectively as possible, so as to reach the greatest possible number of potential tourists. Every tourist business, resort, or region is in competition with other tourist destinations, and it is the firm or organisation that keeps its distribution costs (and hence its product costs) down that will be the most competitive. Price/cost is not the only criterion, although it is important. The product must be attractive and marketed in an effective way if tourists are to be persuaded to buy it.

Product Life Cycle

If the sales of the product are plotted on a graph, a successful product – in this case a hotel resort or airline – will show an upward curve on the sales chart. This will continue until the market is saturated and the number of consumers (tourists) will either remain static or even decline, showing a downward curve (Figure 10.1). This cycle, from the introduction of a product through to its demise or saturation is known as the *product life* and this may be measured in years or decades. The life of the product can be extended in two principal ways:

 i. by finding new markets for the product; or
 ii. by redeveloping the product to meet changing tastes and preferences.

Market Segmentation

This is a term for the process where companies or organisations will identify particular groups within the population who are potential buyers for the tourist product, and the marketing strategy will target these market segments. Market research should help to identify these target markets. These segments are made of four broad groups:

 i. the youth market;
 ii. the family market;
 iii. the senior citizen market;
 iv. the special interest market.

The tourist market can also be grouped by region, with a concentration of marketing effort on the main tourist generating regions. The main markets are those countries or regions who provide, say, over 30 per cent of the main tourist flows. The pricing policies, promotional campaigns and advertising will focus on these areas. Then there are the secondary markets who provide some tourists to a particular destination, but who have considerable potential traffic which is at present going to other destinations. Finally, there are targets of opportunity which are new, rapidly growing economies who are historically of little significance as generators of tourists, but these emerging markets may be attracted to existing tourist destinations.

Figure 10. 1: The Product Life Cycle

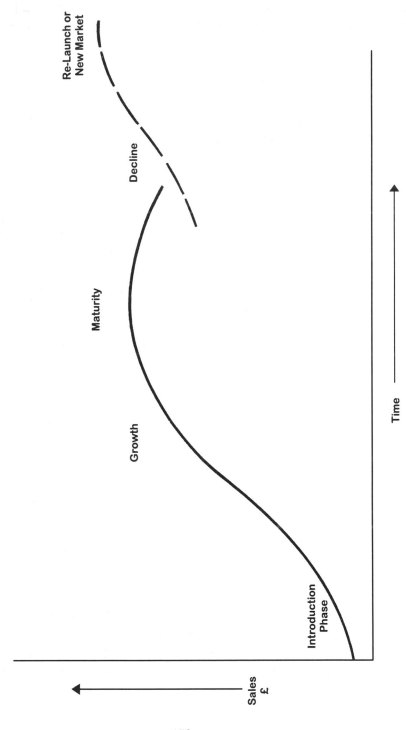

Pricing Policy

This is a further crucial element in any marketing strategy. In order to arrive at the most effective price, the following information is needed:

i. the cost of producing the product;
ii. the planned volume of sales;
iii. the prices charged by competitors;
iv. other external factors, such as interest rates, fuel surcharges;
v. consumer views on prices;
vi. the level of investment required to produce the target sale to achieve a marginal rate of return on that investment.

A number of pricing policies may be used, varying according to the nature of the tourism product and the forecasted life cycle of that product. Where a tourist business or region is trying to break into an established market, a policy of lowering prices and, hence, profit margins may be introduced, with the longer term aim of gradually increasing prices once a market share has been established. This is known as *penetration pricing*.

Promotional pricing may be used to attract customers for a new product or to revive flagging sales of an old product. Here a lower price than normal would be introduced.

Where there is high initial investment and an early recovery of this is needed, the organisation may introduce high prices and then progressively lower them as competition increases. This is known as *skim pricing*.

Pricing policy can also be used as a planning tool if, for example, a region, resort or hotel wishes to concentrate on an up-market clientele, it may deliberately choose to impose high prices as a means of controlling the influx of tourists.

Selling the Product

Having done the market research, developed a product, identified market segments, established a pricing policy and made customers aware of the product, it must be sold to them. Making a sale is the final part of the communications mix. If the seller is a retail travel agent, he or she has to identify the client's needs and suggest the best destination for that tourist. If it is an inclusive tour, does it provide the right kind of accommodation, at the right price and in the right location? Are the travel arrangements satisfactory? If the seller is promoting/selling a particular product they need to convince the customer that the product will meet their needs and at a price they can afford. They need to know the product in detail and the strengths and weaknesses of competing products. Selling the benefits of a particular product is an important part of the sale. As soon as the seller is aware that the customer is willing to buy, they should seek to close the sale and to ask for the business.

Preparing a Marketing Strategy
The first step in preparing a marketing strategy is to establish the main goals and objectives of the firm or organisation. In the case of tourism marketing there is generally a combination of:

i.   increasing the market share of the product;
ii.   increasing the profits from tourist spending;
iii. developing new tourist markets;
iv.   reviving declining tourist products.

These are general long-term objectives and there is often a difference in objectives between those of the national or regional tourist organisation and the individual business, which is usually selling a specific product to a specific segment of the market. Small tourism businesses often do not have a marketing plan and usually have not undertaken any market research. These are the most vulnerable elements in the tourism industry.

There is an element of risk in any marketing strategy in that expenditure has to take place on developing a tourist product and marketing that product *before* the business or organisation is in a position to measure the success of the strategy. Forecasting the outcome of particular strategies is an important element in market research and can be used to predict not only the probability of success of a strategy, but also the degree of risk involved.

There are six main stages in preparing a marketing strategy. These are:

i.   *Identify the target market segments.* This relates to the age, socio-economic profile and region of origin of consumers (tourists) and decisions on whether a high volume mass market or low volume high spending exclusive market is desired.

ii. *Identify the consumer's profile for these market segments.* Market research among the target population can identify their preferences and those aspects of the product mix which have most appeal.

iii. *Identify the key factors which influence the segment's decision to buy a holiday.* Is it price? Is it conditioned by the image of the product? Is it the availability of distribution channels? Is it influenced by socio-political factors?

iv   *Establish the pricing policy.* This has already been discussed, but it is important in relation to whether the strategy is aimed at new markets, fighting off competition from other tourist regions, optimising income year-round or changing the image of the product.

v.   *Relate the marketing mix to the factors which most influence the client's decision-buying process.* This may involve a review of the product mix, the distribution mix and the communications mix in the light of factors that persuade the consumer to buy a particular tourist product. If he or she knows little about the product, there is clearly a case for looking at the effectiveness of the communications mix.

vi. *Identify the main groups of clients.* There are usually two or three groups of client. In the first stage of the distribution mix there are the retailers (travel agents) and the wholesalers and general tour operators. They will require particular discounts or special offers in order to promote and sell the product. In the second group there are the tourists themselves, and the marketing strategy must cater for them also. Finally, there are the business travellers who are influenced by differential pricing but more concerned with factors such as reliability, comfort, frequency of service and quality of service.

Measuring the Performance of a Marketing Strategy

In any marketing strategy it is necessary to build in a control and evaluation mechanism so that the organisation can measure the success of its policies and, if need be, change them in the light of new information. One effective method is to keep weekly and monthly sales (and booking) figures and plot them on a graph to show:

    i. weekly and monthly sales, compared to previous years;
    ii. cumulative sales to date, showing performance over the year up to the present (perhaps against target figures);
    iii. deviations from a regression line which shows long-term trends.

If these sets of indices are plotted, the graph will show a Z shape (Figure 10.2). This provides a clear picture of this year's performance compared to last year, when measured by monthly sales and cumulative sales, and should show that the long-term trend is up, static or in decline. Clearly this technique is readily applicable to an individual business and less so to a tourist resort or region as a whole, *unless* there are detailed statistics available on tourist numbers and spending over a period of years.

An alternative method is to tabulate the weekly/monthly budget forecast of sales and the actual sales for the same period. By measuring the shortfalls or surpluses that occur, you can modify the marketing strategy. *Analysis of variance* is a commonly used statistical method, and for more detailed consideration of this see Gregory (1971).

The tourist industry is continuing to grow as new firms, new destinations, new kinds of tourist product and new markets are developed.

For example, Chapter 6 discussed the impact of de-regulation of coach and air transport and forecast changes in aircraft technology in the 1990s. Both of these developments are already having a significant impact on the tourism industry. Chapter 13 includes references to time-share, theme parks and inner city tourism. All the evidence points to the dynamic and fast-changing nature of travel and tourism and underlines the need for effective marketing. This growth in activity brings with it increasing competition as businesses seek a greater market share. It is clear that any tourist business – from the largest company or national tourist office to the small family business – must develop a marketing strategy if it is to survive and prosper.

Figure 10.2: A Typical 'Z' Graph

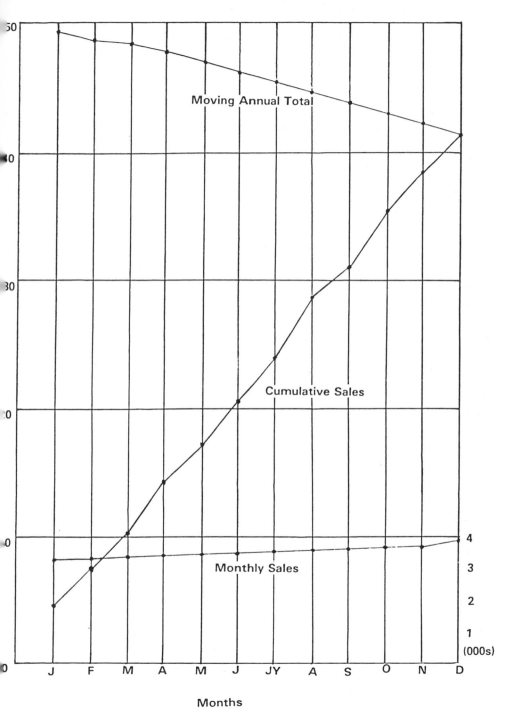

Any marketing plan should include the following elements. In developing a tourism product it should be evaluated for its:

Strengths   (i.e. how does it compare with other, similar products?)

Weaknesses   (i.e. where is it deficient compared with competing products?)

Opportunities   (i.e. what new markets or market segments are there for this product?)

Threats   (who are the main competitors and what are they doing in the market-place?)

In addition to the acronym **SWOT** which sums up the evaluation process, the business of marketing revolves around four P's:

Product   This can be summed up as the scenic, climatic, cultural, historic features that attract tourists; the range of services to transport them to and from their destination, and the facilities to accommodate them during their stay here.

Price   This is of crucial importance in marketing tourism because of the high level of competition between many tourist products. Pricing may be used as a marketing tool, to establish a niche in an existing market, to fight off competition to retain market share, or to present an image of exclusiveness. Pricing policy is usually not static and can vary according to the nature of the tourist product.

Place   This is not only the resort or tourist attraction, it means all the locations where the potential tourist can buy the tourist product. Thus, high street retail travel agents and direct sell tour operators who are selling tourist products are a key factor in the marketing process. Tourist Information Centres and other points of sale are also included under 'Place'.

Promotion   This includes advertising, production of brochures, public relations and sales promotion and is the most recognisable of the four P's. It is often taken to be synonymous with marketing but is only *part* of the marketing process.

Each of these P's has a key role to play in evolving a marketing strategy. However, to be successful they must be seen as part of an overall decision-making process which aims to match the needs and wishes of market segments with particular tourist products, to sell the product as effectively as possible and to maintain or increase market share for the firm or organisation concerned.

Measuring the Effectiveness of Destination Marketing

A central question that has been asked by national tourist officers for decades is, how does a tourist destination measure its marketing effectiveness? What factor or factors persuade tourists to visit one destination in preference to others? One way of producing an effective marketing evaluation system is to devise a meaningful set of performance indicators, and indicators of successful outcome. Performance indicators that can be used include:

- Market share changes
- Expenditure (cost) per visit attracted to the destination
- Ratio of industry funding to national tourist office funding
- Public Relations yield ratio

In the international tourism business, there is evidence of a direct relationship between effective promotion of a destination and the number of visitors to it that can be attracted from a highly competitive market.

An analysis of a number of major destinations between 1981 and 1991 shows that areas with the strongest growth are those which have made a major investment in their marketing budgets since the early 1980s. The winners during the 1980s, measured by the growth in tourist arrivals, were Hong Kong and Australia, with a growth of well over 100 per cent, followed by Singapore 89 per cent and Greece 66 per cent. Given the slowing down of growth of international tourism over the past two decades, it is clear that gains in market share are likely to be at someone else's expense. Each share in the Economist Intelligence Unit's *International Tourism Reports* table is published showing the winners and losers in the world's top twenty tourist destinations. Table 10.1 shows the changes in market share over this period.

Table 10.1: Regional Growth in Tourist Arrivals, 1981 and 1990

	Arrivals (mm)		% change
Country	1981	1990	1981/90
Hong Kong	2.5	5.9	136
Australia	0.9	2.2	144
Singapore	2.8	5.3	89
Singapore	2.8	5.3	89
Greece	5.6	9.3	66
France	30.5	50.0	64
UK	11.4	18.0	58
Canada	12.8	15.3	20
World total	288.8	429.3	49

Source: EIU, *International Tourism Reports*

A second performance indicator of marketing effectiveness is the expenditure on marketing which can be divided by the number of visitors attracted, to provide a crude measure of yield per dollar/pound spent.

A third variable that can be used is a measure of the effectiveness of co-operation between commercial and national tourist organisations, as a means of extending the range and scope of the marketing budget, to obtain more per dollar spent. A trend that has emerged over the past decade is the increasing collaboration between national tourist boards and the private sector in developing joint promotions and marketing campaigns. Joint ventures are seen as a clear benefit to both the national tourist organisation and the private sector, which makes up over 90 per cent of the tourist product.

Investment in promotion is not the only criterion for marketing effectiveness. Whilst the bottom line measure is usually taken as a growth in the number of arrivals from abroad, this is not necessarily an adequate measure of the performance of a marketing campaign. It would be more effective to consider changes in market share, the marketing cost per visitor attracted, the public relations yield ratio, and the scale of collaboration between public and private sector promotional campaigns, as performance measures and indicators of relative success.

Conclusions

The tourist industry is continuing to grow as new firms, new destinations and new markets are developed.

The growth of de-regulation of transport (see Chapter 6) and the emergence of new tourist generating countries, underline the continual need for effective marketing. This growth in activity brings with it increasing competition as businesses seek a greater market share. It is clear that any organisation in the tourist industry, from the National Tourist Organisation or the multi-national company to the small tourist business, should have a marketing strategy if it is to prosper.

ASSIGNMENTS

1. You are marketing consultant charged with preparing a marketing plan for a new company seeking to develop exclusive package holidays to selected, long-haul exotic destinations. Prepare a proposal setting out your choice of destinations and market segments. Identify the strengths and weaknesses of existing competitors.

2. You are the owner/manager of a large hotel in a downtown location in a major resort. Your room occupancy is below average and you have a suite of large rooms on the ground floor that are greatly under-used. Suggest how you might develop a marketing plan to increase your occupancy levels and the usage of your ground floor rooms.

Chapter 11

Tourism Impact Studies

1. The Economic Impact of Tourism

Learning Objectives:
After reading this Chapter you should understand:

- The impact of tourism on the economy of a town or a region;
- The multiplier effect;
- The main methods of measuring the economic impact of tourism;
- The importance of tourism to the national economy.

Introduction
Throughout the last two decades the British Government has recognised that tourism has the ability to generate employment and income faster and more effectively than other sectors of the economy. The tourist industry has supported and encouraged this potential.

This Chapter considers:

- The economic impact of tourism on the economy.
- The means of measuring economic importance.
- Assessing the consequences of tourism on the economy.
- The implications for the future planning and development of tourism.

Tourist Expenditure
Tourist spending is made up of several components which are linked to the different stages in the purchase of a holiday package. If it is an inclusive tour a tourist will have paid for the holiday in his or her own country and the bulk of this money will remain with the operator and retailer and carrier. A proportion will go to the hotel in the tourist region.

The main spending in the tourist region will therefore tend to be on:

- Meals and drinks out.
- Entertainment.
- Car hire or travel.
- Gifts and souvenirs.

However, measurement of economic impacts is more complex than this in that income comes, not just from visitor spending, but also from the wages and salaries from those working in the tourist industry, the profits that the tourist businesses make and the interest on capital borrowed to develop tourist projects.

METHODS OF MEASURING THE IMPACT OF TOURISM ON THE ECONOMY

1. On Regional and Local Economies

The concept of measuring the economic benefits on regional economies of particular activities by means of particular models is not new, and appears in books and articles on regional economic analysis going back over the past 40 years. However, the application of these models to tourism as an economic activity is much more recent. For a general introduction to methods of regional economic analysis, two useful references are W. Isard – *Methods of Regional Analysis* (1970) and H. Richardson – *Elements of Regional Economics* (1970).

There are three main methods generally used and these vary in their applicability and effectiveness.

These are:

- the economic base method;
- input-output analysis;
- the multiplier method.

a) The Economic Base Method

This method divides the economic activities of a region into those that are *basic* and *non-basic*. The *basic* activities are considered to be those exported to other regions and which bring income and generate jobs in the area in which they are based. The *non-basic* sector depends on, and services, the basic sector and the size of the *non-basic* sector is dependent on the level of economic activity in the *basic sector*.

It is, therefore, a very simple model, which is based on 3 assumptions:

- all economic activity is either basic or non-basic;
- economic performance can be measured by the performance of the basic sector;
- there is a constant relationship between the size of the basic sector and the size of the non-basic sector.

If the number of jobs provided by the basic and non-basic activities can be identified, then it is possible to establish the ratio between them and to calculate the number of new jobs created in the non-basic category, following a growth in exports (in this case tourism).

This method is limited in its application not least because it is difficult to identify all the basic and non-basic activities. It overlooks the fact that firms may have activities that are both basic and non-basic, and that there may be linkages between basic and non-basic operations. Also, it is questionable whether the non-basic sector *is* entirely dependent on the basic sector and whether the ratio between the two sectors remains constant. In the case of tourist activity, as a region grows, a proportion of the domestic population may consume the local tourist product and alter the basic/non-basic ratio.

b) Input-Output Analysis

This is based on the concept that the economy of a region (or place) can be divided into producing sectors and consuming sectors. Input-output analysis attempts to model the inter-relationships between the producing and consuming sectors of the economy.

A detailed account of the methodology of input-output analysis is provided in Isard (1970), but the broad concept is developed by producing a matrix of transactions between the producing and consuming sectors. As Table 11.1 shows, the producing sector forms the rows on the vertical axis and the consuming sector the columns on the horizontal axis. It is possible, by using this matrix, to discover how much each industry purchases from other industries and how much of the output of each economic activity is allocated to other industries in the region. Although Table 11.1 shows three main sectors, these could be disaggregated into indivudual industries within each sector to produce a much more detailed and complex transactions matrix.

Table 11.1: A Transactions Matrix

Producing Industry	Consuming Industry					
	Sector 1	Sector 2	Sector 3	Sector 4	Final Demand	Total Output
Primary	20	130	20	10	20	200
Manufacturing	80	50	70	150	50	400
Services	30	10	10	10	180	240
Other	30	20	100	100	200	450
Value Added	40	190	40	180		
Total Input	200	400	240	450		

The main problems associated with applying this method to regional economic analysis generally, and to the tourism industry in particular, are that it is dependent on identifying the representative set of industries and calculating constant coefficients to explain the transactions between them. It is also dependent on having available extensive data sets on regional income and employment levels, in a sufficiently disaggregated form to identify particular facets of the tourist industry at a local or regional level. In may tourist regions the economic theory is in advance of the data needed to apply it.

c)   The Multiplier Method
The concept of the *multiplier* has been used by economists since the 1930s at least, but it was Keynes who provided a much more precise application of this approach.

The *Multiplier concept* is based on the premise that initial spending within a region will inject additional cash into the flow of income in the regional economy, and thus increase the regional income. The size of the income multiplier is based on the proportion of the additional income that is spent *within* the region to be received as income by other businesses who, in turn, will spend a proportion of this income within this region and so on. The more that the initial injection of cash is re-spent within the region, the greater will be the rise in total income.

However, not all this income will be spent or, if spent, remain within the region. There will be 'leakages', for example, savings or spending on goods and services from other regions and with each successive iteration, there will be a certain amount of 'leakage' out of the system and the amount of additional income generated will decline.

The application of the multiplier method to estimates of the regional economic benefits of tourism was developed during the 1970s by B. H. Archer (1973), D. R. Vaughan (1977) and others. These studies identified visitor spending by carrying out extensive, on-site questionnaire surveys, together with information from particular local businesses that were thought to be either representative of the local tourist industry or related to/dependent on the local tourist industry.

These surveys generally attempted to identify three separate sets of data on:

- *direct spending*, that is expenditure of visitors on services/facilities provided by hotels, restaurants, shops and other local businesses/ facilities;
- *generated spending*, which is indirect spending resulting from the further purchase of goods and services by the tourist businesses in which the visitors have spent their money;
- *additional spending* by local residents of the income they have earned, directly or indirectly from visitor spending.

For each type of visitor, a profile was prepared showing the impact of spending and the successive stages that this income progressed through as it circulated in the local economy. For example, if a family spend £500 in a local hotel, the hotel will, in turn, use this income to pay for the wages and salaries of staff, buying food and supplies, paying laundry bills and banking the profit. Some of these purchases or services will be provided by local businesses who will, in turn, use this income to pay wages, meet other costs and keep the residue as profit. Table 11.2 shows a hypothetical example and shows that, by using the multiplier method in this way, for every £500 spent by a visitor, £145 is generated as additional income. So, in this case, the multiplier would be 0.29.

In addition to direct visitor spending in hotels and local facilities, such studies have attempted to survey the main business activities related to tourism in order to produce a coefficient which will reflect the additional income generated. After both types of survey have been completed, the end result is a composite multiplier as an index of all three types of income generated.

The approach developed by Archer (1973) and others is based on a concept that is in itself simple, but which requires extremely complex data collection and analysis to apply in practice. For multiplier analysis to be used in a meaningful way, the economic data must accurately reflect the range of monetary transactions that take place within the local economy. The previous chapter discussed data collection briefly in the context of market research. The same principles apply. The first stage is to identify what local economic data already exists and in what form. Any new data should provide information that will clearly show the impact of tourism spending within the local economy. Such surveys must cover a representative sample of the visitor and local business population and be undertaken over a sufficiently long time-scale to reflect any seasonal or cyclical elements in spending patterns.

Because of the need for highly accurate data at a disaggregated level, such studies using multiplier analysis are usually confined to a local or sub-regional level. They involve time-consuming interviews and visitor surveys and would be expensive to replicate on a larger scale. For this reason, studies of the economic impact of tourism at a national or supra-national level have used different measures.

Table 11.2: The Tourism Multiplier in Action

Action	Expenditure	Income
1. *A family spends in a hotel*	£500	
2. *The hotel in turn spends this money on:*		
Purchases of goods and services	255	
VAT	75	
Taxes	45	
Rates	10	
Wages and profit locally	115	*Direct Income*
3. *The suppliers spend their income on:*	65	
Goods for resale, and	30	
Other services	15	
Taxes	5	
Rates	5	
Wages and profit locally	10	*Generated Spending*
4. *Direct and Generated Income*	125	
of this £105 is re-spent	105	
5. *Additional Income*	20	*Additional Income*
TOTAL INCOME =	145	
For every £500 spent by a visitor, £145 is generated as additional income so in this case the multiplier would be 0.29.	$\frac{145}{500}$	

2. Tourism Impacts on National or Supra-National Economies

Tourism as an economic activity at national level is generally measured using three criteria:

- Its contribution to overall economic activity.
- Its contribution to overall employment.
- Its contribution to the Balance of Payments.

a) Contribution To Overall Economic Activity

The two most useful measures are the ratio of tourist receipts (income) to Gross Domestic Product and tourist expenditures to Private Final Consumption. The tourist receipts of a country generate economic activity and are, therefore, a measure of economic production of that country. Tourist expenditures (i.e. consumption) are part of the overall consumption (Private Final Consumption). Not all countries or tourist regions possess economic data that measure these components accurately, but the annual reports of the OECD on *Tourism Policy and International Tourism* contain a wide range of economic data for the member countries that can be used to calculate the proportion of tourist income and expenditure, compared with total income and expenditure.

Between 1975 and 1995, the proportion of international tourist receipts in the GDP of the OECD member countries has increased steadily, particularly in the United States, Germany and Spain. In terms of dollar expenditure, the main tourist generating countries confirmed their economic impact on international tourism, with volume growth led by Germany, Italy, the United States, Japan, the United Kingdom and France. The greatest percentage changes between 1992 and 1991 were those of Italy (up 42 per cent) and Turkey (up 31 per cent). Aggregate expenditure for all OECD countries amounted to $226 billion in 1992, up 14 per cent from the previous years. Expenditure progressed most sharply in Europe (up 16 per cent over 1991).

International tourist expenditures as a component of Private Final Consumption was most important in Germany (over 4 per cent), Denmark (4 per cent), and the Netherlands (over 4 per cent). However, over recent years the travel account expenditure as a proportion of Private Final Consumption in all member countries of the OECD has remained relatively stable. The income and expenditure from international tourism is only part of total tourist activity, and in order to calculate the total contribution to overall economic activity it is necessary to collect further data on:

- International tourist income and expenditure;
- Intra and extra – regional tourist income and expenditure;
- Domestic tourist income and expenditure.

Moreover, estimates based on direct contribution of tourist spending do not provide a complete picture. Tourist spending makes an indirect contribution to economic activity as the initial income is respent within the national economy.

b) Contribution to Employment

It is difficult to measure the total number of jobs dependant on or generated by the tourist industry, as the effect of spending by tourists is seen across a wide range of occupations and felt directly and indirectly. There are three particular problems when relating tourism to employment:

i. The tourist product is very diversified and covers a wide range of economic activities, many of which provide services used by the local population. The censuses of employment usually include hotels with restaurants and other catering and do not distinguish between those firms which mainly service the tourist and those which do not. Transport is often put as a single category without the tourism element being separated out.

ii. Employment statistics tend to cover employees only and often fail to register employers or self employed. Many tourism businesses are small businesses, run by families or owner-managers, and they form the major proportion of total employment in the industry.

iii. Tourism is a seasonal activity and its importance as an employer will fluctuate with the seasonal changes in visitor numbers. Most studies linking tourism to employment are based on expenditure data for three sectors of the economy:

- Direct employment in businesses that sell goods and services directly to the tourist.
- Indirect employment in manufacturing and wholesale distribution firms that supply goods and services to tourism businesses.
- Investment related employment, such as employment in construction and the construction industry.

In the United Kingdom the earnings from tourism have increased steadily since the mid 1970s, and studies of direct and indirect tourist spending suggest that jobs in the main tourism sectors have grown from 1.25 million in 1985 to 2.88 million in 1991. Over the same period, employment in manufacturing fell by 15 per cent and jobs in the service sector generally grew by 9 per cent. During a period of limited economic growth tourism has performed very favourably in creating jobs compared with other sectors of the economy.

c) Contribution to the Balance of Payments

A country such as Britain receives significant income from spending by overseas tourists. In 1977 overseas earnings from tourism amounted to £2.3 billion. By 1990 this had quadrupled to over £9.9 billion from overseas earnings. This is known as an 'invisible export', as it contributes to the national economy. However, in 1994 around 20 million Britons took summer holidays abroad, spending money on tourist goods and services in other countries. They were therefore 'importing' these services. The contribution of tourism to the overall Balance of Payments of a country is the *difference* between the amount which overseas visitors spend in that country and the amount that the same country's residents spend overseas, and shows the net surplus or deficit on the tourism account. Figure 11.1 shows the contribution of tourism to the Balance of Payments between 1980 and 1994.

In developing countries with limited potential for exporting manufactured goods, and which are reliant on low cost primary products and imported high-cost products, the development of tourist facilities can greatly improve their Balance of Payments position, by bringing a considerable influx of spending into the local economy. In this context tourism can have a stabilising effect, by decreasing the deficit on their overall Balance of Payments.

Before the collapse of Communism, most Eastern European countries sought to encourage the inflow of western tourists, whilst placing restrictions on the foreign travel of their own nationals, with the aim of improving their Balance of Payments and importing much needed hard currency.

If the foreign exchange earnings of the tourist industry in the UK are compared with other leading export industries, it can be seen in Table 11.3 that, between 1984 and 1994, the foreign exchange earnings from tourism more than doubled. Tourism is clearly seen as by far the leading invisible export for the UK now.

Figure 11.1: Balance of Payments and Tourism Exports

Tourism compared with other exports 1980-1994

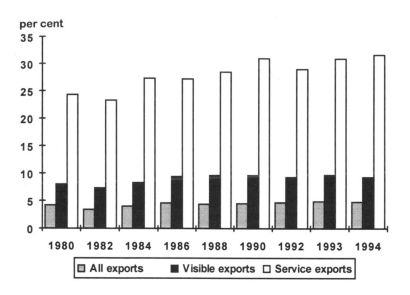

Table 11.3: Tourism Compared with Other Exports 1980-1994

	1980	1982	1984	1986	1988	1990	1992	1993	1994
All exports	4.2	3.4	4.0	4.6	4.4	4.5	4.7	4.9	4.8
Visible exports	8.0	7.3	8.3	9.4	9.6	9.6	9.3	9.7	9.3
Service exports	24.3	23.3	27.3	27.2	28.5	31.0	29.0	30.9	31.6

Sources: *Economic Trends* and *International Passenger Survey*

For some years the Tourism Committee's statistical working party of the OECD has been working to apply a System of National Accounts to identify the economic importance of tourism, principally in monetary terms. The OECD claim that this is the only available framework for coherent analysis of the economic contribution of tourism, because it brings together commodities, supply and use and sets them against activities and final users. In 1991 the OECD adopted a manual on Tourism Economic Accounts. This provides a basis for the compilation of data on production, consumption, value added, gross fixed capital formation, and employment in the tourist industries. It is currently under trial but it is hoped that the OECD will use this system as a basic tool to assess the importance of tourism to member country economies.

d) Other Approaches to National Income Accounting

The measurement of the economic importance of tourism has attracted the increasing interest of governments across the world and, in Canada in 1994, they released the first results of a new analytical tool for the tourist industry. This was the production of Tourism Satellite Accounts, which is a means of using established principles of national income accounting to measure the importance of the tourist industry. This claims to be able to measure the economic activity generated by tourism in a country through the demands for commodities created by tourism in that country and the production required to meet that demand. The concept emerged during the 1980s and was developed by the Canadian National Task Force on tourism data. The Tourism Satellite Account identifies several layers of information which are then measured to provide an overview of tourism activities. Answers are sought to the following questions:

- How important is tourism demand for commodities produced by a country?
- Which industries benefit from tourism?
- How much direct and indirect value-added is generated from meeting tourism demand?
- How much tax revenue does the government receive from tourism?
- How much employment depends on tourism?
- How important is tourism to a particular national economy?

This collects and organises tourism data in the form of economic transactions between producers and consumers of tourism products and services. It also enables a government to examine both the supply and demand sides of tourism within a balanced accounting system. The full details and methodology of this approach to measuring economic importance of tourism has been described in 'The Tourism Satellite Account' published in *National Income and Expenditure Accounts, Quarterly Estimates*, second quarter 1994 (catalogue number 13-001) by the Canadian government. One major reservation is that the specific results of the Canadian Tourism Satellite Account cannot be directly applicable to other countries, because they are based on Canadian data and really relate to the Canadian experience. At present the world tourism organisation is looking at this approach with a view to its possible adoption as a future new international standard. Similarly, the organisation for Economic Co-operation and Development is considering the expansion of its current manual for Tourism Economic Accounts to include aspects of the system, as developed by Canada.

ASSIGNMENTS

1. Using sets of data from a recent OECD Annual Report on tourism policy and international tourism:

   - Assess the impact of tourism on the economies of four contrasting member states over the past 10 years.
   - Plot the balance of payments between 1985 and 1995 of two member states.

2. Using the further reading referred to in the text, apply the application and multiplier analysis critically to the study of at least *one* local economy.

Chapter 12

Tourism Impact Studies

2. The Impact of Tourism on the Environment

Learning Objectives:
After reading this Chapter and the references contained within it, you should have a clear understanding of:

- the types of impact that can occur;
- the methods of measuring the impacts of tourism development upon the environment;
- policy measures that have been developed to conserve the environment;
- methods of planning and managing tourism to reconcile conservation and development.

Introduction

There has been a growing awareness of the socio-cultural and environmental impacts of tourism on a region and that disbenefits can occur through developments, which are often overlooked in the search for economic benefits of tourism. A large-scale seasonal influx of visitors can mean that, by sheer pressure of numbers, the visitors to fragile environments risk destroying the very attractions that they come to see. In coastal regions the rapid growth of a tourist infrastructure in the form of hotels, condominiums, shopping malls and roads, can transform a landscape in a short space of time. Because any discussion on the environmental impacts of tourism can risk being influenced by value-judgements, it is necessary to adopt an objective approach when measuring impacts. This chapter seeks to describe and explain the types of impact that can occur, the methods of measuring these impacts, the public policy response (in the form of planning and control measures) that has evolved to conserve the environment, and management approaches designed to reconcile the inherent conflict between conservation and development.

Types of Environmental Impact

Tourism impacts on the environment in a number of ways. There is the visual intrusion of large numbers of parked and moving vehicles; the presence of large numbers of people on beaches, footpaths or lakesides. There is noise, pollution and overcrowding. There is destruction of vegetation, visual intrusion of new buildings; developments out of scale with existing buildings. There is the impact on the vegetation and the wildlife; and on the ecological system as a whole. Overall, there is a very real risk that, if unchecked, tourism development will lead to conflicts over the use of land.

For example, in the coastal dune areas of North West England, and on the coasts of Holland and Denmark, trampling has caused the loss of stabilising vegetation leading to sand blows inland, the collapse of a fragile ecosystem and the inundation of farmland. In the Dutch dune system, because of its importance as a sea defence, no public access is allowed to beaches, except on a few board walks. In Norway and Sweden the increasing spread of second homes in the mountain areas which lack sewage systems has led to pollution of local rivers and streams, (Council of Europe 1971).

The nature of the tourism impacts is associated with the nature of the tourist resources. With natural resources, i.e. beaches, national parks, lakesides or forests, it is the ability of the resource to absorb the tourist that is the first measure of impact. This has been measured in relation to the *capacity* of the resource. There are three different kinds of capacity: physical, environmental and ecological.

Physical Capacity is the easiest concept to grasp because many tourist facilities/resources will have absolute limits on the number of tourists they can accommodate. Usually other constraints will intervene before this is reached. For example, approach roads will become congested or car parks full before the beach reaches its maximum capacity.

Environmental Capacity. This is the maximum level of tourist use that an area can accommodate before visitors perceive a decline in their attraction to that place and move on elsewhere. This is the most abstract and least tangible measure of capacity, but is an important influence on visitor behaviour. This level of capacity is very personal and varies with the season, prevailing weather, and type of tourist activity – so a wide range of capacity levels exist using this as a measure. Burton (1974), in her work on Cannock Chase, established that 10 to 50 cars in sight represented a critical level of use at which people first perceived the environment was crowded.

This concept has been studied in different tourist environments to produce national standards of capacity. Dower and McCarthy (1967), in their study of Donegal, identified a range of resources critical to the development of tourism and estimated the capacity of each to take people at any one time. Using studies by Furmidge (1969), Houghton-Evans and Miles (1970) it is possible to produce a range of estimates of environmental capacity, see Table 12.1 below:

Table 12.1: Suggested Space Standards for Environmental Capacity

Type of recreation area	National environmental capacity
Major scenic route	20 persons per mile
Minor scenic route	4 persons per mile
Major scenic feature	20 persons per mile
Major historic site	30 persons per mile
Woodland area	100 persons per square mile
Picnic area	60 persons
Enclosed land	50 persons per square mile
Rough or hill land	5 persons per square mile
Coast or lake shore (basic level)	50 persons per mile
Attractive and accessible coast/beach	400 persons per mile

Ecological Capacity is the maximum level of tourist use that an area can accommodate before ecological damage or decline occurs. It is affected by geology, soils, vegetation cover and terrain of an area and the seasonal intensity of tourist use. A person on horseback has more effect than one on foot. When people come in vehicles, especially the 4-wheel drive variety which gives them much greater accessibility to fragile landscapes, the wheels of these vehicles can destroy the vegetation cover and expose heath and stone. This has happened in parts of the New Forest where damage to the vegetation and to trees has occurred, and access to water and food for wild animals has been restricted.

In her work *The Recreational Carrying Capacity of the Countryside* (1974) Rosemary Burton points out that, because the concept of carrying capacity is little understood, and, because it has not been translated into a set of practical planning guidelines, attempts to manage environmentally sensitive areas are often frustrated. Although this work was undertaken over 20 years ago, the findings are just as relevant today because of the continuing need to understand and plan for the impacts of tourism on the environment.

Case Studies of Environmental Impact

1. Spain
In the 1950s and 1960s, Spain was developed as a major destination for mass market package tours. By the late 1970s, the growth of domestic and international tourism produced a seasonal influx of over 56 million tourists, concentrated in parts of its Mediterranean coast.

The Spanish authorities, when faced with this huge inflow of seasonal visitors, took two policy decisions. Firstly, they sought to maximise the income from tourism. Secondly, they wished to minimise the damage to the environment. In order to assess the nature, scale, and distribution of tourism impact, several studies were carried out during the 1970s to measure:

- the capacity of the tourist regions;
- the existing levels of tourist use of these regions (i.e. their market share).

The aim was to identify those tourist regions with the greatest pressures of visitor use.

The tourist capacity of the leading holiday regions was calculated using the following formula:

$$\text{Tourist Capacity} = \frac{\text{No. of Beds + No. of Restaurants + No. of Commercial Licences}}{\text{Normal Population (000's) x Land area (Km}^2)} \times 100$$

This index produced the following table of leading tourist regions:

Region	Tourist Capacity	Rank
Costa Brava	27.7	1
Majorca	13.6	2
Costa del Sol	10.5	3
Grand Canary Island	8.0	4
Barcelona	6.7	5
Madrid	4.5	6
Murica-Alicante	3.6	7
Tenerife	2.3	8
San Sebastian	2.0	9
Santander	1.0	10

This can then be related to the market share of the various regions as a proportion of total tourists to Spain.

Region	Market Share (%)	Rank
Majorca	35.2	1
Murica-Alicante	7.4	2
Madrid	7.5	3
Barcelona	6.8	4
Costa del Sol	6.4	5
Costa Brava	5.5	6
Tenerife	5.1	7
Great Canary Islands	4.7	8
Santander	0.8	9
San Sebastian	0.7	10

It can be seen, from this limited example, that some regions with a more limited tourist capacity (such as Murica-Alicante) had a greater market share than other regions, such as Grand Canary which possessed greater capacity. Certain localities, such as Murica-Alicante or the Costa del Sol, were faced with a substantial influx of tourists over a limited period in the year. This led to a range of problems, including acute congestion, especially on the coastal strip, inadequate infrastructure, environmental damage and overloading of local services. Recent publicity has highlighted the response of the Spanish authorities to the spread of development, especially on the coastal strip of the Costa del Sol, where no new development is to be allowed within 100 metres of the shoreline and buildings erected without planning permission may be demolished.

2. Languedoc-Roussillon

The development of this stretch of the South of France was described in detail in Chapter 9. Over a period of 20 years a 180 kilometre stretch of the French Mediterranean coast was transformed from a remote rural region of lakes, salt marshes and uninterrupted beaches into the second most important tourist region in France. There were few roads and the local infrastructure was limited. Six new resorts were built, with a total capacity of 2 million visitors and moorings for over 20,000 boats. A network of major roads and water supply installations was developed. Between the six resorts, the natural vegetation and original landscape was to be preserved and protected so that the local flora and fauna would remain.

But tourism development on this scale will have a considerable impact on the environment. How do we measure this impact? Is it a beneficial impact or a detrimental one? Was the original environment worth preserving? How can we best plan for tourism development so as to minimise its impact on the environment? How can the remnants be best conserved? In any assessment of the impact of tourism on the environment these are some of the questions that must be answered.

Methods of Measuring Environmental Impact

The original work on environmental impact studies was developed in the United States, the stimulus being the National Environmental Policy Act

(1972) which required Federal Authorities to identify and measure the environmental impacts of proposals and to disclose the results to State and local bodies and the public. Several methods of environmental impact analysis have been developed, and three of those most adaptable to measuring tourism impacts are outlined below.

(i) Overlays

This is the most simple method of EIA and consists of a series of map transparencies overlaid to show the geographic extent and intensity of impact of proposed developments. An area can be divided into grid squares and, within each square, information can be displayed showing the potential impact of development proposals on environmental factors. This can bring out significant conflicts between development and the environment. At a manual level there is a practical limit to the number of overlays that can be effectively superimposed upon one another. However, the use of computer graphics could overcome this problem and a wide range of overlays could be interrelated to identify interactions.

(ii) Matrices

A matrix can be constructed to show the impacts of the proposed developments (on the horizontal axis) on the individual characteristics of the existing tourist region (on the vertical axis). Within each cell of the matrix, it is possible to assess the level of the individual impacts (Figure 12.1) with a score ranging from 1 to 10 representing the increasing size or magnitude of the impact. For example, a proposed hotel complex or condominium development might lower the existing water table by several inches, or introduce the risk of pollution within the network of local rivers and lakes. This would produce a high score as a measure of the environmental impact. One criticism of this method is that it only takes account of the *immediate* impacts and is not sufficiently sophisticated to account for secondary and successive levels of impact.

An impact matrix should take account of both the development and the operational phase of a tourism project, and the scale of individual impacts may vary between these two phases. If at all possible, impacts should be measured objectively using quantitative analysis so that the end product of

Figure 12.1: Environmental Impact Analysis Matrix

CONSTRUCTION PHASE

	SCENERY	LAND USE	RESIDENT POPULATION	TOURIST POPULATION	TRAFFIC MOVEMENT PATTERNS	NOISE AND DISTURBANCE	ECOLOGICAL CHARACTERISTICS	ARCHAEOLOGICAL CHARACTERISTICS	POLLUTION	POWER SUPPLY	SERVICES	SEWERAGE	EXISTING SETTLEMENT
Land Needs													
Population changes													
Noise from plant													
Traffic Noise													
Transport of material													
Polution													
Increased Traffic													
Water Discharge													
Transport of Employees													
Labour Needs													
Site use													

CHARACTERISTICS OF EXISTING SITUATION

OPERATIONAL PHASE

	SCENERY	LAND USE	RESIDENT POPULATION	TOURIST POPULATION	TRAFFIC MOVEMENT PATTERNS	NOISE AND DISTURBANCE	ECOLOGICAL CHARACTERISTICS	ARCHAEOLOGICAL CHARACTERISTICS	POLLUTION	POWER SUPPLY	SERVICES	SEWERAGE	EXISTING SETTLEMENT
Land Needs													
Population changes													
Noise from plant													
Traffic Noise													
Transport of material													
Polution													
Increased Traffic													
Water Discharge													
Transport of Employees													
Labour Needs													
Site use													

CHARACTERISTICS OF EXISTING SITUATION

an impact matrix would be a summary indicating that a proposed tourism development would produce:

- gains or losses;
- short-term or long-term effects;
- reversible or irreversible effects;
- local or regional impacts.

Models

The view that matrices are cumbersome to construct and only measure first order impacts, led to the construction of dynamic simulation models. The environment is seen as an open or closed *system* and models are constructed which predict the effects of changes brought about by tourism developments on this environment. The system can be seen at successive intervals of time as a series of calculations are carried out to predict successive impacts on the environment. The construction of such models generally requires considerable data about the environment and the proposed development, and this may require time and technical expertise that is not available. Provided such data is available it is possible to construct complex mathematical models to deal with large complex development proposals.

ASSIGNMENTS

1. Using a stretch of coast line, a beauty spot or a country park within your locality, attempt to measure the following:

   i) The impact of visitors on the area.

   ii) The types of visitor amenities/facilities provided and their location/distribution.

   iii) The existing local policies for visitor management.

2. Using reports of the National Park Planning Authorities in Britain, compare the approach to the *planning* and *management* of any two national parks in Britain. Also identify and summarise what you see as the key issues relating to tourism and conservation within those areas.

Chapter 13

Sustainable Tourism

Learning Objectives:
After reading this Chapter and the source material referred to in it, you should undertstand the nature, scope and elements of sustainable tourism, and the key issues to be addressed in managing the impacts of tourism.

Introduction

The World Conservation Union has defined sustainable development as:

A process which allows development to take place without degrading or depleting the resources which make the development possible. This is generally achieved, either by managing the resources so that they are able to renew themselves at the same rate as which they are used, or by switching from the use of a slowly regenerating resource to one which regenerates more rapidly. In this way resources remain able to support future as well as current generations.

In this context sustainable tourism is seen as a model form of economic development which will improve the quality of life of the host community; provide a high quality of experience for the visitor; and maintain the quality of the environment on which the local community and the visitor depend.

There are three main principles of sustainable development:

● Social and cultural sustainability ensures that development increases people's control over their lives, is compatible with the culture and values of people affected by it, and maintains and strengthens community identity.

- Economic sustainability ensures that development is economically efficient and that resources are managed so that they can support future generations.
- Ecological sustainability ensures that development is compatible with a maintenance of ecology, biological diversity and resources.

Sustainable tourism encourages an understanding of the impacts of tourism on the natural, cultural, and human environments. Sustainable tourism also encourages decision-making among all segments of society, including the local population, so that tourism and other resource users can exist together. It includes planning and zoning which ensure tourism development appropriate to the carrying capacity of the ecosystem. Cultural tourism enhances local community esteem and provides the opportunity for greater understanding and communication among peoples of diverse backgrounds. Environmentally sustainable tourism demonstrates the importance of natural and cultural resources to a community's economic and social well being and the importance of preserving them. Sustainable tourism monitors and manages the impact of tourism and seeks to develop reliable methods of environmental accountability to off-set any negative effects of tourism development.

Policy Responses to the Environmental Impact of Tourism

With the growth in tourism on a world scale, not only are more people using the coastal and inland regions of countries for tourism, they are travelling greater distances, impacting on a greater area and spending more time there in greater numbers. Over the past 40 years there has been an increasing concern for the quality of the environment and the need to conserve scenery and wildlife in areas of great natural beauty. During the 1990s there has also been an increasing concern about the social and cultural impacts of tourism on the host community and this has emerged as a key concern in developing sustainable tourism. At the same time, there has been growing demands for more land for urban development, for roads and factories, for water supply, mineral extraction and many other land uses. The remaining land must also be used for farming, forestry and many other needs.

In order to meet these conflicting demands on the use of land and to conserve areas with fragile ecosystems or of great scenic value, most countries have developed a hierarchy of planning controls. The major landscape resources are usually conserved in National Parks, with the Yellowstone National Park in the USA the first to be established in 1872. The United States National Park Service Act of 1916 sums up the role of National Parks.

To conserve the scenery and natural objects of wildlife therein, to provide for the enjoyment of the same, in such a manner and by such means as will leave them unimpaired for the enjoyment of future generations.

The Netherlands has three National Parks, which are similar in concept to those of the United States. In Britain and Germany, by way of contrast, most of the land in the National Parks is in private ownership and has normal land uses such as farming, forestry and mineral extraction. In England and Wales the designation of an area as a National Park enables special planning legislation to be used to control the use and development of this land. The National Park Authority has powers to plant trees, clear eyesores and to provide facilities for tourists such as car parks, camp sites and information centres. Following the *National Parks and Access to the Countryside Act 1949*, ten National Parks were established in England and Wales. The 1949 Act also provided for the designation of areas of outstanding natural beauty (AONB's) of which 33 have now been recognised (see Figure 13.3). Following the *Countryside Act 1968* local authorities in England and Wales have the powers to establish country parks and picnic sites. These are much smaller, but nevertheless attract recreational facilities and are sited in pleasant countryside within easy access of the major conurbations. One underlying reason for their establishment was a belief that they would help to relieve pressure from the National Parks, which were faced with a growing influx of car owning visitors who could reach with ease the remoter, more fragile landscape areas.

The most successful examples of conservation are in the United States and Holland where land ownership and management are in the hands of one authority. In Britain, a quasi-public body, The National Trust, has

Figure 13.1: National Parks, AONBs and Stretches of Heritage Coast in England and Wales

acquired many thousands of acres of countryside and coast and protects them in the face of development pressures. Otherwise, in Britain, the National Parks have a chequered history as a means of controlling land use, especially mineral extraction.

The most successful measures to reconcile tourism development with environmental conservation have come about through the development of management plans for tourism regions. Sustainable tourism is the sensible use of resources and is concerned with the quality and quantity of many resources and maintaining their presence. Underlying this, is a general view that, if the natural resources are not conserved, they will deteriorate or be destroyed, and then the tourists will leave, perhaps never to return. This would have disastrous effects on a local regional or national economy.

Planning for Tourism Environments
The key to the successful integration of tourism in the environment lies in the planning and management of any proposed development. As part of the sustainable development approach to planning tourism, environmental and socio-economic impacts should be considered throughout the planning process, so that the negative impacts are prevented, or at least minimised, and positive ones reinforced. Projects should also be subject to an environmental impact assessment (EIA) to ensure that no serious problems will emerge from the development. As well as being integrated into the planning and development process, these impacts need to be continuously monitored and managed so that, if any negative impacts emerge, they can be identified and addressed before they become a serious problem.

In planning for tourism environments we must be conscious of the variations in environmental sensitivity associated with the main types of destination. These are outlined below.

Coastal Areas Including Beaches, Marine Areas and Wet Lands
Many beach areas have the potential carrying capacity for relatively high volume tourism, whereas marine areas and wet lands have more fragile

ecosystems and are better suited to small scale tourism. Often in coastal areas there is competition for the use of prime coastal sites with residential, industrial or harbour development, or for other commercial uses.

Mountain and Wilderness Areas
Mountains, forests, moors, deserts, savannahs and other types of wilderness area are mostly visited by tourists interested in natural history or special interest activities. These areas have fragile ecosystems and limited carrying capacity. One potential conflict is with the growth of activities, such as downhill skiing, which is a high volume activity and has a major impact with all its infrastructure on the environment.

The Inland Rural Areas
Farmland, woodland, lakes and riverside environments can provide locations for small scale recreation developments, second homes and farm holidays. Careful planning is required to ensure that these prime farmland and forest land areas are not degraded by tourist facilities and that the water areas are protected from pollution.

Urban Areas
Towns and cities with their cultural events, museums, monuments, historic places, shopping, entertainment and conference facilities can attract and manage large numbers of tourists. The existing infrastructure may have sufficient carrying capacity for visitors, or the capacity can be expanded with benefits also being provided for the local population. However, particularly in historic towns with narrow streets and many old buildings, the influx of too many visitors can lead to congestion and reduced access to amenities.

Small Islands
Small islands are often attractive tourist destinations because of their beaches, coral reefs, sea life and scenic beauty. But, small island environments are highly vulnerable to the negative impact of tourist development. Carrying capacity is usually limited. There can be a very real conflict between the need for conservation and the pressure for economic development, as tourism can be seen as providing much needed jobs, income and improved infrastructure.

Given these different kinds of tourist environment, in order to protect those locations or regions with scarce or fragile environments, a three-fold planning programme needs to be agreed. This consists of:

- Increasing the capacity of regions or tourist resorts which are already adapted and committed to large scale tourist use.

- Creating new resources for tourism, using reclaimed or undeveloped and disused land in the immediate hinterland of our cities and conurbations.

- Developing multiple use of the same resource.

The overall objective of this approach is to divert pressure as far as possible away from those fragile tourist environments with limited carrying capacity and where the impact of development could be catastrophic.

i) Increasing the Capacity of Existing Tourist Resorts/Regions

Wherever possible the aim should be to improve the capacity of existing resorts and holiday areas to accommodate more tourism. This will relieve pressures on more fragile areas, but will also involve the reappraisal of the use and effectiveness of existing tourist resources and the development of management measures, which are outlined later in this Chapter. The advantage with this approach is that these destinations are already well known to the public and are likely, therefore, to receive the first impact of any increased demand for tourism. As demand is often seasonal, measures to extend the season can also help to minimise peak season congestion.

One example of this approach can be seen in the state of Goa, which is on the west central coast of India facing the Indian Ocean. It has a coast line of 106 kilometres, and 65 kilometres consist of sandy beaches. The government's policy since the late 1980s has been for the controlled expansion of tourism development. In 1988 there were 850,000 tourists, most of whom were domestic travellers. The tourist resources within Goa include these extensive beaches but also a scenic natural environment of palm groves, forested inland hills and distinctive cultural and ethnic attractions. However, the major attraction to Goa for foreign tourists is the quality and extent of the beaches and this, together with labour supply and infrastructure and social impact issues, were the primary considerations in a carrying capacity analysis undertaken for the state government. An analysis was made of the existing distribution of tourist arrivals and the preferences of domestic tourists, and a standard was derived of an average density of 40 square metres of beach area per tourist sun-bed. It was also decided that not more than 70 per cent of the beach, or 46 out of the 65 kilometres,, should be developed in order to:

- Protect the coastal villages and their surrounding areas.

- Protect the general landscape character of the area.

- Avoid continuous built-up development along the coast line.

- Cater for the recreational and other needs of the local inhabitants.

Application of this carrying capacity resulted in an overall proposal for a maximum development level of 46,000 tourist sun-beds. This was based on assumptions of future accommodation occupancy rates which will vary between domestic and foreign tourists. The capacity allowed implies a level of 4.1 million tourists arriving annually, which is five times the 1988 level of tourists visiting the region. Based on the present level of under employment and unemployment within Goa, and the projected growth of population and employment in other sectors of the economy, it was felt that inadequate labour supply exists to serve this projected level of tourist development.

ii) Creation of New Tourist Resources
This can take two forms:

- The reclamation of land from the sea, by means of polder or barrage schemes.

- The development of derelict or under-used land around our major towns and cities, especially in, or adjacent to, the main tourist destinations.

The reclamation of Ijsselneer and the Delta scheme in Holland have created a great number of tourist opportunities for camping, water sports and natural history. The proposed barrage scheme for Morecambe Bay and the Wash in England, for Cardiff Bay and also in Southern France, would provide new resources for water based tourism activities.

Throughout Europe there are many thousands of hectares of disused mineral workings, former railways, derelict canals and disused airfields that can be reclaimed/redeveloped for tourism uses. Sand and gravel workings can be reclaimed for water based tourism. Many of the country parks in Britain and the regional parks in France include derelict mineral workings or industrial land that has been reclaimed. In Britain disused railways have been converted to long distance footpaths and bridleways and disused canals have been restored and now provide facilities for cruising, walking and other activities. Much of the derelict industrial land and mineral working is within easy reach of major towns and cities and, if it can be reclaimed and put to tourist uses, this will help to relieve the pressures on more distant and more fragile environments. Developments in some of Britain's inner city areas are a case in point. In London a nine mile stretch of former docklands has been transformed, as part of a major development project to provide a wealth of manmade and water based tourist attractions. Similar schemes have been developed in Bristol, Birmingham, Liverpool, Swansea and Newcastle-upon-Tyne. However, reclamation of under-used land or restoration of derelict land is not the only answer, and may not be possible in every case. In order to protect and conserve the environment, it is also necessary to integrate tourism with other land uses, especially water supply, forestation and nature conservation.

iii) Multiple Use
The reservoirs and their catchments in upland Britain service tourist attractions and provide opportunities for walking, sailing, camping and fishing. The Keilder reservoir is a good example, where a major new tourist development scheme was provided in the 1980s centred on Keilder Water and the surrounding forest area. Sports facilities, accommodation and related facilities all formed part of an ambitious development plan, which was jointly sponsored by the Forestry Commission, The Sports Council, the water authority and the neighbouring local authorities.

In Britain the Forestry Commission has successfully integrated tourism with forestry and now provides opportunities for many activities including scenic drives, picnic sites, camping and fishing. Britain now has seven Forest Parks where these activities are encouraged. In parts of upland Britain the Forestry Commission has developed and built holiday villages. In the Netherlands over 10 per cent of the holdings of the state forest service are managed for tourism and the service has built roads, camp sites, view points and picnic areas. In the United States many of the forest areas in the National Parks play a similar role and see now conflict between the need for timber supply and the provision of amenities for tourists.

Managing Tourist Environments

There are three key principles to be followed in environmental management:

- To maintain the carrying capacity of the tourist area or attraction.
- Provision of adequate infrastructure to serve tourism, as well as general community needs.
- To establish a socio-cultural programme which will provide a structured approach to conserving specific aspects of the area's cultural heritage.

The most effective means of resolving potential conflicts between tourism and the environment is by applying good management practice. Three aspects of management need to be considered.

- Traffic management
- Land management
- Visitor management

i) Traffic Management

Tourists often travel by car to, or within, their holiday destination, and the large numbers of moving and parked cars are one of the most immediate impacts of tourism on the environment. For many years traffic management has been recognised as a necessary means of controlling the movement and access of vehicles in our major towns and cities. In tourist regions the same principles need to be applied if the impact of traffic is to be minimised. This should take the form of traffic design and highway engineering. Traffic design includes the provision of one way systems, speed limits, limits on access to remote areas, and restrictions on car parking. In some areas cars may be banned altogether. In the Peak District National Park an experiment was carried out in the Goyt Valley, where rural roads were closed at weekends to all vehicles except mini buses carrying visitors into the Valley from car parks located around its perimeter. This scheme was possible because the Valley had limited access by road and had no resident population.

To compensate for restrictions on motor vehicles, the planning authorities could provide scenic drives, picnic areas and view points at other locations. In some cases new roads may need to be built by-passing environmentally sensitive areas. The Susten Pass in Switzerland, between Innertkirchan and Wassen, and the Deutsch Weinstrasse, from the French border to Mainz, are good examples of such purpose-built routes.

ii)   Land Management

This relates to aspects of design and maintenance and, by a mix of persuasion and financial incentives, encouraging private bodies to provide amenities for tourists on their land. A circulation pattern may be necessary to direct and control flow visitors through a site, and this may involve the erection of signs, fences and barriers, additional landscaping and planting schemes. It may be necessary to change the visitor access points and circulation routes on an annual basis, to minimise the effects of trampling on the vegetation, and to introduce a programme of planned maintenance for the site. It is important to know the number of visitors that a site can support before services in the form of car parking, access, water and sewage disposal, risk becoming overloaded. There is a need, therefore, to monitor visitor numbers so that controls can be introduced, if overcrowding or congestion is to be avoided. Good visitor management techniques are essential in order to control the impact of tourism on the environment.

iii) Visitor Management

The most effective techniques of visitor management are usually unobtrusive, but persuasive. Visitor management involves two actions:

- Preventing or restricting access to environmentally fragile areas.
- Directing visitors to those areas that can accommodate them.

The most immediate control on site usage can be by limiting car parking provision, since in Europe and the USA most tourists will use their car to visit the coast or countryside, and most stay close to their car when they arrive there. In the Huron-Clinton system of regional parks around Detroit, there is a system of notifying potential visitors that a regional park is "full", and most Americans appear to be prepared to move on when they know a park is full.

Management by price is another control mechanism, particularly for the private sector. A variation of this approach is to have a variable system of pricing related to the seasons and to prevailing visitor numbers. Also, in Britain, the National Trust has introduced a management approach based on tickets which have a limited time to visitor attractions which are particularly popular. Time management may be more widely used.

The use of barriers, such as ditches, screens or mounds to deter people, when confined with direction signs to the visitor attractions, can help to control the spread of visitors in a recreational area. A scheme for the interpretation of the site is an essential element in the approach to visitor management. Guided tours or walks, exhibitions, self guided trails or guide leaflets can all be used to direct visitors to those parts of the site that can accommodate them. If the tourist resource is sufficiently large, it may be possible to zone different localities for a range of uses – from the intensive gregarious activities around the main beach or lakeside area – to the less gregarious scenic drives or small picnic areas, and the remoter parts, which are accessible only on foot and which are some distance from the main visitor facilities.

In order for these planning and management measures to succeed, there is a need for continued co-ordination of efforts between central and local government and between the public and private sector. In many cases the works needed to conserve the natural environment and to manage it effectively require capital investment from central government, if they are to succeed. This raises issues related to the capital cost of financing tourist developments, especially in National Parks and scenically important countryside and coastal areas, and the revenue costs of managing them. Should the tourist generating areas (i.e. the major towns and cities) pay for the up-keep of the rural and coastal recreational areas that they use and rely on? In the public sector, should site management costs be financed by admission charges, so that the burden of maintaining and conserving sites rests on those who use them? In the not too distant future we may have to find the answers to these and other difficult questions, if our environment is to be preserved for future generations. The popularity and success of many private sector visitor attractions does indicate the ability and willingness of people to pay. These are complex issues and no clear solution has as yet emerged.

Managing the Negative Impact of Tourism Development
The underlying principle for sustainable tourism development is to manage the natural and human resources so as to maximise visitor enjoyment and local benefit, whilst minimising the negative impact of tourism on the destination site, community and local population.

James Thorsell, in a training manual prepared for the World Conservation Union, has identified a list of specific factors which can lead to negative impacts and has indicated possible mitigation measures for local tourist areas. These are set out in Table 13.1.

One good example of managing the negative impact of tourism development can be seen at Crater Lake National Park in the United States. Between 1910 and 1925, thirty separate structures were constructed at Crater Lake National Park near the Lake crater's edge. Seventy years later these facilities are inadequate and substandard. Now, on peak days, between 1,000 and 1,500 motor vehicles move through this congested area. Tourists on foot at the crater rim are faced with the sight, sound and smell of this heavy traffic.

Table 13.1: Managing Negative Impacts of Tourism

Factor involved	Negative Impact on environmental quality	Possible mitigation or corrective action
Overcrowding	• environmental stress on humans • changes in animal behaviour in wildlife areas	• limit visitor access • expand carrying capacity
Overdevelopment	• creation of rural slums • habitat loss • destruction of vegetation • land scars and watershed interference • aesthetic impact of power lines	• disperse visitors to other areas and attractions • upgrade and rehabilitate • apply land use planning and zoning regulations
Noise pollution	• irritation to wildlife, local residents and visitors	• conduct awareness campaign • establish regulations • limit visitor access
Litter	• wildlife depends upon garbage • aesthetic clutter • health hazards	• conduct awareness campaign • establish regulations • provide litter containers at appropriate places
Vandalism	• mutilation and destruction of facilities • loss of irreplaceable historic and cultural treasures	• conduct awareness campaigns • establish regulations • increase surveillance
Airport noise	• environmental stress to humans and animals	• consider altering take-off and landing patterns • establish land use controls near airports
Overcrowded roads	• environmental stress to humans and animals	• increase availability of public transportation
Off-road driving	• soil, vegetation and wildlife damage	• limit access • establish or improve enforcement regulations
Powerboats	• disturbance of wildlife, especially during nesting season • noise pollution	• restrict access and use • implement environmental education programme
Fishing and hunting	• competition with natural predators • resource depletion	• restrict access • implement environmental education programme
Foot safaris	• disturbance of wildlife • trail erosion	• install or modify trails • restrict access and use • implement environmental education programme
Souvenir collection	• removal of endangered natural items such as coral, shells, horns, rare plants • disruption of natural processes	• environmental education and awareness campaign • legal restrictions
Firewood collection	• habitat destruction • mortality of small wildlife	• environmental education and awareness campaign • use alternative fuels
Unauthorised feeding of wildlife	• behavioural changes and dependency	• environmental education and awareness campaign
Construction of billboards	• spoils the view	• establish regulations

Source: *Protected Areas in East Africa & Training Manual*,
James Thorsell, Gland, Switzerland: IUCN

After a public consultation exercise, there was consensus for the rim village to remain the focal point for overnight accommodation, visitor facilities and interpretation, with the area around the crater rim to be restored as a more natural and pedestrian environment. An environmental impact assessment was prepared for this development plan. Four main conclusions were drawn after this assessment.

- The Crater Lake ecosystem was to be enhanced with a reduction in the potential of pollutants from waste water, cars and snow ploughs entering the lake ecosystem.
- The natural environment was to be increased by reducing the developed area from 32 to 12 acres, allowing for the restoration of about 20 acres to more natural conditions. The village would be redesigned to concentrate most use in areas designed to handle heavy use. There was to be a reduction in vehicle movements and elimination of 6,000 feet of roads and parking areas.
- The rehabilitation of Crater Lake Lodge will have a long term beneficial effect in maintaining the historic building and general cultural environment.
- The socio-economic environment will be improved as the regional and local economy and state tourism will benefit from the plan.

Managing Socio-Economic Impacts

The social, cultural and economic impacts of tourism, both positive and negative, are all closely related. It is important that, as well as the environmental impact of tourism development, any planning should take account of the socio-economic impacts so that benefits are maximised and problems minimised. In recent years tourism has often been criticised for its negative socio-cultural impacts, particularly in small and traditional communities. But all types of modern development bring socio-cultural impacts on traditional communities and this includes newspapers, television and general economic development. In addition to the problems generated by new tourist development, socio-cultural impacts result from socio-economic differences between residents and tourists, whether they are of the same or different cultural backgrounds. Impacts can also result from significant cultural differences between residents and tourists. Conflicts can arise between residents and tourists because of differences in customs, religious values and patterns of behaviour.

An important principle of sustainable tourism is to regard community involvement in tourism as an essential element of any planning policy, in order to reinforce the positive impact of tourism and to minimise any negative aspects. This will enable residents to have a better understanding of the tourism development and to have participated in the decision making processes. It is also important that the local community has an input in deciding the form and scale of tourism that are appropriate for the local environment and society. This may well mean developing tourism on a gradual basis, allowing residents to adapt to the new developments, as well as monitoring the social and cultural impacts and adopting any necessary remedial measures. As part of this process it will be important to conserve the local culture and to maintain the authenticity of local dance music, drama, arts and handicrafts. It is also important for the major tourist operators and companies concerned with inbound tourism, to educate the tourists concerning local customs and culture, as well as informing residents about the tourism development. One approach towards optimising the economic benefit of tourism to the local community is to give a much higher level of training for residents to enable them to work effectively in all levels of tourism. This will provide greater employment for local people and, through training, provide higher quality services for tourists.

Principles for Sustainable Tourism
At the Globe '90 Conference held in Vancouver, Canada, an action strategy for sustainable tourism and development was put forward. It incorporated eight key principles for sustainable tourism.

- Tourism, planning and development should be part of the sustainable development strategy for a region. Tourism planning and development should be cross-sectoral and integrated, involving different government agencies, private corporations, citizen's groups and individuals, so as to provide the widest possible involvement and benefits.
- Agencies, corporations, groups and individuals should follow ethical and other principles which respect the culture and environment of the

host area, the economy, the traditional way of life, traditional behaviour and political patterns.

- Tourism should be planned and managed in a sustainable manner, with due regard for the protection of the natural and human environment in the host area.
- Tourism should be undertaken with equity in mind to distribute benefits and costs fairly among tourism promoters and host peoples.
- Good information, research and communication on the nature of tourism and its effects on the human and cultural environment should be available before, and during, development, particularly for local people, so that they can participate in, and influence the direction of, developments.
- Local people should be encouraged and expected to undertake leadership roles in planning and development, with the assistance of government, business, financial and other interests.
- Integrated environmental, social and economic planning analysis should be undertaken, prior to the commencement of any major projects.
- Throughout all stages of tourism development and operation a careful assessment, monitoring and mediation programme should be conducted in order to allow local people and others to take advantage of opportunities or to respond to changes.

ASSIGNMENTS

1. Using a country park, stretch of coastline or beauty spot in your locality, attempt to measure the following:

    i.   the impact of visitors on the area;
    ii.   the types of visitor amentities/facilities provided in the location;
    iii. the local policies for visitor management.

2. Using the reports of the National Park planning authorities in Britain, compare the approach to the *planning* and *management* in any two National Parks in Britain.

3. Using an example, either from the developed or developing world, demonstrate how the principles of sustainable tourism can be successfully applied.

Chapter 14

New Developments In Tourism

Learning Objectives:
After reading this Chapter and the additional references, you should have an understanding of:

● Current innovations in tourism development;
● The factors influencing the changing preferences of tourists in the 1990s;
● The tourism potential of our industrial heritage;
● New approaches to the tourist market.

Introduction
Innovation is the one word that best describes the development of tourism in the 1990s and which separates this period from the main phases of expansion of the tourist industry in the 19th century, or the years immediately after World War Two. In North America and Europe the traditional tourist market is approaching saturation point, and the major tourist businesses and tourist destinations are competing for a market share of a relatively static market. In this situation, very often a destination that increases its market share will do so at the expense of another major competitor and, in this competitive environment, it is the innovative entrepreneur or organisation who can identify new markets or new preferences for tourists who will become the market leader. This Chapter attempts to identify new and emerging trends in tourism in the 1990s, and discusses the lessons to be learned from them. It also looks ahead to developments that will be emerging beyond the millennium.

Innovations in Tourism Development
The traditional image of a tourist destination is a resort town set amidst attractive scenery, with a variety of day-trip opportunities within easy access. The resort is usually located on the coast and has relied on sun, sea and sand to attract its clientele. However, during the 1980s and

1990s new types of tourist destinations have emerged. These are based on quite different types of product and demonstrate new approaches to tourism marketing.

Part of this Chapter examines how new tourism products have been developed and considers their role in helping to promote new tourist destinations, particularly areas not traditionally associated with tourism. These include:

- Open air museums/industrial heritage areas.
- Inner city redevelopment, including water based projects.
- Leisure and speciality shopping in indoor resort complexes.
- The garden festival concept.
- Theme parks.
- Time-share.
- The information technology revolution that is reshaping the industry.

Open Air Museums/Industrial Heritage Areas

The long term decline in manufacturing in Europe and North America, since the early 20th century, has left a rich heritage of industrial artefacts. Many are buildings and structures that are worthy of preservation in their own right. Some, because of their historic associations or their setting, are worthy of preservation and interpretation for the benefit of future generations. Throughout the 1980s and into the 1990s, many local authorities have increasingly come to recognise the tourist potential of this industrial heritage, provided the product is developed to a level where it can benefit from major promotion.

The North of England open air museum at Beamish in County Durham is a case in point. This is one of the forerunners of a new museums movement, designed to be a living museum, recreating the industrial social environment present in the North East of England between 50 and 100 years ago. The museum occupies over 300 acres and has a farm with live exhibits. It includes a coal mine, a working tramway, a steam railway and a village, made up of buildings rescued from demolition from various locations in the North East of England. In a row of miners cottages on the site, there are reconstructions of house interiors common

50 years ago. In the West Midlands in 1967, the Iron Bridge Gorge Museum was set up to preserve the industrial revolution. Now the Iron Bridge Museum has an extensive open air site at Blists Hill, as well as exhibits on several other sites in the area.

In South Wales the decline of coal mining synonymous with the area, lead to a diversification into newer types of industry and the rapid disappearance of the traditional mining landscape, through ambitious reclamation programmes. However, more than 100,000 tourists a year visit a Welsh colliery, following the initiative of Torfaen Borough Council. The Big Pit, in the heart of the South Wales valleys, was a working mine until 1980, when its reserves were used up. The local council, together with other organisations, saw the potential in converting part of Wales' coal mining past into a major tourist attraction. The first phase of the project cost £890,000, with money raised from the Welsh Development Agency and tourist board, local authorities, the Coal Board, and heritage associations, and Torfaen Council itself provided £890,000. Soon after the museum opened in 1982, it received a further £500,000 from the European Development Fund. Today the Big Pit Mining Museum is a popular tourist attraction in South Wales with exhibition areas, a blacksmith's forge, engine winding house and so on.

Although each of these developments has produced a major new tourist attraction, on its own it is not sufficient as a catalyst for tourist development. Recent trends in tourism have included more short-break holidays, second and third holidays, and a growth in special interest and activity holidays. In order to attract this potential market, the tourist authorities, who are developing industrial heritage projects, need to consider the tourist product as a whole. Because, often, these are not located in traditional tourist regions, most of these areas lack a range of adequate accommodation and infrastructure to provide a network of information and tourist facilities. This requires investment in major hotel development schemes, development advice schemes for small businesses and a network of local tourist information centres. Given this level of commitment required from local planning authorities and regional trust boards, there is a growing realisation for the potential of the industrial heritage for short-break and special interest holidays. In a similar way the Civil War battle field sites in the United States, and particular locations such as Gettisburg or Bull Run, are seen as open air museums which attempt faithfully to replicate the major conflicts in the American Civil War. These are now major tourist attractions in their own right and have visitor centres, battle field drives and souvenir shops.

Inner City Tourism
i.   Water Front Developments
The industrial heritage theme is also seen within the various water-based development projects which have been completed in various parts of Britain during the 1980s and early 1990s. London, Bristol, Liverpool, Hull and Newcastle all have extensive dockland areas full of empty industrial buildings and waste land. The regeneration of London docklands was an ambitious project which covered over nine miles of riverside land and four main sites – the Surrey Docks, Wapping, The Isle of Dogs and the Royal Docks. The government invested over £450 million to provide a new infrastructure, including the Docklands Light Railway, new roads, river services and the new London City Airport, which was designed for short take off and landing aircraft. In addition, the private sector invested over £2 billion in this development. The existing waterscape of the docklands has been used as a backcloth for a mix of commercial, residential, retail and leisure developments. New museums have been planned for the area, including a Victorian Life Museum and the Great Eastern Railway collection in the Royal Docks. Marina developments have encouraged sailing and wind surfing. The planting of thousands of trees and the development of riverside foot paths and new retail/leisure complexes will transform this part of London by the year 2000.

On Merseyside the development of the region was initiated in the 1980s with the establishment of the Merseyside Development Corporation, the development of an Enterprise Zone and Free Port and the introduction of Urban Development Grants. Within the Enterprise Zone (the Isle of Dogs in London's dockland is a similar designation), there was up to 100 per cent capital allowance against corporate tax for capital expenditure on construction, and exemption from local rates until 1992. No planning permission was required for developments which conformed to the published scheme. Central government Urban Programme Funds were used to attract private finance in joint ventures in Liverpool to develop Beatle City (£1 million), as well as the refurbishment of the Adelphi Hotel. The Merseyside Development Corporation has invested several million pounds in the South Docks, providing an infrastructure that will, in turn, attract private investment. They have also established the Tate Gallery for the North in the former Albert Dock as well as mixed office and residential development.

The increasing involvement of the public sector in such developments in the 1980s followed from experience of similar projects which were introduced in the United States from the late 1970s. In 1977 the US government passed the *Housing and Community Development Act*, which was designed to assist severely distressed city communities containing pockets of poverty and facing economic deterioration. A programme of public and private investment was developed and, by 1982, over $2.2 billion of federal aid was spent on the Urban Development Action Grants Programme. The best known of the US projects is the revitalising of the inner harbour area of Balitmore. The Harbour Place Development transformed a decaying, derelict inner city area into a major tourist attraction, as well as a thriving commercial and conference venue. In similar ventures, New York's South Street and Toronto's harbour front have been transformed, through a mixed development bringing speciality shopping, entertainments, conference facilities and hotels. In Toronto one hundred acres of disused derelict harbour front have been converted into a new residential and market place area. In Australia, in 1984, the New South Wales Government announced the redevelopment of the Darling Harbour area as part of a $2 billion Australian project. Based on the Baltimore model, a festival market place was built with a new exhibition centre and business development, a maritime museum and a monorail link with downtown Sydney. The scheme achieved in five years what took twelve years in Baltimore. The Darling Harbour project now employs 10,000 people and attracts several million visitors a year.

Encouraged by these developments, the English Tourist Board recognised the potential of inner city waterfront sites and sought to act as a catalyst for change during the 1980s. It was closely involved with around thirty waterfront projects. Projects now completed include Ocean Village and Town Quay at Southampton, the historic dockyard area of Portsmouth, the inner city canal area of Birmingham and the Gloucester docks area, where the National Waterways Museum was completed in 1991. Similarly, in Swansea and Hull, ambitious marina and harbour front residential developments have been completed with European Community funding assistance.

ii.   Other Inner City Initiatives
In February 1980 the English Tourist Board announced a major programme to use tourism as a means of regenerating inner city areas. This scheme had three main objectives:

- To create local partnerships dedicated to inner city redevelopment.
- To get key tourism projects off the ground.
- To give practical guidance on how a wide range of local interests can be accommodated by the tourist industry.

The English Tourist Board took the view that tourism in London and the South East was approaching saturation point, and that the future of the industry relied on an expansion of tourism throughout the country, particularly in non-traditional tourist destinations. ETB took the view that tourism needed to be seen as an important element in city plans, with the encouragement of the redevelopment of inner cities as places that people would visit for leisure and tourism, because their townscapes and environments are pleasant to look at and, because they often contain a wealth of potential tourist attractions. One good example was in the West Midlands where the Black Country Corporation, the Heart of England Tourist Board and the English Tourist Board helped to raise the area's profile and attract inward investment. A major £300,000 million retail and leisure complex was developed at Wednesbury on the site of a former 125 acre steel works. Sandwell Mall is now a major attraction of the West Midlands and includes department stores and a variety of leisure facilities, employing over 800 people.

- By 1991 there were 26 tourism development action programmes in progress and 11 new programmes were agreed.   These included

Wiltshire, the Black Country, Castlefields in Manchester, Hemsby and the Upland Cumbria Initiative. The English Tourist Board's Cities programme, launched in 1988, led to a large number of local area initiatives which continued in the early 1990s to include Leeds, Nottingham and Leicester.

A Department of Environment study of the potential for the development of tourism in inner city areas drew a number of conclusions from these projects.

- They can exploit the disadvantages of inner city areas and turn them into opportunities. In situations where there are redundant docks, old buildings and abandoned 'heritage', tourism projects can provide several different types of benefit in a single project; they can improve the environment, create jobs and change perceptions of the area.
- As well as the direct employment generated by inner city projects, economic benefits are created, resulting from visitor spending elsewhere in the town or city in question.
- Such tourism projects are strongly associated with the re-use of empty buildings and derelict land. Many of the projects involve conservation and local heritage.
- Projects which form part of an overall area-based approach to regeneration seem more likely to generate image changes and to attract inward investment.
- Eighty per cent of these schemes would have been unlikely to proceed without inner city grant assistance from central government. The 20 projects in the DOE study supported some 1,200 permanent jobs.
- None of the local authorities in question had tourism strategies in place when the projects were first developed, although it quickly emerged that the potential of tourism was identified though the late 1980s and formal policies and strategies were developed.
- It is clear that such tourism projects are an effective use of inner city funding and produce significant benefits for inner city residents, workers and local businesses. They have the potential to produce jobs for inner city residents and to create benefits through the secondary effect of visitor spending.
- Such tourism projects flourish in old buildings and areas of historical

importance. The opportunity cost of using these areas for tourism or leisure developments is often minimal, as viable alternative uses are difficult to find.

iii.   Leisure and Speciality Shopping in Indoor Resort Complexes

The future will see the development of large-scale mixed retail and leisure projects with tourism as the unique selling point. In northern latitudes, in Europe and North America in particular, all-weather complexes of this type will become the indoor resorts of the future. Shopping is an important adjunct to tourism. Annual visitor surveys of tourist expenditure, by overseas visitors to the UK, regularly show that expenditure on shopping accounted for 37 per cent of total expenditure, emphasising the synergy of tourist investment within mixed development schemes.

West Edmonton Mall in Edmonton, Alberta, Canada provides a model for indoor resorts of the future. In 1981 it was originally intended to be a standard shopping centre, but the owners decided to develop a theme park, an amusement park and shopping complex all under the same roof. It contains 836 shops, covers over 5 million square feet and cost over US $600 billion to build. At the centre of the development is a 2½ acre lake with a replica Spanish galleon and four submarines (more than the Canadian Navy) that take visitors on an underwater ride through waters with live sharks and octopuses. The roof is 16 storeys up. A 10 acre water park has also been built, with a Fantasyland Hotel. The whole complex employs 15,000 people and, in 1994, tourists attracted to West Edmonton Mall and Canada Fantasyland spent over $700 million. There is parking for 30,000. It now acts as a major visitor attraction in its own right and, on autumn weekends, over 400,000 visitors come to the Mall, nearly half of them from outside Alberta. Many come from the United States on short break holidays. A third of visitors are now specifically attracted to Edmonton from the United States and the rest of Canada because of the West Edmonton Mall. It is now estimated that the Mall attracts over 5 million visitors a year. Of these, almost 2 million travellers a year visited Edmonton just to go to the West Edmonton Mall. These visitors spent over $112 million on shopping, $88 million on food and accommodation and $26 million on other goods. It is clear that such major shopping and theme and tourism leisure developments can have a significant economic impact on their locality. A 1992 study predicted that there could be eight or ten such 'mega-multi-malls' in North America by the year 2000. The success of the Mall of America in Bloomington, Minnesota has suggested that this trend is well underway.

Similar, but slightly smaller, very large indoor shopping and themed leisure complexes have been developed on Tyneside (the Metro Centre) and at Sheffield (Meadowhall). The Metro Centre and its associated recreation facilities, including the indoor Metroland Amusement Park, has set new standards in the UK for mixed retail and leisure use. This indoor centre, with a 3 million catchment population within 1 hour's drive has 3 miles of shop front, 2,500 restaurant seats, 10 cinema screens, a 28 lane bowling ally, public houses and over 40,000 square feet of themed entertainment. It is already a significant tourist attraction, bringing shoppers from throughout the north of England and from as far afield as Scandinavia. The £230 million Meadowhall project, on a 130 acre site in the Don Valley near Sheffield, provides over 200 retail stores in an enclosed shopping mall, offering 1.25 million square feet of retail and leisure space. There are themed malls with barrel vaulted, glazed roofs and an associated range of themed leisure facilities in a 15,000 square foot pavilion. Adjacent to junction 34 on the M1 motorway, Meadowhall serves a population of over 9 million people within 1 hour's drive providing 11,000 car parking and 300 coach spaces. It is clear that, in the UK, the evolution of both regional shopping centres and inner city developments is moving closer to the North American experience.

In the Netherlands, the company Center Parcs opened up the Tropicana leisure centre in Rotterdam in July 1988. With the Tropicana project, the company has adapted its experience of indoor resorts to create an all-weather, sub-tropical leisure complex within a city conurbation. Tropicana comprises a sub-tropical pool (with waterfalls, slides and rapids, interspersed with terraces and bars), saunas, a revolving restaurant, a Dutch market and several fast food outlets. Tropical trees, plants, shrubs and flowers have been imported from many parts of the world including 120 Fan Palms, which all help to create an exotic atmosphere. Over 600,000 people visit Tropicana each year and the whole complex acts as a major day visit destination for the whole of the Netherlands.

iv.   The Garden Festival Concept

Garden Festivals began in Germany in the 1950s and have been held regularly there since that time. In 1980 a festival was held in Montreal, Canada.   These festivals take part in parks especially created for the occasion and which will remain afterwards as an area of enhanced landscape capable of attracting new investment.   In Germany, garden festivals (which last for 6 months) typically attract between 4 and 8 million visitors.   In 1983 over 10 million visitors came to the Munich Festival.

In the United Kingdom the Garden Festival idea was used to assist with the reclamation of derelict industrial sites or those that had been badly polluted by industrial usage. It was felt that the Garden City concept and the resulting landscaping would help to introduce attractive development opportunities, particularly for the private sector. Government grants were available for the reclamation of derelict land and a series of bi-annual garden festivals was planned. The first UK garden festival was held in Liverpool (1984) on an abandoned dock and rubbish tip, then in Stoke on Trent (1986) on the site of an abandoned steel works. This was followed by a Glasgow Garden Festival in 1988, again on a former dockyard site; and then 1990 saw the Gateshead Garden Festival using a former coal dock and its surrounding area. Finally, in 1992, the Wales Garden Festival was located at Ebbw Vale on an abandoned colliery site. Further funding was provided by the local authorities in these areas and the agencies who were promoted at the festivals. In addition goods and services were provided by exhibitors and sponsors.

Each garden festival was organised and promoted by separate boards. At Liverpool and Glasgow the day-to-day control was the responsibility of the respective Development Agencies.

It is evident that, without the impetus of the garden festival concept, some of these sites would have remained as derelict land and the visual improvements to the landscaping and site access works would not have been done. Sadly, in most instances, not enough thought was given to their continued long term role as tourist attractions, with events and attractions remaining after the festival year. But their general success has paved the way for the garden festival concept in the UK and has proved that large numbers of visitors can be attracted to such events. For further analysis of the garden festival concept, recommended reading can be found in the Department of Environment's study *An Evaluation of Garden FestivalsI,* published in 1990.

v.   Theme Parks

These are perhaps epitomised by the Disneyland developments in California and Florida where, on several hundred acres of land, a series of fantasy worlds have been created. These offer rides, amusements and a wide range of fast food outlets, capable of meeting the needs of 10,000 visitors in a single day. The development of a park on this scale is usually designed around a theme or themes. In Disneyland the themes are Adventureland, Main Street USA, New Orleans Square, Frontierland, Fantasyland and Tomorrowland. The phenomenal success of this concept since its development in the late 1950s has spawned many imitations world-wide.

The forerunners of the theme parks in the USA were the seaside amusement parks, such as Coney Island and Santa Cruz Beach Boardwalk. In its first year of operation in 1956, Disneyland attracted almost 4 million visitors, and its current visitor numbers are around 12 million a year.

There are now 30 theme parks in the United States, with a combined visitor level of over 100 million per annum. The three Disney developments – Disneyland (California), Epcot Center (Florida) and Walt Disney World (Orlando, Florida) dominate the theme park market and, between them, account for over one-third of all visitors to USA theme parks (see Figure 14.1). Most USA theme parks were built in the period between 1950 and 1970, with only two pre-dating this period of rapid growth. The situation has remained fairly static since the mid-1970s, visitor numbers have not grown substantially since then. The theme park market appears to have reached saturation point, and many of the existing theme parks have concentrated on reinvestment, together with the development of indoor attractions.

Figure 14.1: Location of Major Theme Parks in North America

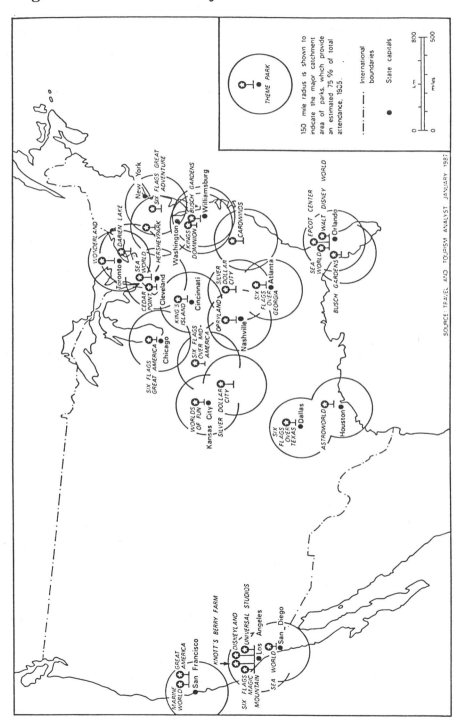

238

USA theme park ownership is highly concentrated, with 21 of the 29 largest attractions owned by just six companies. With corporate ownership, they have been able to achieve levels of capital investment generally not available in Europe. Most US theme parks are visited by day trippers with most of their catchment coming from a 150 mile radius. Americans make over 250 million visits to a whole range of theme parks and amusement parks each year, and visiting a theme park is seen as an important element in holiday planning. Two-thirds of US tourists said that attractions of this kind played an important part in selecting their holiday destination.

Unlike the USA, in Europe during the 1980s, theme parks went through a boom period. Within Europe they are of much more recent origin, having really developed from the early 1970s. The development of large theme parks remains essentially a northern European phenomenon. But, despite the climatic potential of year-round operations in the south of Europe, the population density and propensity of tourists to visit theme parks in Northern Europe suggests that new park development will continue there.

Most theme parks tend to be situated within easy access of large cities and conurbations, for example:

Phantasialand: Cologne and Bonn
Europe Park: Strasbourg and Karlsruhe
De Efteling: Antwerp and Eindhoven
Asterix: Paris
Walibi: Brussels

In general the product is based upon a number of themed areas with a distinct European flavour; themed rides; life theatre or music shows; and a selection of food and beverage outlets retailing foodstuffs which are linked in to the themed areas.

Alton Towers (which was developed as a theme park in the early 1980s), De Efterling (which was developed from the early 1950s) and Phantasialand in Germany dominate the market in their respective countries. The other theme parks generally operate with between

650,000 and 1.5 million visitors. Even with significant investment and new rides, the European theme parks have struggled to maintain their market share over the last decade. Operators are increasingly concerned about the scale of investment needed to add new rides and are looking at other strategies to retain their market share. In addition, there has been a market shift towards attractions providing an educational element to the day visit, with improved presentation, living history and other forms of product enhancement.

Most of the more recent theme park developments have taken place in France in the 1990s, in part encouraged by Disney's opening of a theme park near Paris in 1992. Euro-Disneyland introduced into Europe a successful theme park concept which had been developed by the Walt Disney Company in the United States and Japan over 35 years. It was intended to be the largest theme park development in Europe, with a long-term plan for over 18,000 hotel rooms and 2,000 camp site plots. The Magic Kingdom theme park, which is the centre of the development, opened in 1992, with links by rapid transit rail to the centre of Paris and direct links to the A4 motorway and the station for the high speed rail link from the South of France. But by the end of September 1993, Euro Disney reported a net loss of 5.3 billion French francs, one of the largest losses ever reported by a French company. Of equal concern, Euro Disney ended the financial year with gross borrowings of 21 billion French francs and growing financial problems. In the last quarter of 1993 Euro Disney saw a further fall in operating revenues and an increase in net losses to 553 million French francs. Despite this disappointing financial performance, Euro Disney did succeed as a visitor attraction and the total number of visitors per year to Euro Disney is greater than the combined total of the next four most attended theme parks in northern Europe. Certainly the French government saw the potential for a major theme park development in this location and, in total, the French state and various agencies committed over 2 billion French francs in providing infrastructure services to the Euro Disney resort. Many of the French banks and traditional investors committed a further 8 billion French francs to the development, which was seen as generating potentially over 40,000 direct and indirect jobs.

Despite this potential, by early 1994 Euro Disney was in a serious loss-making condition and it was clear that a major financial restructuring package was needed if the company were to survive. Following extensive discussions between the Walt Disney Company and a consortium of European banks who were the main creditors, a rescue package was announced in June 1994. By August 1995 it was reported that the Park was profit making, and Euro Disney reported net profits of £22 million, compared with a loss of over £60 million in the same period of the year before. The growth was achieved through cutting entrance prices, financial restructuring, an improvement in theme park and hotel revenues and the opening of the multi million pound Space Mountain Ride. This ride, based on a Jules Vernes novel, took two years to construct and is the first white knuckle ride to incorporate three inversions in the dark, where riders simulate a journey to the moon and back.

In 1995 a new rival to Euro Disney emerged in the shape of Port Aventura, a £300 million theme park located 100 kilometres south of Barcelona. This park is managed by the Tussauds Group, which has a 40 per cent share-holding in the project, as well as Anheuser-Busch the US theme park operator, which has a 20 per cent stake. Port Aventura has been built on a site which was a contender for the original Euro Disney Park. Lessons have clearly been learned from the experience of Euro Disney. Prices are much more affordable and Port Aventura is a seasonal operation; it will open on the 1st of May and close for the winter at the end of October. Targets for visitor numbers are also much more modest, with 2.5 million in the first year, as opposed to Disney's 11 million.

Outside of Europe, a company called International Theme Park Services, which is a partner in the American Dream Parks and Entertainment Group, together with Search Asia Investment Holdings Limited, is applying its experience of theme park design and management to developing major attractions in China. The company plans to establish five major theme parks in Shanghai, Guangzhou, Beijing, Chendu and Wuhan. The first two are scheduled to open in 1996. Each property covers an area of around 200 acres with the main park covering 70 acres. An amphitheatre seating 10,000 visitors will be located at each site as well as five themed sections. These parks are intended to appeal to

China's emerging middle class, which is estimated to be over 100 million people by the year 2000.

Finally, the most ambitious and specialised theme park to date is being developed in South Korea, where the world's largest artificial mountain is being built, incorporating an indoor ski jump, expert ski runs and snowboard pipes. This is being planned by British engineers and Anglo-American architects. The £136 million 'Snow Mountain' will be the centre piece of a resort in the city of Inchon, financed by Daewoo the industrial conglomerate. The artificial mountain will contain a choice of four types of ski trail with two four-seater chair lifts and competition ski jumps. 'Snow Mountain' is due to be opened before the end of the century and an artificial snow field is being developed to cover the whole complex, with an air temperature controlled at minus one degree centigrade.

The largest and best known theme park in Britain is Alton Towers in North Staffordshire, which attracts over 1,500 million visitors a year to the 700 acre site. There are over 200 acres of gardens and lakes, 300 acres of woodlands and a series of rides and attractions. The original house – Alton Towers – has been restored and renovated and acts as a backcloth to the main fairground activities of the theme park. Alton Towers is located midway between the M6 and M1 motorways and has a catchment of over 20 million people within a 2 hour journey time.

These theme parks act as tourist 'honey pots' and, by their shear size and drawing power, can attract visitors of a catchment of up to a day's journey time. Often, as has occurred in the United States, the presence of a major theme park will act as an incentive to a related tourist development, particularly the provision of accommodation. The major drawback with Alton Towers as a tourist destination has been the lack of adequate good quality accommodation in the immediate vicinity of the park. This is now being addressed and recent years have seen a marked improvement in accommodation provision in the region. By careful planning and design a large number of tourists can be managed and guided through the theme park, in ways that are referred to in the previous Chapter. The spread of rides and distribution of gift/craft shops, restaurants and fast food outlets can be built into the overall design so that organised routes can be developed in an unobtrusive way.

vi. Timeshare

In the past, the tradition has been for more prosperous people to buy or build second homes, and certain parts of France, Spain and Scandinavia have become synonymous with widespread second home development. However, as these properties are often empty for part of the year, they are costly to maintain, require payment of rates and taxes and risk being vandalised. As an alternative to this, developers hit on the concept of multi-ownership or time-sharing as a way of selling holiday apartments during the recession in the United States in the early 1970s. For a single capital outlay, the buyer gets one or more weeks of fully furnished and equipped holiday accommodation for a given period of years. The cost of purchase varies with the holiday season, the most expensive weeks being at the optimum time of the season. There is also, usually, an annual maintenance charge.

Timeshare has been one of the fastest growing sectors of the holiday market and, despite a lot of negative publicity regarding sales techniques, has grown by 14 per cent a year on average since 1987, in terms of the number of time share intervals sold. The US and European markets have remained at the forefront of the market, although emerging markets, such as Mexico and South Africa, have shown the fastest rate of growth in recent years, although the absolute numbers in these areas are small. Concern over high pressure sales techniques resulted in a European Union Directive being issued in 1994, which insisted that the member states had appropriate legislation in place by 1997.

An analysis of the growth of the world-wide time share industry between 1987 and 1994 shows that world-wide time share ownership has increased by almost 150 per cent, which represents an annual rate of growth of 15 per cent between 1988 and 1994. Ownership in the two largest markets, the United States and Europe, have more than doubled in that period. (See Tables 14.1 and 14.2). By the beginning of 1995, there were 4,200 time share resorts and 3.3 million households owning a time share world-wide.

Within Europe the growth in time share holiday complexes has been most marked in Spain and Portugal, which have been the traditional mass market tourism destinations for northern Europeans. But these are also the areas which have been the source of the greatest number of complaints about the sales methods of time share operators. There has also been significant growth in time share development in holiday complexes within the UK, France, Italy and Germany over this period. Southern Europe very much predominates in terms of time share holiday complexes and France, Italy, Spain and Portugal account for two thirds of all European time share in 1994. Over 3 million Europeans were taking a holiday through their own time share by 1994 compared with less than 1 million in 1987.

Table 14.1: Distribution of World Timeshare Market 1994

	Where owners reside		Where owners own		No of resorts
	No ('000)	%	No ('000)	%	
North America	1,775	53.3	1,595	47.9	1,639
Europe	858	25.7	847	25.4	1,188
Mexico	172	5.2	319	9.6	291
South Africa	162	4.9	161	4.8	142
South America	138	4.1	104	3.1	276
Australasia	84	2.5	84	2.5	117
South-east Asia/Far East	82	2.5	39	1.2	160
Caribbean	9	0.3	139	4.2	202
Other	53	1.6	45	1.4	130
Total	3,333	100.0	3,333	100.0	4,145

Source: Ragatz Associates, *The 1995 Worldwide Timeshare Industry*

Table 14.2: Growth of Worldwide Timeshare Industry 1987-94

	No of owners residing ('000)		% change
	1987	1994	1994/87
North America	850	1,775	108.8
Europe	320	858	168.1
Mexico	40	172	330.0
South Africa	40	162	305.0
South America	0	138	0.0
Australasia	30	84	180.0
South-east Asia/Japan	60	82	36.7
Caribbean	0	9	0.0
Other	10	53	430.0
Total	1,350	3,333	146.9

Sources: Ragatz Associates, *The 1995 Worldwide Timeshare Industry;*
Travel & Tourism Analyst No 2 1988

The most recent development has been that of entire time share resorts. The Marriott Corporation has five time share resorts and is planning more. Club Hotel (a subsidiary of Club Mediterannee) in France, with over 40 resorts, is the market leader in Europe. In France and Italy most of the time share owners are from within the domestic market. In Italy there are about 40,000 time share owners in 45 resorts – either in the skiing regions of the Alps or along the beaches of southern Italy. In the UK about 40,000 of the total 60,000 time share owners have bought weeks outside the UK, mainly in Spain and the Canaries.

There are now two main international time share exchange companies, Interval International and Resort Condominiums International, which is by far the largest, organising holidays in 1994 for about 3.5 million people, making it one of the largest travel companies world-wide. These exchange companies act as 'tour operators' for the owners of time share property, because they not only arrange the exchange of time shares, but also offer a package of travel and other services required by the tourist.

RCI is privately owned, but Interval International (II) was acquired in 1992 by CUC International, a US based membership organisation. This company also provides client incentive schemes and loyalty programmes for banks and other large corporate institutions, mainly in the United States.

In the 1990s in North America, some well known brand names have moved into the time share market, and this could have the effect of improving the image of the industry. One of the most recent entrants is the Marriott Hotel Corporation, which moved into the time share market through its subsidiary Mariott Ownership Resorts Inc (MORI), founded in 1985 through the acquisition of a small time share developer. This firm has now developed 25 large time share resorts in 10 tourist locations in the United States and the Caribbean. It has also recently developed a large time share project in the Costa del Sol in Spain. Since the mid 1980s MORI has sold over $700 million of time shares to over 60,000 people (mainly US families).

The Walt Disney Company also entered the time share business in 1991 through its wholly owned subsidiary Disney Vacation Club. Its initial time share development was on an 80-acre site which formed part of the Disney World resort in Orlando, Florida. It has now announced plans to develop six large-scale resorts in the USA and has outlined plans for a further five in Europe. The Hilton Resorts Corporation has also now moved into the time share business within the USA, and has set up a joint venture with an existing time share development team to form a new company called Hilton Grand Vacations Company. It is currently building 250 time share units adjacent to the Las Vegas Hilton and 200 units in the grounds of the Flamingo Hotel in Las Vegas. It also acquired a 30-acre site adjacent to Sea World in Orlando and intends to build a 360 unit time share development there.

In Europe future time share developments are likely to focus on the Mediterranean, with Greece, Spain and Portugal still being the least represented time share destinations. The main European markets for time share sales will continue to be Germany, the United Kingdom and Scandinavia. Once the European Union Directive controlling time share practices and sales is in place in 1997, it is possible that some of the major hotel chains may seek to move into the time share market, following a pattern which has emerged in the United States in the 1990s.

viii. Information Technology
Tourism, probably more than any other industry, is investing in new technology, especially related to information services, booking and reservation systems and electronic transfer of data from cash (direct debits) to timetables. The cumbersome directories, timetables and airline/shipping guides are rapidly being replaced by viewdata systems.

What is Viewdata? How does it work? Who uses it? Is there more than one system? These are some of the questions that might be asked and there is an array of answers to some of them. Viewdata is the electronic transmission of information onto a computer monitor screen via the telephone network. The scale of the technological revolution is impressive. By 1992, 96 per cent of travel agents in the United States and 85 per cent of agents in France were using computer reservation terminals. By the early 1990s most major CRS providers had expanded their services to include provision for reservations for hotels, car rentals, cruises, railways, tours, sporting events and theatres. Although they were originally designed for the exclusive use of travel agents, several companies, such as Sabre and Worldspan, are offering more user-friendly versions via the commercial computer networks like CompuServe and America On-Line.

One major caveat is that the pace of technological development in travel and tourism in the UK has been so great over the past five years that any description risks becoming out of date as soon as it gets into print. One example is the speed with which the main UK tour operators have developed videotext information systems and computer networks. In 1982 all tour operator bookings were taken by telephone, telex or letter. By the end of 1986, Thomson, one of the big four tour operators, was able to insist that all agency bookings be made electronically. Some operators, such as Horizon or Thomson, have their own networks, but the three main UK videotext networks used in the travel industry are PRESTEL, ISTEL and FASTRAK. Airline reservation systems include TRAVICOM, SABRE and APOLLO.

The growth of videotext to become the major means of holiday reservations has also encouraged the growth of specialised databases covering a large number of subscribing tour operators. They are not confined to late booking, but also used at peak booking periods. The three leading network suppliers ISTEL, FASTRAK and British Telecom Travel Service (which runs PRESTEL GATEWAY) have all invested big sums in preparation for the 1997 season. For example, two of the leading UK videotext operators ABC Electronic and ISTEL, have joined forces to give agents a new on-line service for package holidays and seat-only late availability. The new service, called ABC Travelbank, combines ISTEL's Travelbank and ABC's databases Holidayfinder and Seatfinder, as well as offering instant cross connections to up to 30 tour operators connected to ISTEL. In addition, from April 1988 ABC Travelbank also carried ABC's International Travellers Guide, electronic mail, mailbox and telex facilities brochure requests, flight reservation systems and closed user group facilities.

Over 95 per cent of High Street travel agents now use British Telecom's PRESTEL service, which includes several pages of information supplied by the National Tourist Board (ETB). To enable small operators to access this material, there is a low cost package available. In 1987 the English Tourist Board received more than a million accesses to their PRESTEL pages and processed over 50,000 orders for brochure packs for operators. PRESTEL is used by travel agents as a quick, efficient way of getting news updates and for brochure ordering. For example, 85 per cent of 'top up' supplies of the England Holidays brochure are now ordered via PRESTEL. The latest products on the PRESTEL service include British rail schedules and fares; information supplied by national and local tourist boards; hotel and UK resort information and live reservations; telex and electronic mail services; and a new theatre and concert reservation system.

In the case of the airlines, in order to fend off market penetration by the US systems, the Association of European Airlines called for Europe's carriers to create a single European Computers Reservation System. But differences between two main factions has led to the development of two European-based international networks connecting their computers and the terminals of travel agents. Galileo is being developed by a consortium of airlines including British Airways, KLM, Swissair and Alitalia. Amadeus is the other consortium, set up by Air France, Lufthansa, SAS and Iberia. The aim of each consortium is to provide a complete information and transaction service to travel agents worldwide, to allow for up to the minute information, the issue of full documentation recording and reporting of sales.

The most likely result is that in the UK, for example, Galileo having British Airways as a major partner, is likely to become the major distribution network for travel agents, with a similar picture in Holland, Switzerland and Italy. Other systems will compete for the rest of the European market.

In the past 10 years Computer Reservation Systems in the United States have grown to such a scale that 88 per cent of US airline tickets are sold through them. The growth of US air travel in the 1960s and 1970s and its de-regulation in 1978 encouraged these processes. Airlines discovered that computer technology could help them keep up-to-date reservations and fares more accurately, quickly and cheaply than by taking on more clerical staff. The airlines quickly realised that an industry-wide reservations and fare system could be extended to retail travel agents, especially the larger multiples developing the business travel market.

During the 1960s and 1970s there were several attempts to set up a single industry system, but these largely failed because the two largest airlines – United and American – said they would expand their own internal reservation systems and related products, Apollo and Sabre, and market them to travel agents. From 1976 the race was on to install CRS terminals at travel agent locations, thus getting greater sales exposure. But the impact was relatively limited in a largely regulated market and the three largest airlines United, American and TWA also handled other carriers' transactions.

After de-regulation in 1978, these joint activities ceased, particularly when the airlines began to realise the competitive edge they had in the form of their computerised reservation systems. A huge database is needed in order to process de-regulated fares and routes and the major carriers exploited their CRS's. For example, fees per booking for smaller airlines were raised from 35 cents to $2.75 per booking.

A wide range of incentives were offered to agencies to sign up with the main systems – hardware, software, free lines and so on. The percentage of agencies with CRS went from 5 per cent in 1977 to 95 per cent as of May 1987. In theory, use of automated airline systems did not mean that agents had to lose their neutrality, but in practice they often did, as the airlines through financial penalties or pressure wrote contracts that precluded multiple systems.

In the 1980s this resulted in growing interdependence between travel agents and airlines, high fees for previously very cheap services and agent favouritism. Other non-vendor airlines and agents began to complain on three major issues – fees, display bias and subscriber contracts. Fees were higher for CRS participants who competed with the vendor airlines and lower with CRS participants who didn't compete. Even where fees were paid, there were charges of display bias in that the less competitive airlines were allegedly given better display positions. There was also the 'halo effect', that is higher revenues for airlines from their agents than from non-vendor agents, which led to some substantial incentives being offered to agents. (In a 1985 Congressional hearing, North Western cited an example of the incentives offered to an agent in its territory: $500,000 in cash, a 10 per cent override (on top of the standard commission) for sales on United and five years' free use of Apollo including telephone line charges if the agent would switch from Sabre to Apollo. In 1986 NorthWest resolved this by buying a half share in TWA's PARS system.

However, there are a number of lawsuits pending against United and American and to date the US Government has not acted. Sabre and Apollo between them now account for three quarters of automated revenue from airline ticket sales and CRS is clearly the primary form of marketing airline seats. (See Table 14.3).

Table 14.3: Airline Computer Reservation Systems in the United States

| Airline | American | United | Texas | TWA | Delta |
CRS	Sabre	Apollo	System 1	Pars	Datas II
Revenue ($ millions)	490	325	210	160	140
Profits ($ millions)	190	125	50	40	20

The 'halo effect' of CRS sales is certainly significant and the stronger airlines have found that the system dominating sales has the ability to affect sales. For example, American's Chairman, Robert Crandall, has said that they gained 8–12 per cent in incremental revenue from display preference from Sabre Agents over non-Sabre automated agents.

Vast sums of money are involved in setting up CRS and they are now a major feature of airline strategic planning. American and United have spent about $750 million on Sabre and Apollo development and United has talked about $1 billion worth of new investment in computer systems and personnel. Texas Air is spending $200 to 400 million to make the System 1 CRS more competitive. In fact System 1 has been selected by the AMADEUS Consortium in Europe as the basis for their CRS. Each of the other main CRS's is investing heavily in order to increase, or at least maintain, their market share.

The impact of both de-regulation and CRS's on travel agents in the US has been considerable. The major CRS are looking for retail outlets which can bring them a large amount of business in the fastest possible time, and that often means agents producing a lot of business travel. Although there are over 29,000 travel agents in the US, only 7 per cent of these accounted for 28 per cent of agency sales and the picture has been one of fewer agents doing more business. In many cases dwindling profits have led to consolidation, and many agents have joined or formed chains that are able to offer good national coverage and the kinds of discounts on air tickets, hotel rooms and car rentals that come with volume of business. All CRS vendors are now offering agents PC's and three offer IBM's new PS/22 standard. These SMART terminals offer a variety of accounting and administrative backup as well as the reservations system.

Over the past decade there has been a great increase in travel-related databases developed by specialist firms. Some have themes, such as adventure travel, or cruises. One example is the World Travel File which offers a text-based, menu-driven, on-line electronic database of over 120,000 products and destinations around the world. This database is accessible by over 200,000 travel agency terminals world-wide and 40,000 corporate travel and planners who use the Official Airline Guide. In addition, the airline CRS systems are experimenting with including images and maps as a way of helping suppliers market themselves more effectively. Both Sabre, and Apollo and Galileo are including visual imaging programmes.

Whilst these information services have traditionally depended on using the ISDN telephone network, an increasing number of organisations are looking to the use of electronic computer networks to disseminate information and increased sales. This was initially developed by firms such as CompuServe, and America On-Line (AOL) which serves mainly an American market. In 1992 the British Tourist Authority began an experiment, putting British travel information on CompuServe, and have expanded this to America On-Line. Other tourism marketing organisations who have followed suit include Florida, Singapore and the Netherlands. Until the early 1990s these systems were all text-based but, with the development in computing facilities and the increasing ability to mix graphics with text and to distribute it globally at a small cost, this has changed the whole approach to information technology. The emergence of the World Wide Web on the Internet has transformed access to information on tourism destinations over the past 18 months. Users of the World Wide Web can now access high resolution pictures, video clips and text and data about tourism destinations. The cost of accessing this service is usually that of a local telephone call. By late 1995 the Web was attracting over 4 million users a year. During 1995 many of the world's major airlines, car rental companies, hotel companies, resorts, tour operators, and cruise ship companies and agencies have gone onto the Internet and provide information for users of the World Wide Web.

The race is now on to extend this technology to provide interactive television and home teleshopping. The increasing spread of cable throughout the UK will improve the opportunities for multi-media and video access to be piped through direct to individual homes. As well as home consumers, major companies, for example Thomas Cook, are having discussions with banking partners with the intent of locating its travel kiosks in non-travel locations. These would include CD-ROM and on-line access to global distribution systems and computer networks so that interactive booking of tourist destinations could be undertaken. The Post Office, which has over 20,000 branches in the UK, has also indicated its interest in selling travel within its premises.

Conclusions
These developments in information technology are having a dramatic and radical impact on the way tourism and travel is marketed, distributed, and sold and delivered. The introduction of interactive information systems and immediate electronic booking, together with the development of electronic cash transfer, viewdata information and related global distribution systems may, in time, lead to the disappearance, or at least a reduction in the number of high street retail travel agents. Brochures

from tour operators can be mailed direct to the home, where a teletext/ viewdata/CD-ROM system will enable the consumer to get instant information on holiday destinations and available bookings. He or she can make their own reservation and confirm by electronic direct-debit – all from the comfort of their own home. This will bring a totally new meaning to the term 'armchair traveller'. This change from relatively slow channels of communication to instantaneously accessible digital, graphic and text information which is interactive, has occurred in just the last decade, and technological developments are continuing at a fast pace. The improvements in personal computers, linked televisions, telephones, modems and CD-ROM players have provided a new integrated multi-media communications network. This emerging technology will undoubtedly have a major impact on tourism marketing in the future.

Continuing improvements in aircraft design and the development of engineering projects, such as the Channel Tunnel, will undoubtedly transform holiday patterns. A new generation of wide-body jets has brought down the cost of long-haul air travel and one of the fastest growing destinations in the 1980s was Australia. The biggest growth in travel has been to East Asia and the Pacific, which has more than trebled its share of international tourists over the past 20 years. (WTO 1995) A surge in tourism to these areas has seen China, Hong Kong and Singapore become some of the most attractive destinations. The collapse of Communism in Eastern Europe has also shown some dramatic changes where, for example, Poland has seen a six-fold growth since 1989 and the Czech Republic has doubled its figures of tourists. The UK has seen growth of 60 per cent in bookings for long-haul travel in 1996. Europe's share of both arrivals and revenue has shrunk since 1975 when more than two-thirds (69 per cent) of tourists visited the continent. The past decade has seen the emergence of new tourist destinations, such as Hong Kong and Singapore, and in Eastern Europe countries such as Hungary, Poland and the Czech Republic. It is clear that those national tourist organisations who have invested in developing their marketing and strategic marketing research and increasing their marketing spend per visitor have been the winners world-wide in attracting the main share of the existing travel and tourism market.

It is also clear that the domestic tourist industry must continue to be innovative in the face of increasing foreign competition and, in the travel and tourism industry more than any other, complacency will lead to a decline in business and, ultimately, smaller firms going out of business. Organisations, towns and individual firms must be continually seeking to develop new products, new markets and, wherever possible, to harness new technology to improve operating costs, increase market penetration and improve profit margins. The prospects are bright for the tourist industry in the 21st century. Many parts of the world have yet to realise their tourism potential and many new markets are awaiting discovery.

ASSIGNMENTS

1. Identify what you think are the two most significant innovations in tourism during the 1990s. Give a reasoned justification for your choice, with examples.

2. Using your library, look at a tourist guide from the 1950s and compare it with one written in the 1990s. What are the main differences? What are the most significant changes that have taken place in the presentation and content of tourist guides over the past 40 years?

References

OVER 150 USEFUL REFERENCES ON TRAVEL AND TOURISM

CHAPTER 1

British Tourist Authority, *Annual Reports*

British Tourist Authority, *British National Travel Survey,* Annually

British Tourist Authority, *et al.* (1981) *Tourism in the UK – The Broad Perspective*

Chicago Tribune, Graph, April 18, 1988

Clawson, Marion and Carlton S. Van Doren, *Statistics on Outdoor Recreation Resources for the Future,* Washington, D.C. 1984

Department of Employment, *Pleasure, Leisure and Jobs – The Business of Tourism,* HMSO 1985

Development of Tourism Act (1969) HMSO 1969

Economist Intelligence Unit, *Travel and Tourism Analyst (6 issues a year, covering business information and forecasts for all sectors of the travel and tourism industry)*

English Tourist Board, *Annual Reports*

English Tourist Board, *Regional Facts Sheets*

Frechtling, Douglas, 'US Domestic Holiday Traffic', *Travel and Tourism Analyst*, The Economist Publications, London 1986

Henley Centre, *Leisure Futures*, Published quarterly

International Union of Official Travel Organisations (IUOTO), *UN Conference on International Travel and Tourism*, Rome 1963

International Passenger Survey, (Published annually, usually reported in *British Business*)

League of Nations, *Report on Tourism by Committee of Statistical Experts*, January 1937

Lickorish, L.J., *The Travel Trade,* 1958, Appendix III

National Tourism Resources Review Commission, Report: *Destination USA,* Six Volumes, Washington, D.C. 1973

Organisation for Economic Co-operation and Development, *Tourism Policy and International Tourism,* Published annually, ECD Paris

Time Magazine, 'Travel – A $260 Billion US Industry on the Move' Business Edition, May 18, 1987

Travel Weekly, Travel Market Yearbook, 1987, News Group Publishing, 1986

U.S. Department of Commerce, International Travel and Passenger Fares, 1982, *Survey of Current Business,* 63, No. 5, May 1983

U.S. Department of Commerce, International Travel and Passenger Fares, 1986, *Survey of Current Business,* 67, No. 6, June 1987

USA Snapshots, *USA Today,* December 5, 1984

USA Snapshots, *USA Today,* May 5, 1986

US Travel Data Center, *National Travel Survey* – Full Year Report 1986, Washington D.C., 1987

US Travel Data Center, *The 1986-87 Economic Review of Travel in America,* Washington D.C., 1987

US Travel and Tourism Administration, *Recap of International Travel to and from the United States in 1986,* US Department of Commerce, Washington D.C., 1987

Waters, S.R., *Travel Industry World Yearbook – The Big Picture,* (1995), Child & Waters, New York, 1995

White, K. and M. Walker, 'Trouble in the Travel Account', *Annals of Tourism Research,* 1982

World Tourism Organisation, *Annual Reports*

World Tourism Organisation, *Economic Review of World Tourism,* WTO 1994

World Tourism Organisation, *World Tourism Statistics Annual Yearbook,* WTO 1994

CHAPTER 2

Bennett, E.D., (Ed.), *American Journeys – An Anthology of Travel in the United States,* Convent Station, New Jersey: Travel Vision, 1975

British Travel Association, *The British Travel Association 1929-1969,* British Tourist Authority, 1970

Brittain, J. and E. Wedlake Brayley, *The Beauties of England and Wales,* (Cumberland), London, 1802

Brunner, E., *Holiday Making and the Holiday Trades,* OUP 1945

Burnet, L., *Villegiature et Tourisme sur les Côtes de France,* Paris 1963

Clawson, Marion, *The Crisis in Outdoor Recreation,* American Forests 65(3):22-31, (1959)

Defort, P.P., 'Quelques Reperes Historique du Tourisme Moderne', *The Tourism Review*, January/March, 1958

De Santis, Hugh., The Democratization of Travel: The Travel Agent in American History, *Journal of American Culture* 1(1):1-17, (1978)

Dulles, Foster Rhea, *A History of Recreation – America Learns to Play,* New York: Appleton-Century-Crofts, 1965

Howell, Sara, *The Seaside,* Cassell, Collier, MacMillan, London, 1974

Lennard, R., *Englishmen at Rest and Play*, Clarendon Press, Oxford, 1931

Lickorish, L.J. and A.G. Kershaw, *op. cit.,* Chapter 1

Lundberg, Donald E., *The Hotel and Restaurant Business,* CBI-Van Nostrand, New York, 1984

Lundberg, Donald E., *The Tourist Business,* Cahner Books, Boston, 1974, 1985

Patmore, J.A., *Land and Leisure*, David and Charles, 1970

Smollett, T., *Humphrey Clinker*, Dent

Stephenson, R.L., *Travels with a donkey in the Cevennes*, Dent, 1986

Swinglehurst, Edmund, *Cook's Tours – The Story of Popular Travel,* Blandford Press, Poole, Dorset, 1982

Travel Weekly, Travel Weekly's 25th Anniversary Issue, (May 31) 1983

Travel Weekly, Park Data Show RV's Top Choice, (September 3) 1984

Ullman, Edward L., 1954, Amenities as a Factor in Regional Growth, *The Geographical Review* 44(2):119-132

U.S. Bureau of the Census, *Statistical Abstract of the United States.* Washington D.C., Various Years

Van Doren, Carlton S., 1981, Outdoor Recreation Trends in the 1980s: Implications for Society, *Journal of Travel Research* 19:3-10

Van Doren, Carlton S., 1983, The Future of Tourism, *Journal of Physical Education, Recreation and Dance,* 54:27-29.42

Van Doren, Carlton S., 'The Consequences of Forty Years of Tourism Growth', *Annals of Tourism Research*, 12, 1985

CHAPTER 3

Cohen, Erik., 'Rethinking the Sociology of Tourism,' *Annals of Tourism Research,* 6 No.1, Jan/March 1979

Caribbean Tourism Research and Development Center, 1987, *Travel and*

Leisure's World Tourism Overview 1987/1988, The annual review of the travel industry world wide, American Express Publishing Co, NY, 1987

Education and Training Advisory Council, *Hotel and Catering Skills – Now and in the Future*, Hotel and Catering Industry Training Board, London 1983

Gearing, Charles E., *et al. Planning for Tourism Development*, Praeger Publishers, 1976

Gunn, Clare A., *Vacationscape – Designing Tourist Regions*, Second Edition, Van Nostrand, 1988

Gunn, Clare A., *Tourism Planning*, Second Edition, Taylor and Francis, 1988

Institute of Manpower Studies, *Jobs in Tourism and Leisure*, English Tourist Board, 1986

Mayo, Edward J., and Lance P. Jarvis, *The Psychology of Leisure Travel,* CBI Publishing, 1981

McIntosh, Robert W. and Charles R. Goeldner, *Tourism – Principles, Practices*, Philosophies, Wiley & Sons, New York, 1986

Plog, Stanley, 'Why Destination Areas Rise and Fall in Popularity,' *Cornell HRA,* Quarterly 14, No.4, 1974

Ritchie, J.R., Brent and Charles R. Goeldner, *Travel, Tourism and Hospitality Research,* New York: John Wiley and Sons, 1987

Stengel, Richard, 'Ah, Wilderness!' America's parks have become too popular for their own good,' *Time*, July 11, 1988

Time Magazine, 'Travel– A $200 Billion US Industry on the Move,' Business Edition, May 18, 1987

Travel Weekly, *Travel Market Yearbook*, 1987, News Group Publishing, 1986

Travel Weekly, *Waikiki Beach and Oahu – 1988 Reference Guide* (Supplement), July 11, 1988

U.S. Department of the Interior, *National Park Statistical Abstract,* 1987, Denver, Colorado

U.S. Travel Data Center, *Tourism's Top Twenty* (1987), Washington, D.C. 1987

Waters, S.R., *Travel Industry World Yearbook – The Big Picture, (1995), Child and Waters, New York, 1995

CHAPTER 4
Working group of the National Trust Organisations of the EEC, Fifth

Report on *The Economic Significance of Tourism within the European Economic Community,* British Tourist Authority, 1983

Organisation for Economic Co-operation and Development, *Tourism Policy and International Tourism,* Published annually, OECD, Paris

U.S. Travel Data Center, *National Travel Survey,* (Annually)

Waters, S.R., *Travel Industry World Yearbook* – The Big Picture, (1995), Child and Waters, New York, 1995

World Tourism Organisation, *Economic Review of World Tourism,* WTO, 1986

World Tourism Organisation, *Yearbook of Tourism Statistics*, Annually

CHAPTER 5

American Society of Travel Agents, *ASTA. STAT,* Various issues

Beaver, A., *Mind Your Own Travel Business*, Beaver Travel, 1979

Business Travel News, 1988 Business Travel Survey, Issue 113, CMP Publications, June 6, 1988

Economist Intelligence Unit, *The British Travel Industry – A Survey*, London, 1968

Lickorish, L.J., and A.G. Kershaw, *The Travel Trade,* 1958

The Times, Article in the Business Section 12.1.87

Travel Trade Gazette, Article, January 1987

Travel Weekly, 'The 1988 Louis Harris Survey,' June 29, 1988

Travel Weekly Focus, '1987 Profit Guide,' July 31, 1987

CHAPTER 6

Beeching Report, *The Reshaping of British Railways*

Department of Trade, *Report of Official Inquiry into the collapse of the Court Line*, HMSO, 1975

Daube, Scott, 'Daylight Rockies Service Depust,' *Travel Weekly*, July 21 1988, 24

Lickorish, L.J., *op. cit.* Chapter 1

Official Airline Guides (OAG), *Worldwise Cruise and Shipline Guide* (bi-monthly)

The Travel Agent, 'More Americans Take to the Skies,' October 19, 1987

Time Magazine, 'Travel – A \$260 Billion U.S. Industry on the Move,' Business Edition, May 18, 1987

Transport Act 1980

Transport Act 1988

Transport Review 1994, *Organisational Responses to the deregulation of the insurance industry in Britain,* vol.14, No.4, 1994

Transport Statistics, HMSO, (Annually)

Travel Agent Magazine, 'ABA's Top 100 List Rounds Up Cream of North America's Crop,' March 3, 1988

United States Travel Data Centre – Annual Surveys of Airline Travellers to US

Waters, S.R., *Travel Industry World Yearbook* – The Big Picture 1995 Child & Waters, New York, 1995

CHAPTER 7

Brown, B. and P. Lavery, *A survey of serviced and self-catering accommodation in South East Dorset*, Southern Tourist Board, 1986

Department of Employment, *Action for Jobs in Tourism,* HMSO, 1986

Education and Training Advisory Council, *Hotel and Catering Skills – Now and in the Future*, Hotel and Catering Training Board, 1983

FOA/ECE Working Party on Agrarian Structure and Farm Rationalisation (Several papers on Farm Tourism contained in) *Report of the Symposium on Agriculture and Tourism*, Government of Finland, Helsinki, 1982

Horwath and Horwath, *World Wide Hotel Industry,* 1987

Laventhol and Horwath, *U.S. Lodging Industry 1986,* Philadelphia, 1986

Travel Weekly, 'Study Cites Needs for More Hotel Rooms', November 11, 1985 44 No.103, 1985

U.S. Department of Interior, *National Park Statistical Abstract,* 1987, Denver, Colorado

U.S. Travel Data Center, *National Travel Survey – Full Year Report 1986,* Washington, D.C., 1987

Waters, S.R., *Travel Industry World Yearbook* – The Big Picture 1995 Child & Waters New York, 1995

CHAPTER 8

British Tourist Authority, 1970

Beekhuis, Jeanne V., *World Travel Overview,* Travel and Leisure, 1987-88

Department of Employment, *Pleasure, Leisure and Jobs,* (Ch 4) *op. cit.*

English Tourist Board, *Annual Reports*

Hewett, R., and L.J., Lickorish, *et al. The British Travel Association 1929-1969*, London, 1971

National Tourism Resources Review Commission, Report: *Destination USA*, Six Volumes, Washington D.C., 1973

Organization for Economic Co-operation and Development, *Tourism Policy and International Tourism*, Paris, 1984

United States Congress, National Tourism Policy Act, 97th Congress 1st Session (Public Law 97-73), 1981

U.S. Travel Data Center, *The 1986-87 Economic Review of Travel in America*, Washington D.C., 1987

CHAPTER 9

British Tourist Authority, *Strategy for Growth 1984-88*, 1984

British Tourist Authority, *Guidelines for Tourism to Britain 1991-1995*, BTA, 1991

English Tourist Board, *Financing Tourist Projects*, 1980

English Tourist Board, *Tourism in the UK: realising the potential*, ETB, 1992

Further developments on the Languedoc Rousillion development, see:

Lavery, P., *et al. The Strategy for Hadrian's Wall*, Countryside Commission 1984

Loudry, R., 'Tourism development of Languedoc Rousillion', Paper given at International Seminar, *Physical Planning and Area Development for Tourism*, IUOTO, Geneva, 1973

Lundberg, Donald E., *The Tourist Business*, Cahner Books, Boston, 1974, 1985

Murphy, Peter, *Tourism, A Community Approach*, Methuen, 1985

Tourism U.S.A., Guidelines for Tourism Development, U.S. Department of Commerce, U.S. Travel and Tourism Administration, 1986

Travel Weekly, Waikiki Beach and Oahu – 1988, Reference Guide (Supplement), July 11, 1988

CHAPTER 10

For further reading on Tourism Marketing, see:

British Tourist Authority, *Marketing Opportunities 1992-93*

BTA/ETB, *Insights*, (A series of detailed market research studies of particular aspects of the travel and tourism industry), Annual

Foster, D., *Travel and Tourism Management*, Macmillan 1985

Krippendorf, *Marketing et Tourisme*, H. Lang & Co, 1971

Middleton, V., *Marketing in Travel and Tourism*, Heinemann (2nd edition, 1995)

Wahab, S., *et al. Tourism Marketing*, Tourism International Press, 1976

CHAPTER 11

Archer, B., and C.B. Owen, *Towards a Tourist Regional Multiplier*, 1971

Isard, W., *Methods of Regional Analysis*, MIT, 1969

Organisation for Economic Co-operation and Development, *Tourism Policy and International Tourism,* Published annually

Richardson, H., *Elements of Regional Economics*, Penguin, 1970

Travel and Tourism Analyst, *Measuring Tourism's Economic Importance – A Canadian Case Study,* EIU, 1995

U.S. Department of Commerce, International Travel and Passenger Fares, 1982, *Survey of Current Business*, 63, No.5, May 1983

U.S. Department of Commerce, International Travel and Passenger Fares, 1986, *Survey of Current Business*, 67, No.6, June 1987

CHAPTER 12

Burton, R., *Recreation Carrying Capacity in the Countryside*, MSc Thesis, University of Birmingham, 1974

Ceton, Marvin J., *et al.* 'Into the 21st Century, Long Term Trends Affecting the United States', *The Futurist*, Vol.22:4, July-August, 1988

Davis, Robert S., 'Tuttle Cites the Importance of Regional Structure,' *Travel Weekly*, Vol. 45: 96, November 3, 1986

De Santis, Hugh, The Democratization of Travel: The Travel Agent in American History, *Journal of American Culture*, 1(1):1-17, 1978

Dower, M. and P.E. McCarthy, 'Planning for Conservation and Development', *Journal of the Royal Town Planning Institute*, 53, No. 1, 1967

European Information Centre for Nature Conservation The Management of the Environment in *Tomorrow's Europe*, Council of Europe, Strasbourg, 1971

Furmidge, J., 'Planning for Recreation in the Countryside', *Journal of the*

Royal Town Planning Institute, 55, No. 2, 1969

Houghton-Evans, W. and J.C. Miles, Environmental Capacity in Rural Recreation Areas', *Journal of the Royal Town Planning Institute*, 56, No.10, 1970

Kotler, Philip, Dream Vacation – The Blooming Market for Designing Experiences, *The Futurist,* 18:5, 1984

Organisation for Economic Co-operation and Development, *The Impact of Tourism on the Environment*, General Report, OECD, Paris 1980

Ragatz, Richard L., *Trends in the Market for Privately Owned Seasonal Recreational Housing, Proceedings – 1980 National Outdoor Recreation Trends Symposium, Volume 2*, U.S. Department of Agriculture, Forest Service, Northeastern Forest Experiment Station, Broomall, PA, General Technical Report, N.E.–57, 1980

Van Doren, Carton S., Outdoor Recreation Trends in the 1980s: implications for society, Journal of Travel Research, 19:3-10, 1981

Van Doren, Carlton S., 'The Consequences of Forty Years of Tourism Growth,' *Annals of Tourism Research*, 12, 1985

CHAPTER 13

EEC (Council of Europe), *The Management of the Environment in Tomorrow's Europe*, Strasbourg, 1971

Globe '90 Conference, *Tourism Stream, Action Strategy*, Adopted at Vancouver BC, Canada, 1990

Inskeep, E., *Tourism Planning: an integrated and sustainable development approach*, Van Nostrand, New York, 1991

World Tourism Organisation, *Sustainable Tourism Development*, WTO, 1992

CHAPTER 14

Lavery, P. and McKeough, P., *Indoor Resorts in Europe*, Travel and Tourism Analyst, No.1, 1989

Lavery P. and Stevens, T., *Attendance Trends and Future Developments at Europe's Leisure Attractions*, Travel and Tourism Analyst, No.2, 1990

Taylor, R. and Stevens, T., *An American Adventure in Europe: an analysis of the performance of Euro Disneyland (1992-1994)*, Managing Leisure, 1995

Pollock, A., *The Impact of Information Technology on Destination Marketing*, Travel and Tourism Analyst, No.3, 1995

Index

268

272

Leisure, Travel & Tourism Books from ELM

EUROPEAN LEISURE BUSINESSES: strategies for the future
Brian Eaton
Topical, well-researched case studies on major companies in the European
Leisure Industry - Rank, Stakis, First Leisure, Eurocamp, David Lloyd Leisure,
Allied Leisure, Ladbrokes and VCI, plus the history, strategy
and competitive environment of European leisure.
Illustrations, maps, charts and tables.
Book 288 pp., 1 85450 230 1
Tutor's Manual, exercises, materials and OHPs 185450 430 4

TOURISM & LEISURE IN THE COUNTRYSIDE 2nd ed.,
Richard Sharpley
Material for a full year's course with nine stand-alone chapters on countryside
recreation, management, planning and the law. Level HND and above.
Book, 336pp, 185450 245 X
Tutor's Manual, 1 year's materials, 185450 440 1

TOURISM, TOURISTS AND SOCIETY
Richard Sharpley
An in-depth study of the relationship between tourism and the societies
that both generate and host tourism and tourists.
Includes: the effects of social change on the pattern of tourism
consumption; motivation for tourism; impact of tourism on
host societies; and commoditisation and authenticity.
Book, 288pp, 1 85450 159 3
Tutor's Manual - exercises/notes/OHPs, 1 85450 233 6

TRAVEL AND TOURISM: A NORTH-AMERICAN-EUROPEAN PERSPECTIVE
Patrick Lavery & Carl Van Doren
Overview of the industry and the role of private/public sectors in the UK, USA
and Europe. Level introductory, beginners + on higher education courses.
32, Book, 224pp, 1 85450 125 9

FROM TOURIST ATTRACTIONS TO HERITAGE TOURISM - Pat Yale
From museums to stately homes, castles, palaces and gardens, religious buildings, archaeological sites and ancient monuments, including industrial and transport heritage. A standard reference work for tutors as well as a good, advanced level class text. Level PG Diploma, degree, etc.
Book, 256pp, 1 85450 016 3, second edition 1997

MUSIC INDUSTRY MANAGEMENT AND PROMOTION - Chris Kemp
Music industry management & promotion, plus useful tips if you enter the business. Using industry' terminology, the author's enthusiasm is infectious. Selecting a band; the agent; managing publicity; marketing; managing the venue; staffing, crew & security; the perfect promotion; finance & administration; managing the band/setting up a tour; music events outdoors; record companies; Studio production.
Book 288pp + Single User Program on PC disks, 1 85450 149 6
Network Version on PC disk + Tutor's Manual, 1 85450 142 9

TOURISM IN THE U.K. - Pat Yale
The business and management of tourism. With commentary on UK tourist attractions. Adopted by many colleges and schools as set text for those new to the business of tourism. Level BTEC Nat., A level+.
Book - maps/charts/diagrams, 320 pp, 1 85450 017 1
Tutor's Manual - exercises/notes/OHPs, 1 85450 094 5

TOURISM LAW, SECOND EDITION - Jim Corke
Updated and revised edition of the first text specially written on the law relating to tourism and travel. New material on EC regulations.
Level HND+. 24, Book, 480pp, 1 85450 028 7
24TM, Tutor's Manual, 1 85450 140 2

WATER BASED RECREATION: managing resources for leisure
Fiona McCormack
Comprehensive treatment of the scope and development of water based resources for leisure. Aspects of management, marketing, environmental issues, conservation, conflicting uses, access and future trends. The first encapsulation and full coverage of this important and growing area of leisure management. The author is a qualified and experienced sailor and instructor.
Book, 320pp, 1 85450 154 2, Tutor's Manual 1 85450 152 6

Computer Software (pc disks)

TRAVEL COMPANY BUSINESS - Ray Garnett
Interactive group exercise in business decisions for a Travel Company.
Can be networked. Demo disk available. Level HND and above.
Disk and Tutor's Manual, 1 85450 035 X

INTERACTIVE MANAGEMENT SIMULATIONS - Humphrey Shaw
To improve decision making and presentation skills. Students work competitively
in groups managing a simulated business. Emphasis on the business and
management aspects rather than the subject or industry context.
Disk and Tutor's Manual. Level BTEC, HND+.
Demo disks available. ISSN 0954-030X
Football Manager, 0 946139 24 5; **Property Manager**, 0 946139 29 6;
Restaurant Manager, 0 946139 34 2

Other Business Management Books

EUROPEAN BUSINESS STRATEGY, 5TH EDN
Terry Garrison
24 well-researched & presented topical case studies from Barings Bank to
France Télécom, from Groupe Bull to Crédit Lyonnais.
Level DMS/PG Diploma, MBA.
Book, 320pp, 1 85450 169 0
Tutor's Manual - answers/notes etc., 1 85450 415 0

PEOPLE IN ORGANISATIONS, 5TH EDN
Pat Armstrong &Chris Dawson
A popular introduction to managing people at work. Includes
theory/application, underlying psychology & personnel aspects.
Book, 472pp, 1 85450 240 9
Tutor's Manual, 1 85450 426 6